D0918248

REASONS OF IDENTITY

Reasons of Identity

A Normative Guide to the Political and Legal Assessment of Identity Claims

AVIGAIL EISENBERG

OXFORD
UNIVERSITY PRESS

Great Clarendon Street, Oxford OX2 6DP

Oxford University Press is a department of the University of Oxford.
It furthers the University's objective of excellence in research, scholarship,
and education by publishing worldwide in

Oxford New York

Auckland Cape Town Dar es Salaam Hong Kong Karachi
Kuala Lumpur Madrid Melbourne Mexico City Nairobi
New Delhi Shanghai Taipei Toronto

With offices in

Argentina Austria Brazil Chile Czech Republic France Greece
Guatemala Hungary Italy Japan Poland Portugal Singapore
South Korea Switzerland Thailand Turkey Ukraine Vietnam

Oxford is a registered trade mark of Oxford University Press
in the UK and in certain other countries

Published in the United States
by Oxford University Press Inc., New York

First published 2009

British Library Cataloguing in Publication Data
Data available

Library of Congress Cataloging in Publication Data
Data available

Typeset by SPI Publisher Services, Pondicherry, India
Printed in Great Britain
on acid-free paper by
the MPG Books Group, Bodmin and King's Lynn

ISBN 978–0–19–929130–4

1 3 5 7 9 10 8 6 4 2

for Stefan

Contents

Acknowledgements ix

1. Introduction 1
2. The Identity Approach: Public Decision Making in Diverse Societies 15
3. Multiculturalism, Identity Quietism, and Identity Scepticism 43
4. Diversity and Sexual Equality: The Challenge of Incommensurability 65
5. Religious Identity and the Problem of Authenticity 91
6. Indigenous Identity Claims: The Perils of Essentialism and Domestication 119
7. Conclusion: Reasons of Identity 139

Notes 145
Bibliography 161
Index 171

Acknowledgements

I am grateful to many people, several institutions, and a few funding agencies for the help I received in writing this book. The book initially took shape in 2004 when I was a visiting fellow at the Centre de Recherche en Éthiques à l'Université de Montréal. I am grateful to the people at the Centre, especially Daniel Weinstock and Martin Blanchard, for making that year so enjoyable and productive. I hope someday to have the opportunity to spend time there again.

I am also grateful for the many stimulating workshops and discussions which were organized in the contexts of two research groups to which I belong. First, the Ethnicity and Democratic Governance research group, based at Queen's University, and directed by Bruce Berman, provided several opportunities for me to discuss my ideas with some extraordinary colleagues and graduate students at Queen's University, University of Toronto, University of Ottawa, and at the Summer Institute in Guadalajara, Mexico. In addition, I have benefited from access to the fine researchers and community organizers who participate in the Indigenous Peoples and Governance research group based at the Université de Montréal and directed by Pierre Noreau. Both groups are funded by the Social Sciences and Human Research Council of Canada, to which I am grateful for funding as well.

Closer to home in British Columbia, I am lucky to be a member of a community of scholars at the University of Victoria who participate with me in the Consortium on Democratic Constitutionalism and the Victoria Colloquium on Social, Political, and Legal Thought. I want to thank my colleagues there, especially Michael Asch, Ben Berger, Andrée Boisselle, John Borrows, Maneesha Deckha, Cindy Holder, Matt James, Rebecca Johnson, Hester Lessard, Colin Macleod, Dennis Pilon, Jim Tully, and Jeremy Webber for making the University an intellectually interesting place to work; for helping to organize seminars, conferences, and workshops; and for lending a book or answering a question whenever I ask. Thanks also to Cara McGregor and Elizabeth Punnett for their superb research assistance. I am grateful to the University and my Department for helping to attract such wonderful visitors and postdoctoral fellows. In particular, I want to acknowledge my debt to Else Grete Broderstad, Katherine Curchin, Rita Dhamoon, and Ilenia Ruggia, whose visits to campus were especially helpful to me in thinking through some of the arguments in this book.

This book has been developed in the course of delivering many research papers in different places in the world, some of which have found their way into books and journals which I would like to gratefully acknowledge. In particular, some of the material in Chapter 4 is drawn from 'Diversity and equality: three approaches to cultural and sexual difference', *Journal of Political Philosophy*, 11(1): 41–64; and ideas found in Chapter 6 were initially worked out in a paper published in *Accommodating Cultural Diversity*, Stephen Tierney (ed.), London: Ashgate, 2007. In addition, I have been fortunate to become involved in projects directly related to themes discussed in this book, three of which led to edited volumes: *Minorities within Minorities*, co-edited with Jeff Spinner-Halev; *Sexual Justice/Cultural Justice*, co-edited with Barbara Arneil, Monique Deveaux, and Rita Dhamoon; and *Diversity and Equality*. I am grateful to my co-editors and to all the contributors to these volumes for helping me to think about the arguments that arise in relation identity claims.

I want to thank Monique Deveaux and Barbara Arneil for being such good friends and wonderful colleagues for the last few years, and for the helpful initial discussions we had about this project while we were fellows at the Rockefeller Centre in Bellagio, Italy. Thanks to the Rockefeller Foundation as well for funding the visit.

I owe many thanks to those who have read and commented on different parts of this book and influenced my thinking by posing difficult questions about it. In particular, I am grateful to Lori Beaman, Martin Blanchard, Monique Deveaux, Marilyn Friedman, Xavier Lander, Patti Lenard, Audrey Macklin, Tariq Modood, Wayne Norman, Anne Phillips, Sean Rehaag, Jeff Spinner-Halev, Jackie Steele, Jim Tully, Michel Seymour, and Melissa Williams for their helpful comments and questions. My gratitude is especially extended to Rita Dhamoon, Sue Donaldson, Will Kymlicka, Margaret Moore, and Colin Macleod who read and commented on an earlier draft of the entire manuscript and offered good advice and helpful encouragement along the way. Thanks as well to Dominic Byatt at OUP for waiting patiently for this book to be completed.

My greatest debt is to Colin Macleod with whom I discussed every idea, who read every word of this book (sometimes more than once!), and suggested changes that helped in significant ways to clarify my ideas and sharpen my analysis. Without his enormous generosity this book would have been impossible to write.

1

Introduction

Over the past few years, I have been examining minority rights disputes with an eye to understanding why some distinctive or special practices of cultural or religious minorities ought to be protected and how public officials, mainly legislators, judges, and other adjudicators, should respond to claims for the protection of such practices. What I found is that groups often argue for accommodation or protection of practices by appealing to considerations of identity. Groups offer justifications for their claims by explaining what is important to their identity. Public institutions often view considerations concerning group and individual identity as relevant to their decisions about whether claims ought to be accepted or rejected. Groups 'explain their identity' and public decision makers 'assess identity' in ways that involve raising challenging questions. What ought to be considered central or important about an individual's or group's identity? What standards of evidence ought to be used to make such assessments? How should inter-community disagreement or individual dissent about the importance of a practice be incorporated into decisions about whether practices ought to be protected or prohibited? How should harm be assessed, especially when what constitutes harm may be controversial? These questions are related to what I call identity claims and they flow from a more general question which guides my research, namely, when is it appropriate to allocate entitlements, resources, and opportunities one way rather than another on the basis of something distinctive and important about the identity of a group or individual?

In one sense, there is nothing new or surprising about such questions or assessments. Public institutions have been assessing identity claims for a long time largely because even the most well crafted human rights document is, at best, only a set of abstract and general principles until public institutions translate its principles into substantive decisions for the people to whom it applies. These 'translations' often require assessments of identity. Conflicts over freedom of religion, for example, usually require that public institutions assess facets of religious identity and make decisions about which groups will be considered 'religious' ones and which practices will be considered important to that freedom. Sometimes, these assessments are controversial. But often they take place without much attention being paid to them. To some extent, we expect public decision makers to understand what is at stake for groups before making decisions which involve minority rights, for instance, before deciding to restrict a particular minority practice, if only to understand the consequences likely to follow from their decision. But how they come to understand what is at stake for minorities is only vaguely understood and mostly ignored in normative political theory and public policy analysis.

Recently, this indifference to identity has diminished to some degree. The change has been propelled, in part, by a greater awareness of the role that identity plays in controversies in Western countries concerning the accommodation of Muslim practices, such as religious arbitration and veiling. By and large, the scholarship that addresses these issues suggests that decisions which involve assessing group identity claims are often made in an arbitrary manner, according to the unfounded presumptions and stereotypes held by dominant cultural groups, or based on opaque and otherwise unjustified criteria. These studies have fueled a large and growing literature which points to the hazards of allowing considerations of identity to influence public decision making and generally concludes that assessments of identity claims should not be made at all. Significantly, much normative political theory proceeds as if decisions about cultural or religious accommodation can and should be made without assessing claims related to the identities of the groups involved. Despite the fact that we live in an age of 'identity politics', surprisingly few political theorists feel comfortable with the idea of public institutions assessing claims groups make about their identities. This is true not only of critics of multiculturalism, such as Brian Barry (2001), who argue that cultural minorities have few if any legitimate claims to accommodation. It is equally (though more surprisingly) true of many defenders of multiculturalism who nonetheless go to great lengths to deny that their defence of minority claims rests on any appeal to 'identity'. This is true of both liberal defenders of multiculturalism, such as Susan Okin (1998), Will Kymlicka (2001, 2007), and Anne Phillips (2007), as well as defenders of multiculturalism who are critics of the liberal tradition, such as Nancy Fraser (1997), Iris Young (2000), and Seyla Benhabib (2002). The scholarship is full of ominous warnings about the problems and paradoxes of 'identity politics' and 'recognition'. These include concerns that allowing identity to play a role in politics can lead to cultural essentialism and ethnocentricism, that minorities will manipulate identity for strategic gain, that an identity-sensitive politics facilitates the assimilation of minorities, and that identity politics heightens social conflict. The main message of this literature is that, wherever possible, institutions should avoid assessing cultural or religious conflicts in terms of claims made by minority groups about what is at stake for their identities.

To some extent, I am sympathetic with the suspicions these scholars have about the very idea of public officials basing their decisions on what they discover about a group's identity. What counts as identity is notoriously ambiguous and the history of public officials interpreting minority identity is not a happy one, especially for minorities who have faced officials who refuse to recognize their practices as falling within the ambit of 'religious' ones (see, e.g., Henderson 1999; McLaren 1999; Beaman 2002; and Adhar 2003), or who decide that their communities are not, properly speaking, 'societies' that merit protection (see Asch 2000). But I have become convinced that claims which are made for resources, entitlements, power, or opportunities on the basis of what is important to a group's identity, that is, to its self-understanding and distinctive way of life, have a legitimate place in public decision making and that public institutions need better guidance to assess such claims fairly.

In part, what has convinced me is that often avoiding identity claims magnifies the problems minorities face or forces them to engage in higher stakes political activity and higher risk decision making. The strategies proposed by political theorists to avoid identity are sometimes unsuccessful because identity-related values already inform the normative principles which are used to settle disputes. Despite their claims to treat everyone with equal consideration, public institutions tend to privilege dominant groups. This is the main message behind the 'politics of difference', particularly as Iris Young (1990) and James Tully (1995) have developed the idea, and one with which I largely agree. The unjust exclusion of ethnic minorities, Indigenous peoples, women, workers, and other groups has given rise to institutional biases against these groups. Institutional bias is also an inevitable result of the way in which political institutions, processes, and even concepts have developed historically in particular places. Without a transparent and fair set of criteria to guide public assessments of identity claims, public decision making runs the risk of perpetuating institutional bias as minority claims continue to be assessed according to the stereotypes that inform the cultural values and knowledge of dominant majorities. Without a fair and transparent guide, public institutions risk perpetuating a narrow and blinkered view of human rights and other important entitlements.

To recognize the historical particularities that shape how abstract principles and entitlements are translated and thereby come to have meaning within a context is not the same as holding that normative principles and entitlements are relative to cultural context or that historical context taints their value. Rather, it is to make a claim that context matters because context sets the parameters of practical debates about the sort of considerations which are central to a norm and the kinds of problems that strain a norm or fall outside its meaning. Context shapes how an abstract normative principle is applied in concrete circumstances and therefore when it seems not to fit a situation. For example, what counts as freedom of speech in Canada is partly the result of a limited though nonetheless rich set of conflicts and debates between different groups in Canada and, before that, in Britain and France. Over time, these debates have given the abstract entitlement to 'free speech' a tangible form which, in some ways, is different from its form in other places. A similar observation can be made about what counts as freedom of speech in Germany or in Denmark. The practical instantiation of abstract rights is shaped by particular and, along some important dimensions, different kinds of debates and historical struggles between certain groups and not others, where, as it turns out, different acts may count as protected in each of these contexts and different policies emerge to protect this freedom. To observe that actual public institutions, values, and entitlements differ in this sense is simply to recognize a basic characteristic of the political reality in which abstract principles are translated into determinant and meaningful policies and protections.

A general aim which motivates much of this project is to understand how abstract normative principles and entitlements, which can have an impact on matters important to people's identities, have been interpreted and shaped by the historical struggles, interests, and values of dominant groups, and as a result have given rise to group inequality, including specific forms of colonialism, sexism, racism, and religious discrimination. This concern took shape initially in thinking about what counts as an 'individual right' as opposed to a 'collective right' in Canada where it seemed to me that these concepts were being used to obscure rather than clarify relations between national groups. In the 1990s, it was common in Canada for the strained relations between the majority and national minorities to be expressed in terms of a tension between individual and collective rights and values. Many elites from English, French, and Indigenous communities seemed to agree that the tension between individualism and collectivism mapped nicely onto the main tensions between Canada's French and Indigenous national minorities, which were viewed as more collectivist, and the Anglophone majority, which was seen as more individualistic. Political leaders joined forces at the time to rectify the situation by proposing to amend the Constitution so that it explicitly recognized the existence of both individual and collective rights.[1]

But the real issue in this debate had less to do with any actual tension between individualism and collectivism than with the different priorities of communities which found themselves in very different circumstances. The minority communities seemed to favour so-called collective rights, not because they were more authentically collectivist than the majority, but rather because their ways of life were less secure and they were more worried about the survival of their language and culture. No one rejected the value of a person's freedom. But the communities differed significantly in enjoying the conditions necessary to secure this value and to participate in shaping how it is publicly understood. The majority seemed more individualist only because it could secure all sorts of collective goods, such as language, recognition as a distinct society, and protection of cherished practices, just by being a democratic majority. Moreover, and beyond these observations, my analysis led me to rethink the work that the 'individual versus collective' framework was doing in the debates. The framework emphasized differences in values that were not really there. In some ways, Indigenous communities are profoundly individualistic and in other ways, the English majority has strong collectivist values – what Canadians have called 'a tory touch'. Moreover, the framework implicitly suggested that the reason why these national minorities were disadvantaged in Canada is that they were collectivists while the majority was individualists. Especially striking in relation to Indigenous peoples, the framework rendered what was in many ways a brutal history of colonial domination into a benign problem of difference between the abstract values of different cultural groups (see Eisenberg 1994).

The framework that was widely adopted by scholars of Canadian politics in the 1980s and 1990s exaggerated some differences in values but then failed to capture others. A better framework, it seemed to me, would put the abstract claims about collectivism and individualism aside at least long enough to deal with the concrete claims of each group.[2] The point is not to give up on individual rights or simply to embrace so-called collectivism but to recognize that rights are notoriously abstract entitlements, which often suggest vague mandates, whose meaning depends on how they are interpreted in concrete circumstances. If interpretations of rights continue to be shaped by the preoccupations of an exclusive set of dominant groups and are then imposed on others, or if rights only reflect the preoccupations that arise from one particular and unjust set of power relations, they will be rejected, despite their value, by those who have been excluded or mistreated. So, in order to address concrete issues in a productive and respectful fashion, Canada needed to address directly and honestly the identity claims advanced by national minorities and to resist reformulating the conflict in more abstract terms.

The second concern that persuaded me that identity plays an important role in normative approaches to minority rights is the absence of a convincing response to the growing public anxiety and political backlash against multiculturalism. Ironically, with the global diffusion of multicultural principles as a means of responding to minority rights, the legitimacy of multicultural policies is increasingly drawn into question. Poor integration, cultural enclavism, and sexual discrimination are amongst the leading social ills attributed to multicultural policies. For instance, in the aftermath of the 2005 bombing of the London transport system, British multiculturalism was accused of heightening cultural differences in a manner that contributed to the tragedy. Along similar lines, many critics have argued that sexual discrimination is an inevitable consequence of multiculturalism.[3] Here, the concern is that, if all cultures are patriarchal, then efforts to protect any of them amount to protecting male privilege. The most provocative critics have described multiculturalism as a form of 'legal apartheid' for the vulnerable (Bruckner 2007). But even amongst moderates, cultural accommodation is portrayed as a social barrier for women. The burka remains a magnet for criticism in the Netherlands, France, Britain, and Canada for impeding integration by preventing open communication and controlling women. The 2004 murder of Theo Van Gogh, motivated by his films depicting Islam as sexist, led the Dutch Parliament to pursue an aggressive integrationist agenda towards minorities (see Phillips 2007: 6–8). In 2007, Quebec appointed a Public Commission on Reasonable Accommodation after small towns north of Montreal passed municipal codes, one of which informed immigrants that women and girls may not be stoned, burned, or circumcized in the town (see Bouchard and Taylor 2008). Cultural enclavism and sexual discrimination are especially well publicized in relation to Muslim minorities, and this gives rise to criticisms that multiculturalism contributes to Islamophobia and other forms of racism which further isolate minorities from mainstream institutions.

The main responses to the multicultural backlash have not been reassuring. Defenders of liberal multiculturalism respond by reminding people that multiculturalism is not a panacea for all social ills and that the only defensible versions of multiculturalism are those that uphold liberalism and individual rights. Liberals argue that multiculturalism cannot be used to justify sexual discrimination or any other denial of individual rights because, when properly understood, it is 'a natural extension of [the] liberal logic of individual rights, freedom of choice and non-discrimination' (Kymlicka 2005: 2). But this response begs the question at the centre of many multicultural debates. Most conflicts, including those over dress codes, religious arbitration, freedom of the press, parental authority, the sacramental use of narcotics, medical intervention, building codes, Indigenous rights to whale, fish, or hunt, to mention just a few, often raise questions about whether a disputed cultural tradition or value, in fact, denies to people the kinds of values that rights are meant to protect. Sometimes religious and cultural practices, which are viewed by mainstream communities as problematic, can just as easily be interpreted to be consistent with 'the logic of individual rights, freedom of choice, and non-discrimination' as many mainstream practices can. To be sure, better and worse solutions exist to conflicts involving disputed practices. But the distinction between better and worse does not arise merely by invoking the logic of individual rights. People disagree about what fidelity to rights requires and how to interpret abstract commitments such as freedom and equality, which inform rights. The parameters of their disagreements are not always limited by the values typically debated amongst Western mainstream liberals. But, even within the parameters of mainstream debate, disagreement exists. People disagree about when parental authority goes too far, when speech is hateful, when voluntary behaviour should be restricted, what status animals ought to have vis-à-vis human beings, what is cruel, consensual, or neglectful. Often conflicts arise, not because a discrepancy exists between a minority practice and the 'liberal logic of individual rights', but rather because a discrepancy exists between a minority practice and the mainstream's interpretation of what freedom allows or requires in a particular case. To point to the logic of rights only underlines what one set of participants views the debates to be about. This tells us little about the diversity of interpretations that inform conflicts and nothing about how to solve them.

A second unsatisfactory response blames the growing public anxiety about multiculturalism on the misuse and abuse of the concept 'culture'. Culture is a notoriously ambiguous concept. What is considered 'cultural' is, as some suggest, 'cultural', as is the current infatuation with the political importance of culture (Scott 2003). Moreover, the concept of culture is often used to explain too much and ends up overemphasizing and reinforcing differences between bounded groups (Dhamoon 2007), explaining away 'bad behavior' like criminal conduct (Volpp 2000), nurturing stereotypes (Phillips 2007), and underemphasizing the overlapping and fluid nature of most groups thereby denying the 'hybridity' of people (Benhabib 2002). The current scholarship in political theory recounts many disputes involving minorities where culture is used and abused. It is unsurprising then that most attempts by public institutions to define or assess cultures are destined to be controversial.

Rather than confronting these problems, the critics of culture often argue that the public anxiety about multiculturalism is the result of an incoherent set of commitments by liberal-democratic states. They claim that, on one hand, multiculturalism presents itself to anxious members of the public as a form of relativism whose advocates are willing to accommodate all sorts of group differences simply because they are important to someone's culture. On the other hand, countries which have adopted multiculturalism as official policy, for example, Canada, the Netherlands, and Britain, impose strict and, in the context of this view, seemingly arbitrary limits on accommodating group differences and thereby appear to fail to live up to their multicultural commitments. In some circles, multiculturalism is thereby interpreted as a scam of sorts, that is, as a means to alleviate guilt and shame about how minorities have been treated while garnering the power of dominant groups (Povinelli 1998; Markell 2003), as a marketing ploy to entice a cheap labour force of immigrants (Day 2000; Abu-Laban and Gabriel 2002), and as a smokescreen to divert attention from problems which are more difficult to solve like poverty, racism, and imperialism (Gitlin 1995; Žižek 1997; Bannerji 2000).

I have considerable sympathy with the concern that multicultural commitments are in some ways disconnected from the reality of how minorities are treated in states committed to multicultural principles, but less sympathy for the suggestion that multiculturalism is irrevocably a means to shore up the power of dominant groups. There is no denying that what counts as culture is often ambiguous and that the state has a hand in shaping cultural identity, just as it has a hand in shaping identities based on race, class, nationality, and gender. The question though is how should democratic institutions respond to claims advanced by minority groups for rights, resources, powers, or opportunities when these claims are based on something distinctive and important about the group's identity? Many critical positions taken against multiculturalism are paralysing because they suggest that *any* public policy which takes seriously the cultural practices or values of minorities will essentialize, 'domesticate', or 'manage' cultural minorities in the interests of majority groups. Others which are strident in their criticisms of multiculturalism, propose solutions that give rise to some of the same questions that multiculturalism hopes to resolve, such as whether policies which favour individual rights, voluntarism, agency, and consent are able to bear the weight of the collective and communal commitments that groups advance as identity claims and which they argue are central to their well being. Even amongst the staunchest critics, who argue that multiculturalism lends itself to reinforcing racism and neo-imperialism within western societies, few suggest that efforts to ensure cultural equality ought to be abandoned entirely. Instead, they either argue that such efforts are hopeless or they propose solutions which ask that we live up to a particular version of multiculturalism that addresses problems of social injustice.

This book offers a third response to the crisis in multiculturalism. A largely unanticipated consequence of the normative theory and political commitments associated with multiculturalism over the last twenty-five years is a dramatic increase in the number of claims that minority groups make in order to secure protection or accommodation for aspects of their cultural, religious, indigenous, or other identities. These identity claims are not entirely new. Rather, what is new is the number of claims, the opportunities to make such claims, and the publicity they get. Multiculturalism has invigorated identity claiming both in the sense that it has mobilized groups to advance claims by framing them in terms of their identity and in the sense that it has motivated governments to increase the number of venues, that is, the laws, institutions, protocols, conventions, and procedures by which these claims can be heard and assessed. At the same time, multiculturalism has heightened a general public awareness of how these kinds of claims are interpreted and of problems associated with relying on elite and hegemonic public institutions to interpret them. As mentioned earlier, there is nothing particularly new about the fact that public institutions assess identity claims. Such assessments have been an aspect of public decision making for a long time and many approaches taken by institutions to assessing identity claims have been shaped by some of the same concerns raised by critics today. But, the dramatic increase in identity claiming and the heightened awareness of how identity claims are being interpreted (and by whom) means that this kind of decision making is, understandably and properly, the subject of intense scrutiny. Unsurprisingly, it is sometimes found wanting.

The general aim of this book is to develop a set of fair and transparent normative criteria to help guide the resolution of conflicts informed by identity claims. One of my initial objectives is to show that identity claims are frequently assessed by public institutions, though not always in a transparent or fair manner. Societies that protect minority rights cannot avoid interpreting, assessing, and thereby 'reasoning about' minority identity. In fact, coming to grips with the kinds of values and practices which are important to the identity of a particular minority group is often a way to draw majority norms into question, to tackle stereotypes, and to arrest the tendency of hegemonic groups to over- or under-interpret identity-related differences. Conversely, attempts to avoid the assessment of identity, several of which are surveyed in this book, often distort minority claims by translating issues which are presented in the first instance as matters concerning the significance of a claim to a person's identity into an abstract discourse with a more established pedigree in normative political theory, such as rights discourse, discourses about democratic proceduralism, or the more specific and specialized tests used within legal culture and by courts. The argument here is not that rights, democratic procedures, or legal tests are unhelpful to sorting out disputes which involve minority claims. Rather, the problem is that often these discourses are informed by implicit and unfounded assumptions about what is of value or important to the identities of those advancing claims.

One result of the rise in identity claiming by minority groups over the last twenty-five years, and the cause of much public anxiety, is the discovery that widely used public discourses by which disputes have been conventionally settled are biased either because they purposively exclude and disadvantage some groups, or for the more benign and inevitable reason that they have been shaped by the preoccupations of majority groups in light of a limited number of historical, cultural, and religious experiences and values. Structural and institutional bias in public discourse has been uncovered thanks in part to the mobilization of minority groups and the rise in identity claiming that has followed multicultural policies. But the promise of multiculturalism is unfulfilled in practice if public institutions lack the capacity to assess identity claims fairly. The best response to the backlash against multiculturalism is not now to extract identity from decision-making discourses. In fact, doing so will worsen the problems of institutional bias that decision makers mean to avoid. Rather, good public decision making in democratic societies committed to equality and diversity relies on decision makers who have access to fair and transparent criteria by which to assess identity claims and to reassess the existing apparatus of public decision making to ensure that it reflects a fair-minded approach to the claims of different peoples and their ways of life.

In addition to these general considerations, three more specific reasons ground the need to develop criteria by which identity claims can be assessed in the public sphere. The first reason has to do with what respect for people requires of public institutions. When public institutions have the capacity to consider identity claims fairly as one kind of reason for distributing opportunities, entitlements, and resources one way rather than another, they show respect for the people advancing such claims by acknowledging the *prima facie* validity of the ways of life developed by communities to distinguish themselves and to survive. Communities develop practices to ensure their survival and continuity in light of the circumstances they have confronted, sometimes including their conflicts with dominant groups and the state. These practices are often seen by communities to reflect their distinctive relation to important values, their ingenuity in the face of adversity, and their commitment to secure their way of life into the future. Minority practices are often viewed by their members, sometimes even members who do not partake in the practices, as a reminder of what their communities have done to protect a distinctive way of life. Public institutions need the capacity to acknowledge not only the value of these distinctive ways of life and the practices which help to sustain them, but also the circumstances under which these ways of life will be jeopardized by public decisions that conflict with them.

The second reason to develop criteria by which to assess identity claims is to engender institutional humility about the fairness of public practices and values of decision making. Identity claims advanced by minority groups often provide a perspective from which to reveal bias, inequality, and even oppression that masquerades as fair principles which are purported by some to be neutral when it comes to religious, ethnic, gendered, or racialized differences. We ought to be sceptical about the neutrality of any political institution along these lines because, like legal entitlements and political values, institutions have been shaped by the experiences and interpretations of dominant groups.[4] Majority identity is already politically significant within public decision making. To develop criteria by which to assess when identity claims legitimize entitlements is to inculcate in public decision making a practical and healthy scepticism towards the neutrality of public institutions and thereby to check majority arrogance about the fairness of long-standing practices, institutions, and ways of interpreting values. The point of institutional humility is to reveal and respond to inequality in the access that majorities and minorities have to participate in shaping public institutions and in how they are treated by these institutions.

The third reason to develop criteria by which to assess identity claims is pragmatic. Identity is a powerful mobilizer. It resonates with people. People understandably care about how the distribution of resources and entitlements bears on their community's survival or its capacity to sustain practices central to its identity. But identity is also an ambiguous and fluid sort of thing. Many different interests can be advanced as identity claims. Therefore, a tendency exists today for identity claims to proliferate in the public sphere. Groups will often choose to publicize their claims as identity claims. Institutions could refuse to hear their claims or require claimants to frame their claims in terms other than identity. They could treat claimants as though they are suffering from false consciousness and explain to them that their identities are constructed, contingent, and more flexible than they might suppose. But, on one hand, there is no guarantee that doing so will thereby eliminate substantive assessments of a minority's identity in more covert ways. And, on the other hand, there is still the pragmatic problem, namely, how should public institutions respond to laws and policies that currently invite groups to argue their cases in terms of how an aspect of their identity generates a claim to distribute resources, entitlements, power, or opportunities one way rather than another. Identity is not the only nor, in many circumstances, the best way to advance the claims of vulnerable minorities. Nonetheless, what is needed is an approach that responds to the identity claims groups advance in a manner that can be applied by actual institutions.

The position developed in this book aims at reanimating basic normative values like equality and freedom in relation to the legitimate identity claims made by minority groups. This does not mean that every minority group can legitimately require that its own understanding of equality or freedom is honoured by public institutions. Rather, it means that when public institutions render decisions that restrict group practices, they do so for reasons that are transparent, that appear fair to a diversity of peoples, that substantively assess what is at stake for a group's identity, and that consider what is at stake for different groups and individuals who might also be involved in particular conflicts.

In the context of contemporary political theory, this goal attracts criticism from all corners. The critics of identity claiming fear that direct engagement with such claims will impair everything from political analysis to political compromise. Identity politics is said to give rise to a plethora of incommensurable claims that tax democratic institutions. Identity-based analysis is charged with obscuring racism and excusing sexism. It is said to license biased or arbitrary decision making which places the very integrity of people within the ambit of political contestation and thereby raises the stakes of deliberation. Identity claiming is also accused of covertly assimilating and domesticating Indigenous peoples and of trading in essentialist notions. In short, the critics worry that a politics which highlights identity claims is risky and dangerous.

The challenge I take on in this book is to explain how the considerable benefits of identity claiming, namely, respect, institutional humility, and pragmatism, can be realized while steering clear of the dangers emphasized by different critics. Public decision makers need to examine on a continuous basis how particular and exclusive values shape abstract principles and political institutions in ways that treat minority groups unfairly. They can only do this effectively by directly addressing the challenges and risks of doing so.

This book examines how public institutions actually assess identity claims and how they might do so in a manner that is transparent, reasonable, and fair while meeting the challenges posed by doing so in contemporary politics. I begin, in Chapter 2, by assessing what an identity claim is and outlining an approach, consisting of three conditions, by which identity claims can be publicly assessed. In general, the approach suggests that identity claims should be vindicated if compelling evidence exists that (1) important and otherwise unrealizable dimensions of a group's or individual's identity will be severely jeopardized in the absence of granting the claim; (2) the practice is suitably validated through legitimate processes internal to the community and, where relevant, between communities; and (3) the claim, if protected, will not place people at risk of serious harm. I call these the jeopardy condition, the validation condition, and the safeguard condition, respectively.

Chapter 3 identifies two broad theoretical responses to identity claiming that provide important challenges to my approach. I label these responses 'identity quietism' and 'identity scepticism'. Although they offer different analyses of the terrain on which identity claiming takes place, both favour forms of politics that avoid direct engagement with identity claims. Quietists defend the normative commitments of multiculturalism while maintaining that issues concerning the accommodation of cultural minorities can be settled without actually examining the claims advanced by minorities about their identity. I argue that identity quietism often fails and that, despite their official disavowal of identity claiming, defenders of multiculturalism implicitly invoke identity considerations to understand how conflicts ought to be settled. I illustrate the failure of quietists by examining the debates over religious arbitration in Canada. Identity sceptics are more successful at avoiding identity but they do so by rejecting the normative commitments of multiculturalism. Their wholesale scepticism towards the possibility of assessing identity claims fairly is unfounded. Nonetheless, identity sceptics pose four interesting challenges to identity claiming.

I take up these challenges in Chapters 4 through 6 and explain how they can be answered and therefore, how the general approach to identity assessments I develop can be vindicated. Chapter 4 looks at whether identity claims cause a proliferation of incommensurable claims as some critics worry. I examine the 'challenge of incommensurability' in relation to conflicts between claims to gender equality and claims of vulnerable communities to protect their sexist practices. Chapter 5 examines the role of authenticity as displayed in the need to distinguish between 'genuine' and 'fraudulent' identity claims which is one of the chief concerns raised in the context of cases about freedom of religion. Chapter 6 takes on the challenge posed by essentialism which is often considered endemic to identity politics. It also examines whether a method of decision making which assesses the claims of minorities in relation to their identity will disempower or 'domesticate' groups that are already vulnerable. These two challenges, essentialism and domestication, are explored in relation to approaches adopted nationally and internationally to assess identity claims advanced by Indigenous peoples.

This book draws upon resources from both normative political theory and from the actual practices of institutions within the public arena in developing criteria for the assessment of identity claims and identifying the challenges that such an approach faces. 'The public arena' refers to public debate and decision making that takes place primarily through political institutions such as legislatures, legal institutions such as courts, judicial commissions, and human rights tribunals, and institutions of public deliberation and debate such as news and media outlets. The approach that I outline is, admittedly, better suited to institutions where public decision makers, such as judges, can ensure the three conditions of jeopardy, validation, and safeguard are fairly and accurately applied. But the intention here is to design an approach which can be more broadly applied. It is concerned with what public institutions, in general, can do in democratic contexts to ensure that different peoples are treated fairly and have an equal role in shaping how public institutions work. Regarding identity, the overall analysis is informed by two questions. First, when is it appropriate to allocate resources, entitlements, power, or opportunities one way rather than another on the basis of something distinctive and important to an individual's or group's identity, that is, to its self-understanding and distinctive way of life? Second, how should such claims be assessed? The basic point I make here is not that identity claims are always the best way for minorities to advance claims for resources or entitlements, nor that such claims should have more power than claims which rest on other forms of injustice. Rather, I wish to show that identity claims have a legitimate role to play in public decision making and ought to be taken seriously in order to show respect for persons, to instantiate humility in majority-dominated public institutions (and thereby change them), and to respond to the current climate of claiming.

Public institutions provide a rich yet imperfect source of practical guidance for understanding how identity is used and assessed as a basis for claims made by minorities. They rarely accept the force of minority identity claims at face value. Nor do they usually treat identity claims as beyond the pale of public interpretation and deliberation. Instead, they often take identity seriously. This observation is meant less as a defence of the current practices of public institutions than as an observation about the complexity of the task at hand. Even though public institutions have a wealth of experience in addressing identity claims directly, much of this experience has not been the subject of sustained scholarly attention in normative political theory. This study is meant to address this gap and in the course of doing so to provide some guidance as to the benefits, drawbacks, and possibility of the public assessment of identity claims.

2

The Identity Approach: Public Decision Making in Diverse Societies

In the previous chapter, I identified three reasons why identity ought to be considered a legitimate basis to advance claims for entitlements, resources, and opportunities. The first reason is to ensure that institutions treat people with different identities respectfully. Institutions which have the capacity to take seriously, listen attentively to, and consider the merits of identity claims are better able to show respect for the people advancing these claims. The second reason is to engender a sense of institutional humility about the fairness of public practices, values, and processes of decision making. Identity claims advanced by minority groups often provide a perspective from which to reveal bias, inequality, and partiality that masquerade as fair decisions and neutral principles. Institutions with the capacity to assess when identity claims legitimize entitlements are better able to detect errors in their previous decisions or bias in decision-making procedures. These two reasons ground the moral force of identity claims. A third reason why identity ought to be considered a legitimate basis to advance claims for entitlements is that identity claims are increasingly ubiquitous in the public sphere and so a pragmatic need arises to develop institutions able to respond to them fairly.

This chapter elaborates on these reasons and then provides an overview of the theoretical framework for interpreting and assessing identity claims developed in this book. It examines the meaning and ambiguities of identity in political and scholarly debates, and the widely held position that identity and identity claims have no moral force. Most normative political theorists argue that because identity claims are ambiguous, socially constructed, and socially reified, they either ought to be treated like other interests and compete for resources in the political sphere (rather than being the basis for legal entitlements) or they should be considered a form of evidence of group oppression or unjust exclusion from the political community (but, again, not as a basis for an entitlement to protection for a specific practice or activity related to identity). Here, both of these positions are shown to be unsatisfactory. The position I develop, which I call the identity approach, maintains that identity claims sometimes have moral force in democratic politics and requires that just institutions are designed with the capacity to assess these claims fairly.

THE UBIQUITY OF IDENTITY POLITICS

The current legal and political context is perhaps more congenial than ever to considering claims for the protection of groups on the basis of identity. In the last twenty years, institutions, declarations, and conventions have emerged at the national and international levels, and many existing ones have been reformed to address claims for the protection of cultural, religious, and linguistic identity. We find these commitments written into the *Charter of Fundamental Rights of the European Union* (2000),[1] *The Draft Declaration on the Rights of Indigenous Peoples* (1994),[2] the *International Labour Organization Convention No. 169* (1989),[3] the *UN Convention on the Rights of the Child* (1990),[4] as well as the *Declaration on the Rights of Persons Belonging to National or Ethnic, Religious and Linguistic Minorities* (1992),[5] to name a few. Similar trends are evident at the state level where national and linguistic minorities have convinced many governments to pass laws and amend constitutions in ways that offer symbolic as well as more substantive recognition to minorities.[6]

Where laws or constitutions do not explicitly entrench protection for culture, indigeneity, or other aspects of 'identity', minority groups often advance claims for such protection by arguing that their other basic rights are not adequately protected unless some specific aspect of their way of life is legally or politically accommodated. In some cases, groups have mobilized national and international campaigns to ensure that their identity is considered in the context of public decision making about, for example, property rights, museum exhibits, banking regulations, the regulation of drugs or food, and myriad of other concerns. For instance, in Britain, the Netherlands, Denmark, and Spain, religious minorities seek to ensure that religious identity is accommodated in setting European-wide standards about animal cruelty and slaughter, intellectual property, and genomics research. Some of the strongest campaigns to put identity on the table occur in the context of economic trade agreements like the North American Free Trade Agreement, where the protection of cultural and national identities remains an issue of contention between the signatories (see Bernier 2005; also see Van den Bossche and Dahrendorf 2006). Identity is also relevant to the standards used to settle trade disputes. For instance, the World Trade Organization has come under pressure from member states to modify its criteria for assessing food-related disputes to include considerations of identity, not just food safety, in light of controversies surrounding genetically modified foods, artificial growth hormones in animals, and the export of raw milk cheeses (Brom 2004). Efforts to regulate the dissemination of genetically modified foods have been framed in Mexico, for example, in relation to the protection of the identities of Indigenous peoples whose campaigns to protect wild corn strains raise the question of whether food safety can be interpreted to include assurances that trade and production do not jeopardize crops which are integral to a way of life (Stabinsky 2002; Lopez 2008).[7] More broadly, Indigenous groups throughout the world seek assurances that market forces can be regulated so as not to jeopardize resources or activities which are crucial to their identities. And often they want these assurances written into legal regulations, constitutions, and international conventions.

The response of public institutions to these claims, unsurprisingly, is not always satisfactory. But, contrary to recurrent concerns expressed in normative political theory, public institutions rarely simply accept at face value claims that are made on the basis of identity. Rather, institutions grapple, sometimes in complex and sophisticated ways, with the challenges these claims present. In some cases, they develop formal legal tests such as the 'compelling interest test' used in the United States to assess religious claims, or the 'distinctive culture test' used in Canada to assess some of the claims made by Indigenous peoples for constitutional rights. In other cases, less explicit and transparent criteria are used. For instance, the United Nations Human Rights Committee has assessed claims made under Article 27 of the International Covenant on Civil and Political Rights in terms of whether a claim is important to a group's cultural survival. In cases about religious freedom, Canadian courts use the assessment of 'individual sincerity of belief' to establish the importance of a practice to religious identity. These are all highly contentious features of decision making in the area of minority rights and identity politics. It is naïve to suppose that their contentiousness is lost on public decision makers. Legal and political debates often reflect considerable awareness of the problems that arise in making decisions of this sort. Public records reflect that judges critically examine the standards they employ for establishing the veracity of claims, that appointed or elected officials are wary of excluding or privileging particular perspectives, and both are aware of employing biased rules of evidence, imposing arbitrary historical standards, and applying unfair criteria about who counts as a spokesperson for a group.

Nonetheless, it is easy to be critical of how institutions respond to claims of ethnic, religious, and Indigenous minorities because, in many cases, evidence suggests that they have applied biased and confused standards or standards that reflect their own instrumental interests. It is likely that courts at every level, in every state, have applied unreasonable or unfair criteria, at one time or another, to assess the claims of minority groups, and numerous examples exist in which judicial interpretations and political assessments of identity are informed by ethnic bias and stereotypes. What is by now a very large literature in political theory describes some of the most infamous policies and cases to illustrate these failures.[8] These cases illustrate the problems with interpreting and assessing identity claims and frequently are used to argue that the best response to the recent upsurge in identity claiming is to discourage it wherever possible.[9]

Despite the fact that identity claims are ubiquitous in pluralist societies, scepticism surrounds these claims because they are supposed to be too ambiguous and easily manipulated to serve as a basis for minority entitlements or legitimate grounds for distributing resources one way rather than another. These concerns are worth taking seriously. But, none points to the *prima facie* need to abandon all consideration of identity claims. Rather, the concerns often raised show that, in ethnically and religiously diverse societies, judges, legislators, social workers, police, and many other practitioners and pubic decision makers need fair guidelines and structured decision making to respond to clients and claims from minority groups.[10] The concerns often raised in practical contexts of decision making confirm that the assessments of minority identity claims are not always successful or useful and that guidelines are either absent or unsatisfactory. These failures indicate the need to understand more precisely what is important about these claims, how they ought to be weighed against other claims, and under what circumstances they establish entitlements.

WHAT IS IDENTITY?

The term 'identity' refers to the attachments that people have to particular communities, ways of life, sets of beliefs, or practices that play a central role in their self-conception or self-understanding. When people claim that a practice, a place, or an activity is important to their identity, they usually mean that it reflects something important about their sense of who they are or that they cannot realize something important about themselves without access to it. When they claim that an ascriptive characteristic, such as their race, gender, or ethnicity, is central to their identity, they mean that they understand themselves partly in terms of this characteristic.

Even ascriptive aspects of identity, such as gender, ethnicity, or race, have important non-ascriptive dimensions in the sense that people may not identify with features of what, in any given social context, their relation to a group is typically understood by others to entail. People often do not follow what Anthony Appiah calls the 'scripts' of the collective identities that structure possible narratives of their individual self (2005: 23). Or they make of these scripts what they wish and bind themselves to groups in ways that are, at the same time, of their own making and difficult to change without causing real damage to themselves. Stuart Hall uses the metaphor of a 'suture' between the psychic and discursive to describe this aspect of identity (1996: 16). Amartya Sen (2006) makes a similar point when he argues that identities are not prior to one's capacity to reason but instead present people with choices that engage their capacity to reason.

Partly because the substantive content and value of a collective identity vary from one individual to the next, many people argue that identity is an unreliable basis for legal and political entitlements. This is one of the key concerns of Rogers Brubaker and Frederick Cooper, who urge political analysts to move 'beyond identity' partly because identity 'tends to mean too much . . . too little . . . or nothing at all' (2000: 1). The abstract nature of identity is repeatedly mentioned in contemporary debates and across several scholarly disciplines, to confirm its political elusiveness. Sociologists and anthropologists have argued that identity should be treated as a useful fiction, 'a sort of virtual center to which we must refer to explain certain things, but without it ever having a real existence' (Claude Lévi-Strauss in Lévi-Strauss (ed.), *L'identité*, p. 332, cited in Brubaker and Cooper 2000: 9), or as an idea 'without which certain key questions cannot be thought at all' (Hall 1996: 2).[11] In legal scholarship and even legal cases, identity and the related notion of culture, though frequently employed, are not employed consistently and are rarely defined.[12]

Despite this reputation for vagueness, identity is usually used to refer to the attachments and activities that are important to the 'self-conception' or 'self-understanding' of an individual or group. The relation between identity and respect for persons arises because identity refers to the distinctive way in which individuals or groups come to understand themselves in a social context. Identity is 'the background against which our tastes and desires and opinions and aspirations make sense' (Taylor 1994: 33–4). It is the answer to the question 'Who am I?' (p. 34). It refers to the ways in which social properties become embedded in a person's self-conception (Appiah 2005: 65), or crucial to their personality, including their citizenship, gender, ethnicity, language, religion, life projects, and ethical commitments (Copp 2002). Margaret Moore traces the connection between identity self-esteem and respect (2006: 27). Ingrid Creppell examines the mutual influence of tolerance and identity in the history of western political thought and describes identity as 'the relatively persistent but always permeable formation of the self that provides a basic orientation for human agency in acting collectively and individually within a social and political world' (2003: 8).[13]

Rather than viewing identity as definable, many of these scholars – for example, Appiah, Copp, Moore, and Creppell – recognize that some components of identity have ethical status and generate normative commitments because of the close link between identity and self-esteem, integrity, respect, solidarity, and agency. Moore, for instance, argues that identity ought to be taken seriously in politics because of its integral relation to the self, to a person's core moral commitments, and to personal traits that are ascriptive and therefore beyond choice (2006: 29). Appiah is more cautious about using identities to generate entitlements but, nonetheless, he recognizes their importance in providing people with patterns by which to make sense of and organize their lives and by helping people to realize values through a collective sense of themselves (2005: 21–5). Most of these scholars agree that identity is connected to the core moral commitments and patterns of interaction by which individuals orient themselves in the social world. But most of them also contend that identity is too variable, changing, and hybrid to be directly assessed by public institutions or considered the basis for political and legal entitlements.

One means of avoiding some of the ambiguities related to the term 'identity', or at least narrowing the scope of the ambiguities, is to focus on culture and cultural rights. Here, identity is preferred to the concept of 'culture' because the term 'identity' covers more ground in the sense that it can refer to religious, linguistic, gendered, Indigenous, and other dimensions of self-understanding.

Another means of skirting some of these ambiguities is to focus on 'identification' rather than 'identity'. Brubaker and Cooper prefer 'identification' to 'identity' because, they claim, identification highlights the measurable, active, and changeable processes related to self-understanding while avoiding the reification of social categories which occurs when political analysts and activists activate groupness through their use of the term 'identity'. Their concern is that analysts reify groups by suggesting that they have particular identities and thereby treat similar characteristics as coherent, enduring, and foundational aspects of selfhood rather than 'contingently activated in differing contexts' (Brubaker and Cooper 2000: 8). 'Identification' avoids this reification by indicating that only through active identification do identities become significant within political analysis.

In my analysis, the term 'identity' is preferred to 'identification' because identification avoids too many of the complexities which are genuine features of identity politics. The concept of 'identification' gestures towards a normative preference in favour of processes in which individuals are actively engaged. But what it obscures about the conflicted relation between individuals and groups is just as relevant to political analysis even though more difficult to assess. For instance, some people actively defend their practices because they are important to their way of life while others defend the practices of communities to which they are distantly associated even though they have no interest in actively participating in these practices, and still others follow practices like habits, without intentionally 'identifying' with a way of life. Even if there are good ethical reasons to favour the ways that individuals identify with their practices, communities, or ascriptive characteristics, these reasons do not flow from methodological premises about what counts as significant political phenomena related to identity. Identification is an important part of the story, but it is not an adequate substitute for identity.

Many of the contradictions that are supposed to arise in relation to the use of the concept of identity are due to the complexity of the phenomena in question rather than the misuse of the term. To start with, identity applies to both individuals and groups. It is sometimes used to indicate sameness across persons in groups and sometimes to point to the individual's sense of selfhood. This might appear to be a contradictory use of the term 'identity' (as Brubaker and Cooper suggest), but it also accurately reflects one of the key tensions that arises in liberal-democratic politics between individuals and groups. Identity is used not only to refer to the development of collective self-understanding (group identity), but also to refer to the fragmented self 'patched together through shards of discourse' (individual identity) (2000: 8). Again, this is less a contradictory use of the term than an observation that individual selves and groups are fragmented in some ways (signifying the plurality or hybridity of groups), and united in other ways (signifying the individuals' unitary sense of self). Both individuals and groups might be described as unique or distinctive in some ways, although what makes an individual unique or distinctive differs from what makes a group distinctive. What protects individual distinctiveness might be different from what protects group distinctiveness.

What is especially important to this analysis is that both individuals and groups can advance claims for the protection of their identities. Identity claims are claims that entitlements, resources, or opportunities ought to be distributed one way rather than another because of something distinctive and important about the identity of the individual or group advancing the claim. Identity claims are generated by both individuals and groups, sometimes by groups against individuals, and sometimes by individuals against groups.

While both individuals and groups can advance identity claims, their claims tend to be distinctive along two dimensions. First, the identities of groups and individuals are threatened by different kinds of circumstances and, second, different kinds of legal and political resources are useful to protecting individual identity and group identities. In societies that aspire to be liberal, some individual identity claims are mediated through the language of rights. This does not mean that all rights aim to protect individual identity. But liberalism provides an especially rich set of normative resources to understand and elevate what is important to individual identity and how it might be protected. The sort of rights that protect individual identity include those which ensure that individuals have the opportunity to voice their specific opinions, through freedom of speech, to choose their own beliefs, through freedom and religion and conscience, and generally to be treated as equals while also being the authors of their own lives. A political community that values and protects individual identity is one that sets parameters to community decision making so that individuals can dissent and thereby lead their lives, as far as possible, according to their own self-conceptions. In this sense, the historical development of individual rights is one means by which liberal political traditions have attempted to understand and protect values which are integral to how individuals develop identities.

But some rights have nothing to do with protecting identity and, moreover, rights are not always the only or best means to protect identity claims. As mentioned in the previous chapter and explained in more detail in Chapter 4, rights can also distort conflicts involving identity or point to misleading solutions that lose sight of broader values related to how people want to live their lives. Rights are best viewed as one means by which aspects of individual and group identities may be effectively protected. As a means to protecting identity, liberal rights have helped to articulate, in clear and powerful terms, a set of values which is crucial to individual identity, namely that individuals sometimes need protection against community traditions and standards in order to protect their distinctiveness and the means by which they develop a healthy self-understanding. As liberals have argued, individuals should live their lives 'from the inside' and what this means, in part, is that they should shape their own identities. A political system that considers individual identity to be an appropriate basis upon which to advance a claim is one that attempts to ensure, through the distribution of entitlements, resources, and opportunities, that individuals are able to dissent from communities in order to develop their own self-understandings along a variety of dimensions considered especially important to sustaining individual identity.

Similarly, a political system that considers group identity to be an appropriate basis upon which to advance a claim is one that displays some awareness of the possibility that groups may be entitled to special protections, resources, or opportunities in order to ensure that certain crucial features of their identities can be sustained in contexts where a group's practices and self-understanding differ from some or all of the practices of the larger community. As with individual identity claims, some of the claims of groups might be expressed in terms of 'collective rights', but, again, it is important to recognize the limits of this terminology. While most so-called collective rights are related to sustaining some aspect of a group's identity, some group identity claims can be met without recognizing a collective right. For example, religious groups advance identity claims when they argue that the right to religious freedom extends to a religious practice which has not been previously recognized as falling within the scope of the right, on the basis that the practice is important to the group's religious identity. An Indigenous community advances an identity claim when claiming jurisdiction over a fishery or land use because of the importance to the community's identity of an endangered species of fish or a particular place. Sometimes, these claims can be described in terms of 'collective rights', sometimes not.

In one sense, all group claims boil down at some level to claims about individual identity. The distinction between individual and group identity does not rest on or imply that a metaphysical notion of 'group' stands above the individual and generates a separate and distinctive claim to protect group identity independently of individual claims. All normatively plausible claims generated by groups are claims made by individuals on behalf of a way of life that they value. In this sense, conflicts between claims made on behalf of individual and group identities are especially confusing when expressed in terms of a competition between individual and collective rights. But the distinction between individual and group identity claims is, nonetheless, important because it highlights that some entitlements, which are aimed at protecting values central to individual identity, will fail to protect groups. Some values that are central to an individual's identity depend on a collective feature of a distinctive group in the sense that they depend on interacting with others who share this feature or they depend on the security and flourishing of a particular cultural, religious, or linguistic community. For example, an individual's right to use a language is practically useless unless others (and usually many others) share the language and can practice it together. Similarly, some crucial religious practices depend on the presence of a group of believers (e.g. Minyans in Judaism or Spirit Dancing amongst the Coast Salish peoples). And many communities rely on membership rules which need to be collectively enforced and sometimes publicly recognized by those outside the group in order to work effectively.

The political or legal means available to respond to the identity claims of groups share with the identity claims of individuals the goals of enhancing individual well being and respecting agency. Yet, to focus only on individuals or to privilege legal and normative tools, such as rights, by which individuals can advance claims, obscures the group-based nature of many important claims and suitable protections. People face disadvantages which are structural and relational, rather than intentional and direct, and many of these disadvantages target group-based characteristics.[14] The approach developed here recognizes that individuals and communities generate claims based on their identities, but it does so without reducing group claims to individual claims or vice versa. The distinction between individual and group identities preserves the possibility that measures which are required to protect the identity of a group might differ from and even conflict with those which protect individual identity. Usually in such conflicts, the identity claims advanced by individuals are stronger, often because individuals have more at stake when aspects of their identities are threatened by groups. But in some circumstances, the identity claims advanced by groups might be stronger than the claims advanced by individuals and, in all cases, claims must be weighed against and compared to each other. In any case, the strength of a claim is assessed on the basis of criteria which together show what is at stake for the identities of those involved in conflicts rather than merely whether their claims fit into the pre-defined parameters of what counts as an individual or collective 'right'.

INTERPRETING THE NORMATIVE FORCE OF IDENTITY CLAIMS

Most people agree that identities are socially constructed in the sense that any practice, belief, or value which is viewed as part of an individual's or group's identity arises as a response or strategy devised by individuals or communities to organize their way of life and orient them in a social context, or to realize other important values connected to human agency, or the individual's sense of self. But people disagree about what conclusions ought to follow from this fact. Some scholars, Charles Taylor being amongst the most prominent, argue that identities are formed dialogically, that the recognition of identity is a vital human need, and that 'misrecognition' 'can inflict a grievous wound, saddling its victims with a crippling self-hatred' (1994: 26). Others argue that identity and the practices that contribute to identity have no moral status whatsoever because identity merely refers to what groups do, want, or believe rather than how they ought to act or what they ought to value (Barry 2001: ch. 7).[15]

The position here is that the institutional capacity to assess identity claims fairly is an important feature of the background conditions of a just society with fair institutions. This ideal of fairness depends on institutions that possess what I call 'institutional humility' which refers to the capacity of public decision makers to detect the errors of their decisions and the biases in their procedures caused by employing criteria that favour the identities, including the histories and values, of (usually) dominant groups over all others. It also requires that institutions treat the people advancing these claims with respect, which again requires that institutions have the capacity to assess identity claims fairly, because otherwise they will avoid these claims or translate them into terms which are more abstract and potentially distort their meaning for those who consider them most important. Public institutions which are designed with the capacity to assess identity claims are better able to display institutional humility and respect for people. The next section traces the relation between identity claiming, institutional humility, and respect for persons, by showing how two leading approaches to minority rights, both of which reject identity claims, thereby have a weak capacity to ensure that institutions are adequately designed to treat minorities fairly.

Fair background conditions and institutional humility

With few exceptions, normative political theorists who draw attention to the social construction of cultural and religious practices do so in order to argue that identity thereby has no independent moral force. Cultural forms are often considered unworthy of respect because, as James Johnson (2000) argues, they are morally arbitrary strategies devised by people to respond to their social circumstances. Johnson argues that people use symbolic forms of culture strategically to present the possibilities from which others are then invited to choose (p. 414). Whether or not these practices contribute to self-respect, self-esteem, equality, justice, individual autonomy, and the like, is an open question and, in any case, according to Johnson, a question that points to the instrumental rather than intrinsic value of identity claims. In a similar vein, Brian Barry (2001) responds to the current surge in identity claiming by arguing that the fact that some practice is important to a group's identity provides no justification whatsoever for supposing that it ought to continue to be practiced. What people do and what they ought to do are unrelated questions. Therefore, according to Barry, '[t]he appeal to culture establishes nothing... The fact that you (or your ancestors) have been doing something for a long time does nothing in itself to justify your continuing to do it' (2001: 258). What matters to justice, according to this position, is that the background distribution of resources is fair. Against a background of just public institutions, and a just distribution, no individual or group has an entitlement to the protection of some aspect of their identity. We might each prefer policies that favour our way of doing things or seeing the world. But this preference is not a legitimate basis upon which to grant special entitlements.

If public institutions and background social conditions are already just, then these critics are correct that the claims of some people for special entitlements or additional resources are unfounded from the start. But identity claims are not usually advanced by groups whose intention is to alter arrangements that are already fair. Rather, they are meant to be one effective means to draw into question what count as fair background conditions from the perspective of those who are marginalized or otherwise disadvantaged.

A similar project which also employs the perspectives of those who are disadvantaged in order to generate claims for institutional reform is a feature of theories of difference. In particular, Iris Young (1990) used claims of difference to develop an approach to justice that went beyond conventional distributive accounts of justice in order to detect different 'faces' of oppression that, she claimed, distributive accounts missed. She argued, for instance, that while sometimes people experience oppression as ethnic bias or poverty, sometimes their oppression stems from more complex systems of behavior, social structures, and institutional procedures which together make them consistently vulnerable to violence or exploitation. In general, Young argued that oppression is structural, relational, and sometimes occurs through the choices made by the oppressed.[16] And, importantly, it is often difficult to detect: 'the conscious actions of many individuals daily contribute to maintaining and reproducing oppression, but those people are usually simply doing their jobs or living their lives, and do not understand themselves as agents of oppression' (Young 1990: 41–2). Oppression can persist even though institutions appear to be neutral, distribution appears to be equal, and people appear to be choosing rationally how to live their lives. One question this raises is how does one create a perspective that reveals oppression? People who belong to dominant groups may never experience disadvantage or exclusion on the basis of their identity. They may not even view themselves as having a distinctive identity[17] and therefore are unaware that identity is the basis upon which they enjoy some of the privileges that they do. At the same time, members of minority groups may experience seemingly neutral policies as ones which implicitly accommodate the identities of dominant groups but fail to understand this as unfair bias. Because of the obscure nature of unfairness, the question which arises is how can institutions develop an effective capacity to interrogate on a continual basis the background structures and relations of social and political institutions in order to detect oppression that is indirect, systemic, and structural?

In Young's account, the concept of 'difference' is used to highlight the ways in which characteristics typical of particular identity groups, including but not confined to cultural, religious, racial, and gendered groups, have shaped institutions and social structures and therefore how they might provide a perspective from which to reshape institutions in a manner that is more inclusive and just. For Young (2000), the project of reshaping institutions has less to do with identity than ensuring groups were included in the broader democratic conversation. Like many normative political theorists, Young argued that identity ought to be viewed as something that individuals alone create for themselves and of themselves (Young 1997*a*, 2000: 102–8). 'Difference' is preferred to identity because she considered the idea of identity, especially 'group identity', to be politically dangerous.

Clearly, my account departs from Young's with respect to the role of identity in understanding the problem of oppression and possible solutions to it. But putting this matter aside for the moment, Young's perspective nonetheless helps to articulate the question which is central to the development of just political institutions, namely, what ought to count as fair standards and just background conditions in diverse societies given that institutional structures and relations have been shaped in ways that privilege some groups and disadvantage others? This question rests on considerations relevant to institutional humility. To require institutions, which aspire to be fair, to assess identity claims using well thought-out criteria can effectively require them to grapple with how minorities perceive and experience political institutions, and to uncover possible inequalities in the ways that majorities and minorities have access to and are treated by public institutions. Decision makers who are reflective of the dominant majority's position can display arrogance about the essential soundness of their interpretation of basic values and they can be blind to the ways in which unacknowledged assumptions about identity are at work in their decisions. A guided approach whereby identity claims are directly addressed by public institutions can be designed to reveal these biases and thereby engender a healthy degree of institutional humility. In this respect, identity claiming offers democratic communities the opportunity to re-examine the meaning they have attributed to normative concepts, the fairness of standards, and the impartiality of processes and structures in order to determine whether these are interpreted in a way that is inclusive of different perspectives presented by groups with different self-understandings and commitments related to their identities. To dismiss these claims and the opportunity they offer is to forgo one of the promises of democratic equality in diverse societies which is to allow minority voices to participate equally in shaping public values, structures, standards, and processes.

In one sense then, the position developed in this book to assess identity claims is generally in agreement with a position which holds that if institutions are fair and if resources are fairly distributed then no individual or group needs a special entitlement to protect their identity. But it also recognizes that so much depends on what counts as a *just* distribution or *fair* background conditions, and what is considered a *special* rather than a *basic* entitlement, that this way of articulating the position of justice is nearly useless in explaining how the demands of minorities ought to be assessed in a society that aspires to be democratic and fair. A position like Barry's which denies any connection between the structure of just institutions and the identities of peoples governed by these institutions easily begs the question of what counts as justice and fairness and appears to suppose, as I do not, that conditions of justice and fairness are established independently of the deep commitments and values of the peoples to which these conditions apply. This does not mean that identity claims ground the only kinds of commitments and values that ought to shape just institutions. But they represent one kind of important claim, which is distinct from a mere political interest, which public institutions ought to take seriously if they mean to treat people fairly.

Inclusion and respect for different peoples

A second and somewhat different conclusion drawn by normative political theorists who worry about the social construction of cultural or other identities is that the moral force of ethnic minority claims rests entirely on the presence of structural injustice that groups suffer at the hands of the state. For example, Courtney Jung argues that cultural difference fails to generate a normative basis for Indigenous and cultural claims because the identities of groups grow out of and are directly shaped by injustice and exclusion. 'Ethnic groups develop social and political salience', she argues 'because states have used differences of language, "race", and cultural practice to mark the boundaries of citizenship and to organize access to power and resources' (2008: 15).

In Latin America, 'Indigenous identity' is seen, according to this view, as a strategic kind of politics which effectively fulfils the same function as did class politics based on peasant identities in a former era (Jung 2003: 436–7, 460). Several scholarly accounts show that Indigenous activists recognize the wisdom of employing Indigenous identity strategically today largely because international organizations such as the United Nations, the International Labour Organization, and UNESCO, as well as human rights groups, and even Indigenous-based organizations offer incentives for groups to frame their claims in terms of their indigeneity. Indigenous communities understand that in order to attract international-aid funding, or in some cases, tourist dollars, they should emphasize their 'uniqueness' and emulate the standards of indigeneity set according to what is considered 'typically Indigenous' (see Tilley 2002).[18] On some accounts, to invite groups to express their entitlements in relation to something important about their identity invites minorities to 'perform' for the majority's human rights agenda (see Povinelli 1998).[19] Groups are encouraged to display their distinctiveness, internal homogeneity, and cultural autonomy through distinctive dress and other practices even if this display is contradicted by their real-life ethnic experience (Tilley 2002: 546).

Jung's response to this conflicted discourse is to argue that what groups are owed depends not on who they are or claim to be, but on the 'history of exclusions and selective inclusions that is the condition of their political presence' (2008: 16). In other words, claims that are based on something important about a group's identity are important primarily as a means to trace historical injustice and exclusion because markers of identity have been used by the state to exclude and oppress different groups of people. What is ultimately important is not the cultural identity per se but the structural injustice that has employed and shaped identities. According to Jung, structural injustice is uncovered by historically situating minority claims within the contexts in which they have come to have the character that they do. Injustice can then be addressed by using resources, like rights, and specifically membership rights, to provide groups with leverage to participate and transform structures of oppression rather than to recognize difference. Her framework addresses injustice to groups in terms of compensation for past wrongs rather than communal entitlement to the protection of some aspect of cultural identity.

Jung's argument is sensitive to what I have called institutional humility in that it specifies that the fairness of background social conditions and institutions ought to be interrogated using the cultural practices and identities of groups. Cultural practices and identities have no independent moral status but they are the means to assessing the fairness of background conditions. These practices have become markers of identity largely because they have been used by states to exclude groups and diminish their life chances. Cultures and practices have been shaped by histories of injustice and exclusion. Groups are socially constructed. Therefore, under different and more just circumstances, group identities will change.

But the problem with treating cultural practices merely as a means to assessing the fairness of background conditions is that this gives rise to the risk that minorities will not be treated respectfully by political decision makers because their distinctive practices will not be viewed as important to their self-understanding but rather as the product of how others have mistreated them. A strong constructivist position thus conflates two different kinds of claims about identity. One claim is that a minority practice has arisen and assumed importance largely as a result of exclusion or oppression. Jung is surely correct that many practices and values arise or assume importance for this reason. The nomadic nature of Roma lifestyle, the importance of specific lands to Indigenous peoples, polygamy amongst Fundamentalist Latter Day Saints, veiling amongst European Muslims, and probably every Jewish holiday are just a few that come to mind. A second claim, which does not follow from the first, is that because these practices are 'constructed', they are not 'really' valuable. Regardless of how some practices arise, they can be deeply important to the groups who advance them in the sense that the failure of the state to make room for these practices or to take them seriously denies groups something that they view as manifestly and profoundly important about their identities. For instance, many Muslims in the West do not advance claims to wear veils, to have prayer rooms in public institutions, or to have access to religious arbitration in order to manipulate others, even if sometimes these claims are advanced by people whose purpose is to manipulate. Regardless of how these practices arise or whether they could be used manipulatively, they are also deeply important to the identities of devout Muslims and integral to how they organize their families and communities.

The problem with a strong constructivist position is that it assumes the constructed nature of group identities to be evidence that group identities lack real value and therefore should not be the basis for entitlements. This conclusion regarding the value of identity does not follow from the premise that identities are constructed. Moreover, to suppose otherwise runs the risk of discouraging public decision makers from taking seriously the claims groups make about the importance of a practice to their identity. In some contexts, the position will draw the motives of groups into question. If identity claims have no moral force because they are socially constructed, then groups advancing these claims appear either to be suffering from a form of false consciousness in the sense that they are mistaken about what is 'really' important to them, or it might be the case that they are well aware of the strategic construction of their identity and are using their (re)constructed identity instrumentally, for example, to fight against their unjust exclusion from the state, as in Jung's account, or for manipulative purposes to gain additional resources or advantages over others.

Jung is primarily interested in how cultural identity is strategically constructed in order to fight against structural injustice. Her research has focused on political bargaining between groups in post-apartheid South Africa

(2000), and the reorganization of social movements over the last thirty years in Mexico (2008), both of which are contexts of rapid social change where activists have mobilized categories such as indigeneity because 'they are seeking the terms of struggle' not because they have experienced a fundamental shift in their identity (2008: 74, 77). But, in other contexts, the sort of shifts found in South Africa and Mexico are either absent or do not tell the whole story. For instance, Indigenous peoples in Canada, Australia, New Zealand, and the United States have no history of organizing on the basis of a peasant identity, as they did in Latin America, or any identity other than one which emphasizes, albeit in different ways, indigeneity. Their claims for land, for the protection of particular practices, including methods of governance, economic activities, and jurisdiction over resources are a consistent feature of Indigenous–settler conflicts. At the same time, many of these groups live in a social context where their claims to protect particular resources and practices are already suspected as being manipulative strategies by which to gain additional resources unjustly. Especially in relation to claims over scarce natural resources or valuable land, the position that these claims are strategically manipulative or merely of instrumental value to the minority making them often acts as a reason to deny the claim. Without a doubt, people advance identity claims strategically and powerless communities might use whatever strategy works best in order to gain resources. But to suggest that all identity claims are only strategies ignores the meaning they have for some of those who make them and is more likely to distract decision makers from what are surely the more important questions, namely whether a practice is a good strategy, and what a good strategy consists in.

The fact that identities are socially constructed does not diminish their value. Identities and practices important to identities may well arise as a kind of strategy devised to organize a way of life and orient people in their social context, to realize important values connected to human agency or the individual's sense of self, or even to act as a means of resisting or counteracting oppression. But identity practices come to have importance to individuals and groups independently of, or sometimes even despite, their origins. Sometimes, practices are valued by groups partly because they commemorate exclusion and resistance in the face of adversity, because they acknowledge what it means to belong to the group, or because they are integrally related to how communities survive in a manner that is both economic and historically meaningful to them.

Normative theorists have suggested some possible ways of getting at these aims besides focusing on identity claims. But none is satisfactory. Some are better designed to accommodate individual claims rather than group claims. Some focus on structural injustice but fail to respect people in the terms they claim respect. And some offer respect for persons but on terms that provide no perspective by which to assess critically the variety of ways in which social structures might be exclusive and oppressive. For these reasons, the successful and respectful interpretation of normative commitments to equality and individual freedom require public institutions to have the capacity to acknowledge and respond to the identity claims of groups. A framework by which these assessments can be made is set out in the next section.

THE IDENTITY APPROACH

The previous section offered some reasons for resisting doubts about the normative force of identity claims and showed how considerations of institutional humility and respect for persons provide justice-based reasons for taking identity seriously. The challenge now is to explain and defend the criteria that should be used by public institutions to vet identity claims. I want to begin to answer this challenge by outlining the three main components of the identity approach. I suggest that assessing identity claims rests on establishing the strengths of a claim according to three conditions: (1) the jeopardy condition; (2) the validation condition; and (3) the safeguard condition.

The jeopardy condition

The jeopardy condition gauges the strength of a claim in terms of its importance to the identities of those advancing the claim. The strength of claims is assessed along three dimensions. First, stronger claims are ones in which the practice, place, tradition, or value at issue are central and integral to a claimant's identity. For instance, observing the Sabbath is central and integral to the way of life of observant Jews; polygamy is central and integral to the religious beliefs of Fundamentalist Latter Day Saints (FLDS); and fishing salmon is central and integral to the way of life of the Sto:lo First Nation in British Columbia. Conversely, minor religious holidays, newly invented community rules, or practices which are highly idiosyncratic are general examples of the sort of claims which are likely to be weak (though might nonetheless count as an identity claim). With respect to individuals, stronger claims are, again, ones considered integral as opposed to tangential to individual identity. For instance, the right to decide on one's own religious beliefs, to be treated with equal respect, or to raise one's own children would generate strong claims. Conversely, the right to have a view of the ocean, a job in one's hometown, or access to a favourite walking path would generally generate weak claims.

Second, stronger claims are those where, in the absence of recognizing entitlement or additional resources, serious jeopardy, as opposed to mere inconvenience, is the result. For example, the Sami community in Finland might credibly argue that reindeer herding is central and integral to their identity but fail to establish that sharing the land with a quarry development places herding in serious jeopardy. Similarly, an observant Jew might credibly claim that observing the Sabbath is integral to his or her religious identity, but fail to establish the claim to prohibit public transit in his or her neighbourhood during the Sabbath in order to enhance his or her celebration of the day. Conversely, laws in Canada and the United States which criminalize polygamy seriously jeopardize the religious way of life of members of FLDS. Similarly, the claim of the Sto:lo people for salmon fishing rights on the Fraser River in British Columbia is strong in light of evidence which shows that if the Sto:lo were prohibited from fishing salmon on the Fraser, either because other fishers had priority or because wild salmon became extinct, they would not simply change fish or location, and remain the same people. Rather, something central to the identity of the community and integral to its political, social, and familial organization would be lost (Carlson 1996).[20]

The third dimension of the jeopardy condition is that the evidentiary standards used to establish jeopardy must be open and flexible in the sense that decision makers must be receptive to different kinds of evidence for establishing a claim and in the sense that they must have alternative methods to corroborate the claims which individuals make about their identities. The acceptance of Indigenous oral history in land claims cases is an example of courts displaying some openness to different kinds of evidence.[21] Public decision makers often develop alternative methods to corroborate the claims that individuals make about their past, their beliefs, and their practices rather than accepting these claims at face value. The strength of the historical record relayed by oral histories is a function, in part, of how well that oral history is corroborated by other kinds of evidence, including written records, other oral accounts, or archeological findings (see McRanor 1997; Borrows 2001: 86–92). Similarly, cases that involve controversial religious practices often invoke a test to establish the sincerity of claimants both in the sense of whether they present themselves as sincere to the court and in relation to their past history and practices.[22]

The validation condition

The validation condition assesses the strength of an identity claim on the basis of how it is validated by the group. To establish this condition requires examining the social and political processes by which a disputed practice or activity became part of the group's identity and how it is sustained by the group. It also requires considering how a restriction placed on a minority practice came about and specifically whether minorities participated in processes of validation. For instance, the 'duty to consult', which arises as a criterion by which disputes between the state and Indigenous peoples are assessed by international adjudicators and some national courts, contributes to establishing the strength of the validation condition.[23]

The validation condition has at least two further dimensions. First, it requires a fuller account of what might be at stake for a community by considering the decision-making processes by which practices or rules are established as also potentially important to the identity of the group making the claim. The validation condition is therefore assessed partly in relation to whether decision making is democratic or otherwise considered legitimate within the community. Some communities do not have decision-making processes that are stable or widely considered legitimate within the community. The decisions of such processes would generate a weak validation condition. Conversely, some communities decide to follow controversial practices or rules on the basis of decisions taken by legitimate though perhaps fragile decision-making processes internal to their communities. The stability of otherwise legitimate internal processes is potentially undermined when the decisions of minority communities are overruled by external decision makers. For instance, in the case of the *Santa Clara Pueblo Indians v. Martinez* (1978), Audrey Martinez challenged a sexist rule which denied her community membership. The decision of the US Supreme Court found in favour of the community's rule because of how the rule was validated. The Santa Clara Pueblo community had passed the membership rule and reviewed it when it was challenged in a manner that was faithful to how its legal and political institutions legitimately operate. The Court's interference would potentially deliver a blow to the legitimacy of the community's decision-making institutions. In these senses, the community had more at stake in this case than simply a membership rule.

A strong validation condition is not always established by showing that decision-making processes are democratic. In this respect, the identity approach departs from the conclusions reached by those who argue that democratic deliberation provides the only grounds for validating identity claims or rules. For instance, Seyla Benhabib argues that cultural dilemmas ought to be resolved through valid deliberation, which reflects three norms: (1) egalitarian reciprocity; (2) voluntary self-ascription; and (3) freedom of exit and association (2002: ch. 5). Similarly, Monique Deveaux argues, in relation to deliberation amongst different ethnic groups in post-apartheid South Africa, that controversial cultural practices, like polygamy, are legitimate if endorsed by suitably democratic and deliberative processes. For Deveaux, these processes must not impose on deliberants strenuous normative requirements nor adhere strictly to non-negotiable liberal principles. Nonetheless, they must be democratically legitimate and thereby inclusive of all stakeholders, including non-members who nonetheless have a stake in a conflict, ensure against the domination of some by others, and ensure that agreements, once reached, can be revisited (2006: 113–18).

Behabib and Deveaux have each outlined an ambitious set of criteria. If any community process actually met these criteria, its decisions would certainly count as being strongly validated. But the position I develop here is importantly different from that of Deveaux and Benhabib. To start with, a traditional communal method of decision making, which might not be democratic, can also establish a credible validation condition although, depending on how controversial or exclusive it is, it may only establish this condition in a weak sense. The main reason to consider undemocratic processes as suitable means to validate practices stems from institutional humility which not only requires that decision makers be open to the vastly different ways in which communities may govern themselves, but also that they resist arrogantly presuming that their own institutions reflect a democratic standard against which others should be compared. Most groups have complex sets of criteria where decisions have to be endorsed formally and informally by different sets of elites or groups. If the identity approach is going to be sensitive to the different identity claims of religious, ethnic, and Indigenous groups, it has to be able to recognize a suitably broad range of ways in which practices receive community endorsement. Further, unlike the approaches proposed by Deveaux and Benhabib, the identity approach considers community validation only one of three conditions that must be assessed in establishing the strength of an identity claim. The strength of a claim relies on the jeopardy and safeguard conditions as well.

Second, the validation condition is weakened by evidence that shows that people are coerced into adhering to group practices because they are indoctrinated or that they are caught in a collective action bind and would abandon the practice if they had full information about it or if they could avoid other harms. The indoctrination of children provides one much-discussed example of why identity claims, even those that receive widespread democratic endorsement, might nonetheless be weak claims. Colin Macleod argues in his analysis of children's identity claims that, while socialization occurs in all communities and is one means by which communities survive, the identity claims of children ought to be assessed separately from the claims of their parents. Parents cannot simply cite their interest in transmitting their identity to their children as legitimate grounds for denying children access to social and educational conditions important to the development of the moral powers or basic welfare interests of children, because children are still developing a sense of who they are (2006: 150). While the distinction between socialization and indoctrination is notoriously difficult to draw, Macleod argues that decision makers must examine how children are treated in a community in order to assess how they have come to have the identities that they do. If people are indoctrinated from birth into a way of life, are discouraged from questioning that way of life, and are cut off from the means by which they can question it, their decision making cannot generate a strong validation condition. In practice, group claims are usually stronger where communities can show that their members have openly deliberated and decided to adopt a particular practice. But, in light of clear evidence of indoctrination, any process of validation, no matter how seemingly democratic, should count as weakening rather strengthening the validity of a contested practice.

As for collective action binds, some controversial practices are endorsed by community members and considered central to ways of life even though they probably would be abandoned by communities or most of their members if they had a choice in the matter. These practices are validated through individual participation in what amounts to a collective action problem wherein people engage in a harmful practice because they fear bringing about worse harm if they alone abandon the practice.

Gerry Mackie (1996, 2003) describes the practice of female genital cutting (FGC) in East Africa in these terms. Mackie calls it a 'suboptimal practice' in the sense that most women who cut their genitals or their daughters' genitals cease to do so after they receive a moderate amount of information about the health risks and, crucially, if they believe that everyone else in their community will also cease to engage in the practice. State laws in some parts of Africa which prohibit FGC have been largely ineffective in getting rid of the practice. In addition, when the medical risks and harms associated with FGC become widely known, and the myths about it are drawn into question by sources considered credible to community members,[24] individual families are nonetheless powerless to end the practice because they correctly fear that their daughters will be unmarriageable if they alone within their community cease to engage in it. Mackie explains that practices like FGC are sustained because people want to raise their children successfully. Organizations, like TOSTAN, have had success at eliminating FGC by reversing the collective action process by which it is validated. TOSTAN engages in human rights education, provides villages with basic information about women's health and medical dangers associated with the practice, and then organizes communities that desire them to do so, to pledge collectively to renounce the practice.

The validation condition highlights that the strength of an identity claim rests on how it is validated by the group. The condition is established by examining the social and political processes by which a practice or activity became part of the group's identity and how it is sustained by the group. Like indoctrination and coercion, collective action binds weaken the validation condition and, depending on whether the practice is harmful or not, can contribute to undermining the validity of the identity claim entirely. Aside from these dramatic and exceptional sorts of processes, many religious and ethnic practices come into being in ways that are not intentional or readily traceable. They are handed down from one generation to the next through education or family life that do not involve deliberation, democratic decision making, indoctrination, or collective action binds. For these practices, the validation condition might neither contribute to the strength or weakness of the identity claim and so assessing the claim would turn mainly on the strengths of other conditions.

The safeguard condition

The safeguard conditions asked that the strength of a claim be assessed in terms of whether it threatens to generate significant harm. But what constitutes harm is often the subject of controversy. All sorts of harmful or otherwise objectionable practices might nonetheless be viewed as important to a group's identity and even validated by the group. On one hand, if the identity approach focuses merely on establishing whether a practice is important, jeopardized, and appropriately validated, it provides no way to distinguish harmful practices from benign or beneficial ones. On the other hand, prohibiting identity claims which involve harm seems to define many of the most difficult cases away and, as an approach to public decision making, runs the risk of imposing a single and probably controversial standard of what counts as harm.

The problem is not merely that people disagree about what constitutes harm, but that standards of harm are normatively suspect because they have been used by dominant majorities to impose their narrow and contestable interpretation on less powerful groups and thereby caricature them as 'uncivilized', 'savage', or 'misogynist'.[25] Without requiring a defence of particular standards, all talk of harm easily becomes a means by which dominant groups impose their own standards on marginalized groups. This is not to suggest that all standards are equally contestable. But publics which become infuriated by the scarring and snipping of children are the same ones that often turn a blind eye to issues of preventable child poverty in their midst. In so far as good public decision making displays institutional humility, it must be constantly vigilant about questioning the reasons, evidence, standards, and criteria by which harm is being assessed.

This might be an overly permissive approach to take to practices which possibly harm, especially since many real examples of such practices are directed at children. But, in addition to institutional humility, there are three reasons to adopt a broader and more permissive approach to harm. First, as Alison Dundes Renteln shows in her study of cultural defences, the threat of harm posed by minority practices is sometimes illusory. Misperceptions surrounding many practices stem primarily from misunderstandings and xenophobia (2004: 218). Renteln argues that cultural evidence ought to be introduced and assessed by courts partly so that these misunderstandings can be addressed directly.

Second, where harm is not illusory, often it must nonetheless be understood according to a vocabulary internal to a culture. For instance, in designing guidelines to detect child abuse in culturally diverse societies, Lisa Fontes shows that parents from minority groups readily abandon practices to which they are otherwise culturally loyal once they are presented with evidence which establishes for them the harmful effects of the practice on their children or, in the case of potentially harmful folk remedies, once effective alternatives are made available to them. In some cases, social workers need only to explain to parents that their actions present as abuse to their children's teachers and friends in order to convince them to stop the practice (2005: 123).

One conclusion sometimes drawn from these kinds of examples is that efforts to respect cultural practices are often based on an exaggerated sense of the importance of these practices to those who practice them. For instance, Anne Phillips (2007) argues that a striking feature of the success of TOSTAN in eradicating FGC is the discovery that the loyalty to FGC turned out to be paper-thin. According to Phillips, '[t]he reasons village representatives gave for wanting to renounce the practice were much the same as parents the world over might offer....'. Culture had little to do with it and therefore, Phillips argues, '[t]here is no need for a theory of cultural difference to make sense of either the persistence or eventual ending of genital cutting' (2007: 47). But it is unclear to me that the success of TOSTAN discloses a 'paper-thin loyalty' to culture or cultural practices. Phillips is probably correct that when people come to view a practice as harmful, their loyalty to that practice is diminished. But the question is how do they come to view a practice as harmful and how does cultural understanding and loyalty affect that process? What is often clear is that the weight of sheer evidence is not enough to convince people of harm because what appears to some people to be unambiguous evidence of harm, appears to others to be a small price to pay in order to secure a greater good. In Judaism, for example, male circumcision is considered a gate-keeping practice in the sense that men who are not circumcised are generally considered not Jewish. But the loyalty to this practice, no matter how important it is within religious doctrine and to community narratives, is indeed thin amongst Jews who believe that the practice harms babies, boys, and men. No interesting controversy exists about whether the practice causes *pain* to babies. But, for its defenders, any harm related to pain is quickly offset by benefits, both spiritual and social, which accompany the practice. But rarely will the practice be defended despite the fact that it harms baby boys. Rather, its defenders usually argue that it does not harm them. Sometimes people have loyalty to practices that cause pain and some physical suffering. But when they draw the conclusion that a practice is causing harm, they change their loyalty to it.

Following from this, the third reason to adopt a more permissive approach to harm is that prohibiting practices that communities do not themselves view as harmful can and often does reinforce cultural loyalty to them. This is one of the great challenges that TOSTAN has confronted. As studies of FGC in Africa indicate, dependable knowledge will be rejected by communities unless it is presented in a manner that respects the cultural differences of the community and takes seriously the values and practices crucial to the community's identity (Nnaemeka 2005: 29).[26] Taking seriously a community's identity does not require that harmful practices are treated as sacrosanct. In the case of FGC in Africa, understanding the function and importance of the practice in the ways of life of people in Senegal and elsewhere, and the processes by which the practice is validated, is crucial to displaying respect for communities where the practice continues and to addressing the health risks associated with the practice. Respect shapes how evidence is presented to communities, how community pledges are organized, and who is invited to participate in presenting this information. For instance, organizations like TOSTAN recruit local people to educate people about the health consequences of the practice and to explain to community members how, if they choose to do so, the practice can be stopped.

The safeguard condition gauges the strengths and weaknesses of an identity claim on the basis of whether the claim causes harm. In most cases, harm or risk of harm can be mitigated by instituting safeguards. For instance, as discussed in Chapter 3, the risk that religious arbitration will be coercively imposed on women without their full consent is a kind of harm that can be mitigated by instituting monitoring procedures to ensure that people understand their options and that they consent. In such cases, the extent to which the safeguard condition weakens an identity claim can be measured in terms of the costs that the practice imposes through the sort of safeguard conditions it requires. Some safeguard conditions might involve minor costs and be very effective while others might be highly costly and give rise to other risks, costs, and administrative inefficiencies. And in some cases, there may be no way of avoiding the risks associated with the practice.

Beyond these dimensions, the identity approach resists identifying a set of criteria by which to establish definitively that a practice is harmful although, on the basis of cases I have assessed, if I did establish such a list, practices that directly harm children or that are evidently cruel would top it. But even basic considerations about harm involve prior questions, such as who counts as a child or what counts as cruel, about which communities disagree. Rather than pushing these cases aside, the approach here suggests that it is worth revisiting the reasons why practices are prohibited as harmful or unhealthy, whether the harms are contested, and on what terms.

CONCLUSION

The aim of the identity approach is to establish guidelines by which public institutions, which aspire to be fair, can make decisions about whether a group or individual is entitled to additional resources, opportunities, or powers because of the something important about their identity. Using the three conditions of jeopardy, validation, and safeguard as a general template for assessment means that an identity claim should be accepted generally if (1) evidence shows that failure to protect a practice places the identity of a person or group in serious jeopardy; (2) the processes by which a practice is accorded importance in a group are fair, inclusive, or otherwise legitimate; and (3) protection of the practice does not threaten serious harm to anyone. By contrast, there is less reason to protect a practice and claimants will have weaker claims to the degree that the claimant's identity is not jeopardized, the processes of validation are not inclusive, fair, or legitimate, and there is a threat of serious harm if the practice is protected.

One general objection to this project is that the power relations implied by the identity approach and set out in conditions like jeopardy, validation, and safeguard, to assess the strength of identity claims, subordinate minorities, which are often making these claims, to dominant groups, which are usually in control of public institutions assessing these claims. There might be something perverse about requiring of minorities, whose identities have been jeopardized by the actions of dominant groups, that they must now prove to members of these dominant groups (who sit in the courts and legislatures) that their identity is indeed jeopardized.

In response, the identity approach is meant to address structural inequality in public decision making about minority claims. It is not meant to resolve many problems that minorities experience because they have been historically disadvantaged. The approach does not require that only members of an ethnic minority can legitimately assess claims made by members of that minority, although sometimes there are good political reasons for this. In any democratic community, minorities will have reason to advance identity claims and decision makers, some of whom will inevitably be members of different religious, cultural, or linguistic groups than those for whom they are making decisions, will need fair means to assess these claims.

Moreover, where public institutions do not aspire to be fair, the identity approach is useless. Where they aspire to be fair, the approach offers two reasons why institutions should be designed with the capacity to assess identity claims. First, institutional humility matters. Institutions must have the capacity to interrogate their previous decisions, procedures, and background social conditions to detect errors, bias, and exclusion. Identity claims are a key to providing a perspective from which unfairness can be detected. Second, they must be able to display respect for people advancing identity claims and not treat them as though they are being manipulative or suffering from false consciousness about who they 'really' are or what is important to them.

The approach rejects the unqualified valorization of any particular identity claim. According to the jeopardy condition, an identity claim is weak if a group or individual cannot show that its identity is jeopardized, if it advances a claim which is no more tied to its identity than to the identities of other groups, if it refuses to explain the importance of the practice to its identity, or if it cannot provide accessible evidence to establish its importance. Similarly, if a group coerces its members, or some of them, then its claim will be weak according to the validation condition. If it harms them or provides no safeguards against potential harm, then its claim will be weak according to the safeguard condition. Decision makers need standards to distinguish between credible and incredible claims so that groups are not forced into strategic behaviour that distorts their identities and provides them with incentives to advance false claims about themselves.

The purpose of developing a structured approach is to set out transparent criteria which reveal the relevant ways in which identity claims are important to those advancing them while being comprehensible to those assessing them. The jeopardy, validation, and safeguard conditions gauge the strengths and weaknesses of identity claims. Together these conditions serve as a strong standard by which to assess the fairness of public values and processes of decision making in relation to what groups view as important to them. The conditions aim at interrogating the strength of claims on bases that are respectful of differences though not blinded by them.

Finally, this is an approach to *public* decision making in diverse societies and as such, the approach is meant to be a pragmatic response to what might otherwise seem unverifiable claims that people make about what is important to their identity. The aim is to ensure that, as far as possible, the right sorts of claims are recognized and the wrong sorts are restricted without relying on unfair assertions about what counts as a harmful practice or naïve and one-sided suppositions about who gets to decide.

3

Multiculturalism, Identity Quietism, and Identity Scepticism

The previous chapter outlined the general features of the identity approach and examined three reasons why such an approach is important to the fair assessment of disputes concerning the claims of minorities: respect for persons, institutional humility, and pragmatism. It also showed why approaches to public decision making which deny the moral force of all identity claims run the risk of entrenching unfair institutional bias and denying respect to those who view the substance of these claims as profoundly import to their identities.

This chapter considers more fully the reservations, which have been articulated both by the proponents and by the critics of multiculturalism, about according assessments of identity a place in democratic politics. On the one hand, I consider the perspectives of identity quietists. Identity quietists are generally sympathetic to the project of assessing the claims of cultural and religious minorities to protection and accommodation, but they believe that multicultural principles can be applied without recourse to identity assessments. Quietists neither explicitly defend nor reject the concept of identity or the notion of an identity claim. To the contrary, they frequently employ identity considerations in the course of their analyses but do so without labeling them as such or recognizing the difficulties they might present. Their arguments rely implicitly on the possibility that group identity can be transparently and fairly assessed, but they do not expressly articulate how this should be done. For the quietists, questions such as whether the *kirpan* should be accommodated in public schools, whether religious arbitration ought to be legally recognized, whether commercial signs in Montreal should be in French only, or whether the Makah should be exempt from anti-whaling regulations are matters that ought to be decided using a framework informed by the commitments of normative multiculturalism.[1] The quietist's fiction is that multicultural principles can be given content without actually talking about identity. So identity quietists studiously avoid questions and problems that arise when engaging in the assessment of identity claims. As a result, ironically, they cede much ground to identity sceptics who pose a more radical set of challenges.

On the other hand, identity sceptics include scholars from a variety of scholarly perspectives who disagree about many things save one: they all want 'identity' off the public table. Identity sceptics raise deep reservations about the form that politics takes when it incorporates recognition of identity claims and groups, four of which capture most of their concerns. First, some identity sceptics worry about the sheer variety and seeming *incommensurability* of claims that can be made in the idiom of identity. They point to the ways in which identity politics burdens the public sphere and heightens social conflict by giving added legitimacy to the different and divisive values of minorities. Second, sceptics are concerned that identity claims give rise to a politics that values *authenticity* which, on one hand, places what is perhaps the most precious, personal, and least negotiable aspect of a conflict – namely, its relation to one's identity – at the centre of public debate, and, on the other hand, then treats such claims as potentially fraudulent and the groups which make them with suspicion. Third, identity claiming is often strongly criticized for *essentializing* groups by encouraging a historically static view of what identity consists in and one that is one-dimensional in the sense that it reduces whole ways of life to 'essential' practices. Fourth, some sceptics argue that identity claiming *domesticates* minorities because it encourages them to perform their essentialized identities for majorities, and thereby creates opportunities for majorities to assert their dominance over minorities while appearing to accommodate them.

In light of these concerns, little scholarly appetite exists for directly tackling questions about identity despite the ubiquity of controversies that implicate identity claims. Instead, the current state of analysis about identity politics (and assessments of culture in relation to minorities) is characterized by many different anxieties about the role of identity in politics. A strong scepticism about identity claims, about how to take these claims seriously and assess them fairly provides fertile ground for multicultural backlash because in the absence of a set of criteria to guide debates about identity claims, which can directly address these concerns, the reasons to decide in favour or against group accommodation within a multicultural framework are not obvious and often appear to the public to be arbitrary or biased. Multiculturalism appears incomplete and potentially dangerous. Identity sceptics recognize this and, unsurprisingly, are often critics (or at least sceptics) of multiculturalism as well. So, whereas identity quietists tend to think that multiculturalism can proceed without identity, identity sceptics tend to believe that politics should proceed without multiculturalism.

The position developed here offers an alternative to both identity quietism and scepticism. It holds that a meaningful and satisfactory interpretation of the abstract multicultural principles depends upon direct, open, and structured consideration of identity claims. In this sense, an approach to identity claims which requires that they be assessed fairly and transparently complements and completes multiculturalism. Such a guide is built upon the concern that the abstract principles of multiculturalism remain mere aspirational ideals which appear, in different contexts, to be both confusing and unattainable without institutions that are designed to interpret principles concretely, in a way that accounts for the identities of those advancing claims, and thereby in ways that are inclusive, that consider these commitments from the perspectives of different peoples, with different histories and experiences, who have been faced with different struggles but who now live together.

This chapter explains the failure of identity quietism in these respects and the role played by identity quietism and scepticism in heightening public anxiety about multicultural accommodation. It illustrates the role of identity quietism, and its failure, in a set of public debates in Ontario, Canada, over whether decisions reached through religious arbitration ought to be legally recognized by the state. I first explain what happened in these debates and how they exemplify the problems with identity quietism. By eschewing identity claims, participants in this debate created a dynamic which entrenched racist stereotypes, marginalized the Muslim community, and heightened public anxiety about multiculturalism. This kind of dynamic is emblematic of identity quietism and provides the grounds upon which identity sceptics argue that identity has no legitimate role in democratic politics. The chapter concludes by outlining the challenges of identity scepticism, which are each taken up in subsequent chapters.

THE PUBLIC DEBATE OVER RELIGIOUS ARBITRATION IN ONTARIO

In 2001, an Ontario-based Muslim organization called the Canadian Society of Muslims proposed to establish an Islamic arbitration tribunal which would allow Muslims living in Ontario to resolve some civil disputes using the principles of Islamic personal law known as *shari'a.* Unlike other provinces in Canada, Ontario has allowed, since 1991, private, legally binding arbitration over family-related disputes.[2] The legislation, known as the *Arbitration Act, 1991*, followed a trend found in other Western countries, which was meant to make arbitration less costly and less adversarial for members of the public.[3]

By 2003, some religious communities in Ontario – Mennonites, Catholics, Jews, as well as Ismaili Muslims – had already organized arbitration services for their members. The proposal to do so for the general Muslim community, through the Canadian Society of Muslims' Islamic Institute of Civil Justice (IICJ) was, in one sense, consistent with what other communities had been doing for some time (see Mumtaz Ali 2004). Nevertheless, the Ontario public, including many people within the Muslim community, strongly objected to the proposal, specifically in the area of family law and in relation to policies governing divorce and custody. The protests against the IICJ's proposal led the Ontario government to establish a commission which issued a report, known as the Boyd Report (Boyd 2004). After receiving input from over forty public interest groups and hundreds of individuals, the Boyd Report recommended that religious arbitration continue in Ontario along the lines it had been allowed in the past with some modest reforms that increased the transparency of the system, the training and the accountability of arbitrators, and that ensured the consent of parties seeking arbitration.[4] The Report did not discuss or describe the role of religious arbitration in the Muslim, Jewish, or any other community. It did not assess the importance of arbitration to any religious commitments, or the principles, such as those contained in *shari'a*, by which it operates. These matters were left for the public to figure out on its own (Emon 2008).

In the public debates as well, the role and importance of religious arbitration to religious communities was barely mentioned. Instead, the public debate in Ontario focused on the general nature of Canada's multicultural values (see Tibbetts 2004: A5; Rutledge 2005). The question of whether religious arbitration ought to be accommodated was broached indirectly through the more general question of how multiculturalism prioritized different normative values adhered to in Canada. On one side of this debate, Muslim advocates for religious arbitration argued that Canada's multiculturalism is meant to allow cultural groups autonomy over important aspects of their collective life, even, in some cases, aspects that conflict with the values of mainstream Canada. They argued that Muslims were being denied what other religious groups enjoyed and they urged the government commission to pay more than simply lip service to the 'principles of multiculturalism'. In his submission to the Boyd Commission, the leading advocate for religious arbitration, Syed Mumtaz Ali, explained that minority communities expected multiculturalism to be extended equally to all cultural groups 'instead of confining it only to the three charter groups: British, French, and Aboriginal peoples' (Mumtaz Ali 1994: 3). 'In the barnyard of democratic multicultural Canada', he wrote, 'some are more equal than others' (p. 2).

Opponents to religious arbitration, including those from Ontario's Muslim community, did not generally challenge the manner in which advocates for religious arbitration characterized Canada's multicultural values.[5] Instead, they argued that multiculturalism was partly to blame for the conflict in the first place. Like the proponents of religious arbitration, the opponents argued that multiculturalism allows groups some autonomy over their own affairs. But, for this reason, they argued, it ought to be abandoned as Canadian policy. For example, Tarek Fatah, a founder of the Muslim Canadian Congress, denounced the Boyd Report as 'multiculturalism run amok' (Eltahawy 2005). Several critics drew a contrast between, on one hand, the radical legal pluralism of multiculturalism, of which they disapproved, and, on the other hand, a 'one law for all' model: 'the civil law must bend and bend again to accommodate religious differences – even where those religious differences violate the spirit of Canadian equality' (Lithwick 2004).[6] Many argued that multiculturalism goes too far when it allows groups to opt out of adhering to Canadian values like gender equality. In fact, the concern that multiculturalism threatens the right to sexual equality as guaranteed in Canada's constitution was repeatedly expressed. The tension between multiculturalism and sexual equality was played up in the international news coverage as well where it also found a receptive audience. Participants characterized the problem in terms of a general clash between the abstract values of multiculturalism and sexual equality. This seemed to suggest to participants who favoured sexual equality that they ought to reject multiculturalism because it was hostile to their priorities. As one member of the Canadian Muslim Women's Council put it, 'I chose to come to Canada because of multiculturalism. But when I came here, I realized how much damage multiculturalism is doing to women. I'm against it strongly now. It has become a barrier to women's rights' (Homi Arjomand as quoted in Wente 2004).

Following the release of the Boyd Report, the protests intensified. In 2005, the government relented to the pressure and, against Boyd's recommendations, amended its Arbitration Act in a manner that, it claimed, banned private arbitration over disputes within the area of family law.[7]

The character of the public debate in Ontario meant that no sustained discussion or description of the principles of *shari'a* or the role and importance of religious arbitration to devout Muslims occurred in the public debate or in the Boyd Report. In large part, this kind of information did not fit the terms of the debate about the nature and limits of multicultural principles. When information was offered about how religious arbitration works, no public discussion followed about its accuracy or partiality no matter how seemingly controversial the information appeared to be. For example, early in the debate, Mumtaz Ali stated that Muslims 'place their spiritual and social lives in dire peril' when they are required to submit to laws other than those which Allah has ordained (1994: 3). He offered no evidence to back up this statement nor was this claim explained or questioned by those who found it contentious.[8] As for the opponents of religious arbitration, some argued that legally recognizing *shari'a* principles in arbitration will lead down a slippery slope that will eventually legitimate Muslim penal measures in Canada. Again, no one scrutinized the plausibility of these provocative statements or sought an explanation for them.

Indeed, one of the frustrating features of the Ontario debates is that questions about the role and importance of religious arbitration for devout Muslims, how it works, how it is validated by members of the community, and whether it can lead to harmful results were hardly addressed at all. Amidst all the rhetoric about multicultural principles, the discussion never broached the question of why proponents wanted religious arbitration to be legally recognized and whether their reasons were compelling. The information about the role and importance of arbitration to Muslims, whether or how it is jeopardized in the absence of legal recognition, how it is validated, and how it places women at risk of harm was never seriously or carefully assessed in the public debates.

One consequence of the absence of such a substantive discussion is that it was relatively easy for adversaries to advance misinformation about Muslim religious arbitration without being challenged. Mainstream Canadian newspapers printed editorials which picked up various statements made in the course of public debate without questioning them. The editorials compared *shari'a* to incest, claimed that it endorsed chopping off people's hands, and that according to its terms, women are chattels. The practice was repeatedly characterized as coercively imposed on women, without any explanation of whether this coercion is endemic to the practice or an abuse of it. In large part, racist rhetoric and stereotyping filled the gap left by the absence of accountable information about the nature of religious arbitration and its importance in Islam. Public debate was framed in a manner that treated these substantive questions as besides the main point of the debate, as taboo and off the issue. Even those who might have wanted to respond to the rhetoric would have found it difficult to do so because this meant responding to a side issue rather than engaging with the main problem, which instead focused on more general questions about the 'limits of multiculturalism', the nature of sexual equality, or the relation between the two.

Even feminist organizations, which tend to be especially aware of the dangers of racial stereotyping and are savvy about the media's role in distorting nuanced debate, chose to ignore the more concrete questions. They also cast the debate at an abstract level that inevitably skirted questions about the nature, importance, and role of religious arbitration to the identities of religious minorities and the relation between its concrete role and the values associated with sexual equality. The National Association of Women and the Law (NAWL), which helped to organize extensive discussions about the issue, joined with other feminist organizations to form a coalition of groups known as the 'No Religious Arbitration Campaign'. They attributed the success of their campaign specifically to the fact that they focused on women's equality and avoided discussing substantive issues related to religion; to arbitration within the Islamic community; to the way in which *shari'a* works in that community; or to what might be at stake for those who view religious arbitration as important to their religious commitments. NAWL's report on 'Lessons Learned' states: 'Framing issue [*sic*] primarily as a women's equality issue was essential to the campaign's success because it removed the political discourse from a potentially divisive focus on religious freedom'. In a similar vein, '[t]here was a lot of talk of religious pluralism and multiculturalism but we maintained the focus on it being a women's issue. There were many attempts to derail and sidetrack us' (NAWL 2007: 4).

In effect, the Coalition's efforts to keep the focus of debate on the priority of abstract values like sexual equality, and to 'widen the discourse', rather than discuss how religious arbitration works in the Muslim community, presented weak obstacles by which to respond to the racial stereotyping and Islamophobia that emerged in the public debates. As the Report concedes, '[w]e could never [fully] widen the discourse to religious fundamentalism in general. It left the impression that Muslims were the problem and thus fed into Islamophobia' (p. 7). Neither the Coalition's report nor the documentation available from affiliated organizations considered the possibility that to avoid discussing identity and instead to frame the issue in terms of abstract values, in effect, froze devout Muslims out of the debate and exposed them to latent racism.

When debates that involve minority entitlements focus primarily on the meaning and priority of abstract values, without reflecting on the way in which these values are given concrete expression in context, two problems arise both of which are related to institutional humility. First, in the absence of institutional humility, dominant groups tend to attribute general relevance to their principled commitments in ways that fail to reflect on how their own practices are also distant from any plausible interpretation of these principled commitments. In relation to gender, Sarah Song (2007) calls this 'the diversionary effect' because majorities divert attention from their own sexist practices by focusing on the patriarchal practices of minority cultures. In the Ontario debates, a principled commitment to sexual equality shaped the opposition to a minority's practice because that practice was presumed to place women at risk of being coerced into divorce arrangements which would privilege the interests of their estranged male spouses. This diverted attention from the large number of policies adhered to in Canada that place all women at risk in the context of marriage, including the legally enforced practices around prenuptial agreements which operate on the basis of exceedingly thin assessments of what counts as consent.[9]

Institutional humility requires that institutions and public decision makers have the capacity to reflect on the possible ways in which access to public debates is unequal and norms which are putatively neutral are in fact biased. Majorities frequently make exceptions to and place limitations on fundamental rights like sexual equality in the course of balancing different considerations that arise in different situations. The question is whether these exceptions are reasonable or whether they are based on reasons that systematically privilege the cultural preferences of one group over all others. When a conflict is framed as one between a group that champions the abstract ideal and another group that attempts to protect its cultural practices, the group purporting to champion the abstract ideal will always appear superior. But this is a distorting comparison because no group's practices reflect the unadulterated abstract ideal. Issues about rights and practices always involve questions about the context that informs choice, about what is at stake for individuals and for groups, and about what if anything is the price for changing practices and policies. In the absence of institutional humility, debates can be structured so that dominant group norms appear to be universalist and superior and minority groups appear to be self-focused and inferior.

The second problem is that, in debates where decision makers lack the capacity or incentive to interrogate the impartiality of the terms by which they make decisions, minorities have little incentive to participate even if they have a great deal at stake in the outcome. Minorities will withdraw from the debate because matters important to them are treated as off-topic or are distorted by what they view as biased interpretations of abstract values, procedures, or past decisions. Sometimes, even members of a minority community who agree that a practice important to their community should be restricted will not participate for these reasons. In Ontario, the overall effect of avoiding issues of identity was that, except for a few bold commentators,[10] members of the Muslim community withdrew from offering any substantive information about Islam or *shari'a*, including information about the problems with the discretionary ways in which private arbitration works within some parts of the Muslim community. Given the tense atmosphere created by the public debate, the risk was great that discussing, in this context, the real problems that religious arbitration presents in the Muslim community would further fuel the fear-mongering and racism. As described by one commentator, Canada missed a 'golden opportunity to shine light on abuses [within the religious Muslim community] masquerading as faith' (Khan 2005) and instead focused on what seemed to 'really' matter, namely whether multicultural commitments would or should prevail in light of religious and Muslim 'difference'.

In the end, the government prohibited the legal recognition of religious arbitration in the area of family law rather than allowing and regulating it according to the guidelines set out in the Boyd Report. Yet, the prohibition does not actually end the practice or the manner in which the practice can be abused. People can still use religious arbitration to mediate their divorce settlements and any 'abuse masquerading as faith' will continue to victimize the vulnerable.[11] The main difference is that the vulnerable now have recourse to public courts should they choose to break with their religious communities, and often with their families as well, in order to use them. The likelihood of this happening is considered slight.

THE FAILURE OF IDENTITY QUIETISM

The debates in Ontario froze out questions that treated religious arbitration as an identity claim and thereby excluded proper consideration of the views of those who considered this practice deeply important to their identity. To treat religious arbitration as an identity claim requires asking why religious arbitration is important to the distinctive way of life of Muslims. Is it jeopardized in the absence of being legally recognized? How is it validated by those who use it? Does it place some people at risk of harm and, if so, how can this risk be mitigated? Instead of broaching these questions, the Ontario debates largely proceeded as though the issues at stake could be resolved by uncovering the nature and priority of abstract principles like multiculturalism and sexual equality. This manner of proceeding is emblematic of identity quietism which often informs liberal multiculturalism.

Identity quietists approach questions about multicultural accommodation in a manner that implicitly depends on a well-reasoned and transparent assessment of identity claims, yet fail to recognize or defend this aspect of their approach. Quietism unintentionally fuels more sceptical positions on identity politics because, in the absence of engaging in explicit, direct, carefully reasoned, and guided assessments of identity claims, multiculturalism seems, at best, incomplete and even dangerous. In the Ontario debates, Muslim religious arbitration was easily vilified partly because the debate failed to engage directly with questions about identity. Multiculturalism appeared to sanction coercive and sexist religious practices while, at the same time, providing no guidance to determine whether the practices in question were actually coercive and sexist.

Quietists would disagree with this assessment. Instead, they would argue that the Ontario debates were derailed because the public was under the misapprehension that Canada's multicultural commitments could, in principle, be used to accommodate harmful or sexist practices. In short, the public misunderstood Canada's multicultural commitments. As Will Kymlicka notes, Canada's multicultural policy is liberal in inspiration and design. Historically, it 'was seen as a natural extension of this liberal logic of individual rights, freedom of choice, and non-discrimination' and in this sense is distinct from policies that enable 'a group to maintain its inherited practices even if they violate the rights of individuals' (2005: 2). Insofar as Kymlicka's description of Canadian multiculturalism is accurate (and I think that it is), one might argue that the Ontario debates reflect a general public confusion about the nature of multiculturalism and the priority of sexual equality over any claim to defer to oppressive group practices.

But diagnosing the problem in terms of public confusion is unconvincing, not because the public's grasp of multiculturalism is flawless, but rather because the invocation of multiculturalism largely begs the question, which is closer to the centre of this controversy, of whether religious arbitration *is* a natural extension of the 'liberal logic of individual rights, freedom of choice, and non-discrimination' or instead a violation of this logic. Asking this question is a central feature of institutional humility because it asks public decision makers to re-examine the meaning historically attributed to legal and normative concepts, such as rights, in order to determine whether interpretations have been inclusive of different perspectives presented by groups with different self-understandings and commitments related to their identities. At the same time, asking this question suggests that, even at the level of abstract theory, multiculturalism requires – indeed it relies upon – prior assessments of the identities of minorities and majorities when disputes of this nature arise. This implicit reliance on identity is apparent throughout Kymlicka's arguments for liberal multiculturalism, so it is worth briefly considering his arguments more closely.

Kymlicka's position is premised on the importance of individual autonomy which requires that individuals lead their lives 'from the inside'. Individuals must be able to examine their own ends including those ends that they might consider, at some points in their life, to constitute their identity and thus ones which seem impossible to question or revise (1995: 91). The importance of the capacity to examine one's ends, and the need to protect this capacity through individual rights, is derived from the observation that individuals are deeply (though not irrevocably) tied to communities and that these attachments constitute their identity. Although 'no end is immune from . . . potential revision' (p. 91), '[t]ies to one's culture', he argues following Rawls, 'are normally too strong to give up' (p. 87) and 'considerations of identity provide powerful reasons for tying people's autonomy-interest to their culture' (1997:

87 fn. 6). The mark of liberalism, Kymlicka maintains, is the capacity of individuals to reflect on their identity.[12]

Unlike more orthodox liberals, Kymlicka recognizes that the state's obligations go well beyond protecting individuals to the exclusion of the groups with which individuals choose to identify. This is because meaningful autonomy always exists in a context of choice amongst various options (1995: 83). Contexts of choice are found in 'societal cultures' which are cultural communities that are large and 'alive' enough to have practices and institutions that 'cover the full range of human activities' (p. 75). Respect for individual autonomy requires both ensuring that individuals have the capacity to make autonomous choices, such as choosing whether or not to adhere to any particular practice of their cultural community, and ensuring that the conditions are in place to help communities thrive and reproduce themselves so that they are able to provide individuals with a decent range of options from which to choose. As Kymlicka puts it, 'considerations of identity provide a way of concretizing our autonomy-based interest in culture' (1997: 87 fn. 6). What people actually identify with is a concrete expression of their context of choice, or at least one component of it.

One weakness sometimes attributed to Kymlicka's theory is that it fails to provide a sufficiently concrete account of what sorts of communities and types of practices should receive protection (see Forst 1997; Carens 2000: ch. 3 and especially p. 61). At one level, the approach is not meant to promise protection for any particular societal culture. Rather, it specifies that individuals need access to *a* societal culture which provides them with a meaningful range of options. In theory at least, people do not need access to the culture into which they are born or to the particular options and types of meaning that their culture sustains. In reality though, good reasons often exist to protect the actual cultural communities people identify with, the primary reason being that people find it tremendously difficult to switch cultures. The communities with which people actually identify provide a real-life guide to which societal cultures ought to be protected.[13] As Kymlicka puts it, '[i]dentity does not displace autonomy as a defence of cultural rights, but rather provides a basis for specifying which culture will provide the context for autonomy' (1997: 87 fn. 6). In other words, the gap between the generic category of societal culture and the specific communities that are societal cultures and therefore ought to benefit from an array of minority rights is filled by the notion of identity.

While identity does not replace autonomy as a defence for cultural rights, the substantive features of any actual identity does a significant amount of the work, according to this account, in fleshing out the precise ways in which communities ought to be protected. The notion of societal culture can provide only the vaguest guidelines in this respect; the details must be filled out by the complex and rich array of traditions, practices, and values that together make up the societal culture with which any individual or group actually identifies. For instance, the argument for protecting societal cultures requires that a 'range of options' associated with a 'full complement of human activities' is protected. But debates about what constitutes a viable option, or whether a given practice ought to be accommodated, turn not on what the generic understanding of societal culture tells us (because it does not tell us anything about how to answer these questions), but rather on what the identity of the community or the individual actually consists of in concrete terms. The question of what the identity of a community actually consists of involves determining how important any given practice is to the viability of the community, that is, to a community's capacity to continue to provide its members with a viable context of choice. Rainer Forst makes a similar point when he suggests that Kymlicka should be less concerned about a context of choice than about a 'context of identity' because what matters about cultural membership is not the number of choices one's culture provides but 'the historically grown, particular "meaning" a culture bestows on the ethical options open to a person as a member of that culture' (Forst 1997: 66). Only by understanding the meaning and role of a practice in relation to the identity of a community can decision makers determine whether the practice is integral to the viability of a community.

Because cultural meaning and religious significance shape what counts as a viable option, identity is implicated in any discussion of what autonomy actually consists in, as Kymlicka (1997) sometimes seems to acknowledge. Sometimes, it is easy to see the connection, where communities exist around a single sort of practice, and that practice is one whose presence, absence, and relation to options and activities is relatively easy to assess.[14] But most debates and conflicts about whether or not to accommodate a minority claim are not as transparent. They often involve disagreements within, outside, and between different communities about how particular practices and institutions are related to a community's way of life, including how important they are to the community's survival as a distinctive body, and how they shape the capacity of individuals to reflect on their life options and attachments. Questions of identity precede questions about choice and options in the sense that only by addressing questions of identity first can we begin to understand some of the things that count as an option and what meaning they have for the people in question.

Identity quietism fails to acknowledge that we must read into the notion of 'viable option' our own assumptions about the importance and meaning of different cultural practices in order to understand what counts as a viable option in the first place. This is especially clear in so-called hard cases where a practice that is integral to a community appears to conflict with what individual autonomy seems to require. Consider in this regard the following question: if religious arbitration is important to Muslim identity but, at the same time, imposes unfair restrictions on Muslim women, how should the conflict be resolved? The identity quietist's approach resolves such hard case apparently without examining the practice as an identity claim. For instance, Kymlicka suggests that hard cases can be resolved by using the language of autonomy and specifically by distinguishing between practices that are external protections and those that are internal restrictions. Group practices that protect the group from the impact of external decisions taken by the larger society (external protections) ought to be favoured over practices that restrict the liberty of group members 'in the name of cultural tradition or religious orthodoxy' (internal restrictions; 1995: 36). Religious arbitration seems more like an internal restriction and therefore seems less likely to be favoured using this distinction.

This position seems sensible at an abstract level. But, in relation to any actual conflict, it does not offer much guidance. First, the distinction between external protections and internal restrictions is murky at best. Few cases exist where external protections do not entail internal restrictions. Cultural and religious rules about membership, governance, marriage, the distribution of property, and education are all intended to protect communities from external influences. But they work primarily by restricting individuals (often women) about who they can marry; how their children gain membership; and what consequences they suffer if their marriages dissolve (see Shachar 2001). Membership rules are notoriously both protective of communities and restrictive of individuals within these communities. Indeed, most cultural and religiously inspired practices are both protective and restrictive because what is usually required in order to protect minority communities from assimilation involves restricting members, for example, by prohibiting them from eating in places which do not serve *kosher* food, working on the Sabbath, or taking swimming lessons at public pools; or by requiring them to wear a veil, take a sacrament, or wear a *kirpan* (see Spinner 1994).

Second, even if Kymlicka is correct that some internal restrictions are unacceptable from a liberal or democratic point of view, which ones are unacceptable depends on the role that a practice plays in sustaining or undermining the capacity of individuals to reflect on their attachment to groups and the vitality of the group to sustain itself as a context of choice. To clarify how the 'internal restriction – external protection' distinction applies to any actual practice, requires first assessing the disputed practice as an identity claim because no other way exists to determine whether a practice poses a 'serious' internal restriction or whether it provides a 'powerful' external protection. The groundwork for understanding whether a practice poses a serious internal restriction or an important external protection depends on its role and importance for the identities of those who practice it. Its role and importance must be assessed before one can decide what counts as an unacceptable internal restriction or a powerful external protection. But these are not concerns addressed by Kymlicka's approach, and by avoiding these concerns, his approach displays the markings of identity quietism.

The failure of identity quietism arises because quietists do not recognize that substantive dimensions of a group's identity must be evaluated before determining whether liberal principles have been violated. They often also do not recognize that where this sort of evaluation does not occur explicitly and transparently, it will tend to occur implicitly. For instance, in discussing how liberals ought to respond to illiberal minorities practices (Kymlicka 1995: 163–70) such as practices that discriminate against religious dissenters in the Pueblo Indian community, or practices that favour boys and deny girls instruction in reading and writing, or practices that deny women the right to vote or hold office in Saudi Arabia, Kymlicka engages in such an implicit assessment. He presumptively notes that these practices are not external protections because they '*do not protect the group from the decisions of the larger society*' (p. 153; emphasis mine). He subsequently refers to them as 'unjust practices'. Yet, to presume that these practices play no role in protecting groups from the decisions of the larger society and therefore that they are 'unjust', quickly and easily passes over what is certainly a more complicated set of questions. It is easy to suggest that if practices mistreat individuals and have no role in sustaining the group's identity, then they ought to be abandoned. But surely the problem is that such conclusions are often disputed both within groups and between them. Consensus does not exist about whether a disputed practice is indeed unjust. If a consensus did exist, then it would hardly be necessary to impose liberal principles on communities which adhere to the practice, because they would themselves change the practice in light of the fact that it is unjust.

The importance of explicitly, transparently, and fairly assessing the role a controversial practice plays in a group's identity should not be underestimated, especially in approaches, like liberal multiculturalism, which are meant to be sensitive to the ways in which dominant societies have imposed their own narrow interpretations of the meaning and value of particular options and choices on cultural minorities. As Kymlicka recognizes, minorities have been coerced and persecuted not only by liberals devoted to theories of benign neglect or racists who hold irrational contempt and hatred for the Other, but also by dominant liberal-minded communities, which impose their own cultural understandings on minorities in the context of assessing whether these minorities provide a decent way of life for their members. The problem here is not just that cultural bias has led liberals to false universalism, but also that, as important and useful as context of choice and societal culture are in generic ways, neither concept provides much guidance on resolving specific disputes. Resolving disputes such as the one in Ontario requires 'concretizing our autonomy-based interest in culture' by paying attention to considerations of identity. Kymlicka's theory provides some of the reasons why we should care about identity and about minority rights. It is not the goal of his theory to provide a means of assessing identity claims even though any detailed consideration of what should count as a minority right in any given case relies precisely on assessing identity claims and, moreover, doing so in a fair manner. In the absence of bridging the 'identity gap' and establishing a set of identity-focused questions to guide assessments, decision makers can only apply the normative commitments of multiculturalism if they rely on their own unguided assessment of minority identities. This is a high-risk strategy whose success relies heavily on how reasonable and informed decision makers happen to be. A better approach is one that ensures such assessments are done in a transparent way and are guided by fair criteria.

The failure of identity quietism consists in a failure to realize that the assessment of identity claims is a required step to fulfilling the promise of multiculturalism and that avoiding the assessment of identity often has the effect of excluding minority groups as equal participants in the public sphere and in public debate. Many minority rights conflicts, including those over religious practices such as veiling, turbans, *kirpans*, religious arbitration, arranged marriages, and polygamy raise questions about whether restricting these practices, in fact, denies to people the kinds of values that individual rights are meant to protect. Often disputed practices can just as easily be interpreted to be consistent with individual rights and equality as some mainstream practices can. This is not meant to suggest that individual rights are culturally relative. But the distinction between better and worse interpretations of abstract commitments such as individual rights or sexual equality does not arise because a single and uncontroversial interpretation exists of what these commitments mean. To claim that liberal multiculturalism gives priority to individual rights over the claims of cultural or religious groups does not sort out the problem either, because it does not address the different ways in which the values of individual freedom and equality are being interpreted by different groups in relation to their actual practices. Moreover, it says nothing about how to solve conflicts generated by different interpretations when they arise. Despite its fractious character, even the limited and inadequate discussion of identity in the Ontario debates over religious arbitration had a salutary effect: it revealed that mainstream institutional responses to diversity can be facile and that racial stereotyping finds a way into debates that are cast at an abstract level, possibly because they are cast so abstractly. Decision making and debates which attempt to avoid these matters related to identity can engender a false and exaggerated sense of confidence in the adequacy of institutional and public interpretations of abstract commitments and responses to diversity.

Like many debates about multiculturalism today in Canada, Britain, and throughout Europe, the debate in Ontario over religious arbitration quickly became a platform for anti-Muslim racism. It is important to understand why this occurred. Some critics suggest that multiculturalism gives rise to racism, specifically today, anti-Muslim sentiment, because it heightens the salience of culture and thereby easily lends itself to cultural stereotyping and determinism. Anne Phillips (2007) points to disturbing evidence of this sort drawn from numerous public decisions taken about veiling, cultural defences, and forced marriages. Along similar lines, some critics argue that racist narratives coexist comfortably with multiculturalism and that, while multiculturalism is neither effective at addressing racism nor particularly well designed to eliminate it, it is often viewed by dominant groups as evidence that they are not racists because their laws accommodate 'cultural' differences (see Bannerji 2000).

The religious arbitration debates suggest that, although the normative commitments of multiculturalism do not directly contribute to racist stereotyping, abstract public debates about these commitments create space for misinformation to go unchallenged and close off opportunities for the full and equal participation of minorities who may have the most at stake in outcomes. Public debate in Ontario over religious arbitration was framed in a manner that treated substantive questions about the nature of religious arbitration, its role in Islam, and importance to Muslims as besides the main point of the debate and thereby excluded from serious consideration matters which some people viewed as deeply important. Racism flourishes where racialized groups are excluded or discouraged from participating as equals in the public sphere. The integration and equal participation of cultural groups in this sense is the promise of multiculturalism. However, identity quietism impedes the realization of this promise.

IDENTITY SCEPTICISM

Unlike quietists, identity sceptics realize that multiculturalism requires the assessment of identity claims. But they do not favour building an approach that ensures direct and fair assessment of such claims. Instead, identity sceptics insist that identity claims cannot be assessed fairly, that multiculturalism is thereby built on shaky foundations, and that it should be abandoned or radically rethought as a normative orientation to public decision making in diverse societies. Sometimes, identity sceptics propose alternative normative principles to multiculturalism, many of which tend to focus on more familiar (albeit unrealized) political values such as democratic participation (e.g. Fraser 2000; Benhabib 2002; Jung 2008), agency (Phillips 2007), and the fundamental importance of abstract individual equality (Barry 2001). Other sceptics, some of whom consider multiculturalism's normative commitments to usher in a pernicious form of governmentality,[15] offer no alternative to it, but are nonetheless trenchant in their criticisms about the problems with approaches which frame politics and political decision making in terms of identity (Povinelli 1998; Day 2000; Markell 2003; Brown 2006).

Identity scepticism includes a diversity of scholars who tend to agree, for different reasons, that an approach to political decision making which focuses on identity or culture invites the sort of problems that many Western societies are now experiencing in light of their attempts to accommodate religious and cultural minorities. Identity scepticism suggests that the public anxiety and moral panic that surrounds multiculturalism in North America and Europe today arises because multiculturalism raises promises about minority inclusion and integration that it cannot fulfil, it mobilizes minorities communities to make demands about their status and accommodation within Western states that it cannot appease, and it encourages a kind of claiming that further stigmatizes and victimizes those it purports to help. For identity sceptics, identity is either a dangerous political toxin or it is too easily turned against those who are most vulnerable. Either way, it is best avoided altogether.

I see considerable merit in the arguments of identity sceptics even though the position defended here is directly at odds with the conclusions they draw. Identity sceptics take seriously the complicated role played by identity and culture in multicultural politics and theories. Their concerns arise from appreciating, rather than ignoring, the confounding problems and challenges that identity raises. But whereas many sceptics conclude that identity is inherently problematic, constitutes a poor way to advance claims for entitlements, resources, and opportunities, and should not be the subject of public assessments, I think that much more is lost by abandoning identity than is gained by avoiding it. Nonetheless, the sceptics raise some important challenges, four of which are central to understanding how the assessment of identity can proceed in a manner that is transparent and fair and how focusing on identity, rather than ignoring it, is the best way to meet some perennial problems encountered in decision making about minority claims. Below, I briefly outline these four challenges before addressing them more systematically in subsequent chapters.

Incommensurability

According to identity sceptics, identity generates many incommensurable claims and, because of its vagueness and sheer complexity, offers few if any reliable bases upon which to choose amongst competing claims. Sceptics who raise the challenge of incommensurability base their concerns on what they consider to be the defining characteristics of identity claims, namely, that they are opaque, have vague conceptual contents, are unfalsifiable, have no clear semantic reference, are 'monolithic', and non-negotiable. They argue that, in light of these features, it is easy for groups to present their interests and values as matters which are important to their identity. In particular, it is easy for them to use their identity in a manipulative and thereby illegitimate way in order to cut off debate, to signal that their position is non-negotiable, and thereby to intensify what is at stake in a conflict. The concern of some sceptics in this regard is that identity claiming potentially creates a 'deadly serious politics... played out for high stakes' (Waldron 2000: 158). The more one group advances their interests in terms of identity, the more other groups will be inclined to do the same. Therefore, identity claiming is an escalating politics of incommensurable and non-negotiable claims which brings about democratic deadlock or, worse, leads to open hostilities (Weinstock 2006: 23).

The challenge of incommensurability rests on the idea that no politically accessible or coherent basis exists upon which to evaluate conflicting views about how identity matters or about how matters putatively fundamental to identity can be weighed against each other in any given conflict. According to some sceptics (such as Barry, Phillips, Waldron, and Weinstock) identity claims should be avoided and instead politics should be devoted to the assessment of claims to entitlements that are predicated on more transparent and familiar interests. Therefore, the challenge is to show that a transparent method of assessing identity claims can be designed and that it can provide a normative currency by which seemingly incomparable claims about identity can be weighed and assessed fairly.

Authenticity

Many people reasonably assume that only identity claims based on some genuine or authentic dimension of an individual or group's identity merit recognition and accommodation. Yet, several difficulties arise when attempts are made to distinguish reliably between authentic and inauthentic identity claims. One problem is that the authenticity of a practice or belief – that is, its centrality and importance to a person or group's self-understanding – is often understood to rest upon subjective criteria of a deeply personal nature which should not or cannot be assessed by external decision makers. For instance, in relation to claims about religious identity, the authenticity of a belief rests on the rationale that it has for believers who consider it to be true or important. Yet, precisely because authentic beliefs and practices are highly subjective, they are often considered by decision makers to be too easily used in a fraudulent or strategic way to secure privileges or exemptions not otherwise available to people. Therefore, the need to assess the authenticity of practices is perceived to be great, but the possibility of doing so reliably is perceived to be slim.

The challenge of authenticity is especially well illustrated in cases about freedom of religion because the truth or falsity of religious or spiritual claims is generally viewed as highly subjective and appropriately treated as personal and private. State institutions treat the identity claims of religious minorities with suspicion and seek evidence, which may or may not be available, to verify that identity claims are not fraudulent. Minorities defend their claims in ways they believe will be convincing. Sometimes, this means that they distort or oversimplify the rationales for their practices in order to meet the expectations they assume dominant groups have about them. Minorities thereby 'perform' their identities and their performances are built on caricature which easily lends itself to naturalizing, essentializing, and stereotyping. When these distortions are publicly exposed, the minority appears to be making fraudulent claims and the majority's suspicious disposition to minority claims is thereby justified. The challenge of authenticity is to develop an approach capable of distinguishing between genuine and fraudulent claims in a reliable manner and without causing this dynamic.

Essentialism

Many theorists have observed that dominant groups tend to essentialize the cultures of minorities. Some identity sceptics attribute this to the failure of multiculturalism to negotiate identity adequately.[16] They argue that the current trend to find political significance in cultural attachments encourages a narrow understanding of what culture is. This narrow understanding essentializes individuals in the sense that it defines them in terms of their culture and often defines their cultures in crude and static ways. While essentialism is considered endemic to all identity claiming and cultural rights, it is especially well illustrated in relation to policy making about Indigenous peoples. Often, when public decision makers attempt to consider the relevance of 'culture' to the entitlements of Indigenous peoples, they latch on to an exaggerated and highly simplistic understanding of what that culture entails and therefore what ought to be protected about it. An Indigenous community's culture will be reduced to a narrow set of historical practices rather than understood in more dynamic and 'living' terms. Communities can thereby become imprisoned by static, constricting, and unrealistic construals of identity.

The challenge of essentialism is that identity claiming usually characterizes ways of life in narrow and nostalgic ways. Any rights or accommodations that are won on this basis are thereby likely to be insignificant to the more fundamental objective of enhancing the well being of vibrant and dynamic, albeit vulnerable, minority communities. The challenge is to show that identity claims, which are claims to protect practices considered especially important to people's identities, will not simply exacerbate essentialism and can be assessed in ways that overcome the essentialist understandings which sometimes influence decision making.

Domestication

The peril of domestication is again a broad challenge but one that also has special resonance in relation to Indigenous peoples and other communities which have been colonized. Domestication refers to the tendency found within several political accommodation strategies, such as multiculturalism and identity claiming, to undermine the political and legal legitimacy of the broader project sought by some minorities to secure recognition of their right to self-government or self-determination. Sceptics argue that identity claiming diverts public attention and community resources away from the real issue in most conflicts, namely that Western states have illegitimately imposed their rule on communities that were self-governing and territories that were for common use. Indigenous entitlements which are written into constitutions and international conventions usually fail to address this broader problem. Often courts refuse to assess the strength of Indigenous claims to self-determination and instead interpret entitlements in terms of narrow forms of accommodation for discrete cultural practices. Identity claiming is said to reflect this narrow project. The peril of domestication is that identity claiming, at best, secures for Indigenous minorities minor adjustments to existing state policies. At the same time, it disempowers these communities by leading them into costly legal battles that drain their resources and divert their energy from the larger more important project of fighting for their right to self-determination. And finally, identity claiming implicitly legitimizes the decision-making processes which are external to minority communities and controlled by the state or state system which is often responsible for domesticating the community in the first place. The challenge of domestication is to show how identity claiming can proceed without undermining the efforts of communities to advance their entitlement to self-government or self-determination.

CONCLUSION

Despite the good reasons to be sensitive to the problems associated with the public assessment of identity and to be critical of decisions that are made poorly in this respect, public institutions should not avoid the assessment of minority identity in making decisions about minority accommodation. The coherent assessment of identity claims is a central feature of democratic relations in diverse societies. In other words, this is not a side issue but rather the central and most difficult work that institutions do in multicultural contexts. If they do not do this work well – that is, in a reasonable, transparent, and fair manner – then they will end up sustaining an incomplete and distorted form of multiculturalism which is easily subject to backlash.

One aim of this chapter has been to address the charge that identity politics camouflages racism. In order to do so, I have explored the hazard of identity quietism, which is that quietism fails to connect the success of multiculturalism with the presence of a set of criteria that are designed to facilitate the fair and transparent assessment of minority identities. I have also outlined the arguments of identity sceptics and laid out four challenges that arise from the sceptical positions. The chapters to follow examine each of the challenges raised by identity sceptics in greater detail and in the context of how identity is actually assessed by public institutions. If these challenges can be met, as I believe they can, then identity claiming can and should play a role in just and diverse democratic communities.

4

Diversity and Sexual Equality: The Challenge of Incommensurability

In the previous chapter, I distinguished between two kinds of critics, identity quietists and identity sceptics, and explained why identity quietism cannot offer a satisfactory account of what the abstract normative commitments of multiculturalism require in determinate practical settings. Identity quietists suggest that the normative commitments of multiculturalism can be realized without engaging in the assessment of identity claims. By contrast, identity sceptics recognize that identity is central to multiculturalism but are consequently sceptical about the wisdom of multiculturalism as a normative orientation to politics in diverse societies. Identity sceptics have four reservations about an approach to public decision making that is based on the assessment of identity claims. This chapter examines the first reservation which concerns the incommensurability of identity claims. The problem of incommensurability rests on the idea that no politically accessible or coherent basis exists upon which to evaluate conflicting views about how identity matters and how it is to be weighed against other putatively fundamental considerations at play in any given conflict. The chapter examines this challenge in relation to one of the most frequently cited conflicts today in minority politics, namely the conflict between claims to sexual equality and claims to cultural accommodation or autonomy.

The chapter begins by examining the challenge of incommensurability and two general responses to the problem, one which re-expresses important claims, such as those about identity and sexual equality, in terms of rights, and the other which resolves such conflicts by establishing suitable processes of deliberation and democratic decision making. I call these the rights-based approach and the process-based approach. Both approaches seek to avoid entanglement with identity claims and both are often proposed specifically to resolve conflicts between sexual equality and cultural autonomy. I then turn to the identity approach and show how this approach provides a better way to understand and resolve the putative incommensurability of claims for sexual equality and cultural autonomy. By focusing on what is often a common denominator of values at stake in such cases, assessments that focus on identity claims provide a normatively rich but non-arbitrary means of comparing the significance of conflicting practices and values. At the same time, an identity approach cuts through the impasse, which is often generated by appeal to abstract but inflexible normative commitments such as rights, but it does not dodge substantive normative matters by merely deferring to the authority of process.

THE CHALLENGE OF INCOMMENSURABILITY

Incommensurability refers to a conflict between claims that are not easily compared because the claims in question appeal to seemingly distinct kinds of values. The incommensurability challenge potentially applies to any dispute where different kinds of claims are at stake, where these claims conflict, and where they appear to be equally or similarly important. Therefore, the challenge is not endemic to identity politics or identity claiming. Rather, the incommensurability of competing claims or goods is a broad and frequent concern in democratic politics about how to reconcile claims of different kinds in a satisfactory manner.

The potential conflict between sexual equality and cultural autonomy is one example of the sort of conflict which raises the challenge of incommensurability. On the one hand, sexual equality is important and fundamental to the well being of women. Women have a basic right to sexual equality. At the same time, most women fail to enjoy anything close to the legal, political, social, or economic status of men, and one of the main explanations for this is that the cultural and religious traditions and practices that shape women's lives and define their status within their communities are sexist. On the other hand, cultural and religious minorities often have seemingly legitimate claims to autonomy and by extension to protection and accommodation of their key practices. Yet, the gender inequality in marginalized groups often makes it more difficult for such groups to win recognition for their claims to cultural autonomy. Throughout Europe and North America, gender equality has become a favoured basis upon which to judge minorities and a proxy for demonizing minority groups, particularly Muslim minorities (see Phillips and Saharso 2008).[1] The suspicion is that respecting cultural autonomy fosters the denial of sexual equality. In Canada, the United States, and Australia, the status and well being of Indigenous women within their communities has, time and time again, been used to cast doubt on policies meant to strengthen Indigenous self-government (see Nahanee 1997; Monture-Angus 2003; Smith 2005). In this light, claims to cultural autonomy appear to be incommensurable with claims to sexual equality because measures aimed at promoting even modest forms of cultural accommodation appear hostile to the achievement of gender equality, while measures aimed at promoting gender equality appear to threaten the accommodation of minority groups.[2]

Identity sceptics argue that permitting identity claims to play a role in democratic politics is especially likely to generate the problem of incommensurability. Three factors fuel their concern. First, the sceptics believe that identity is an idiom which shields claims from being rationally scrutinized. Many people believe that identity is too complex and fluid to be the appropriate focus of public assessment, especially legal adjudication. For instance, Martha Minow argues that identity is socially negotiated and forever changing 'in relation to others and against the backdrop of social and political structures of power' (1991: 127). As a result, it defies determinative description. Joseph Carens (2000: 15) raises similar concerns in noting that identities are partly subjective, partly objective, sometimes singular, but often multiple, sometimes experienced as given, sometimes as chosen, shifting over time for both individuals and groups, reflecting or sometimes not reflecting cultural differences. In so far as identity is inscrutable in these ways, identity claims appear to be self-validating and subjective which makes them 'interpersonally and socially non-negotiable' (Waldron 2000: 158). This is one of Jeremy Waldron's concerns and is a key to his identity scepticism. The question that motivates Waldron's position is, who is in a better position than I to assess what my particular identity is and what respecting it entails? Cultural and religious traditions are viewed by those who follow them as important to their identities for deeply personal reasons, or based on doctrines and texts whose authenticity rests with the rationales they have for those who follow or practice them and not with external political and legal institutions (p. 170). The claim that something is important and central to my identity is in some important ways opaque to others and ought to remain so.

A second worry is that identity claims are monolithic claims that must either be accepted as a whole or rejected. As a consequence, they present themselves as non-negotiable claims that are not amenable to reasonable compromises of the sort upon which democratic politics depends. The sceptics view identity claims as monolithic because they are related to matters integral to a person's self-esteem and they are vague in terms of their precise conceptual content. According to Daniel Weinstock (2006), identity arguments impede compromise because identity claims mirror claims for self-esteem and self-respect which are about the core of a person. While we 'hold' values and 'possess' interests, 'that around which we construct our identity constitutes who we *are*' (p. 21).

A third concern is that the more demands of this non-negotiable and vague sort find their way onto the public agenda, the greater the chances are that claims will conflict. If, by recognizing the political legitimacy of identity claims, groups are encouraged to present their interests as identity claims, they will burden the public agenda with a host of vague, monolithic, non-negotiable, and thereby incommensurable claims. Moreover, an approach that seeks to determine which identity claim is more important (or more jeopardized) when two or more claims conflict, invites those involved in such conflicts to assert, in highly charged terms, the importance of their (opaque, self-validated, monolithic, and deeply personal) claim to their identity. This is how identity claiming raises the stakes in conflicts and implicitly draws into question the legitimacy of public institutions to decide amongst different and conflicting identity claims (see Minow 1991: 128). An approach that asks public decision makers to choose amongst different identity claims or different interpretations of what is important to the identity of a particular group, places an enormous burden on them which many people argue should be avoided.

An approach that specifically counsels decision makers to be sensitive to identity may invite into the public realm a host of non-negotiable and opaque claims which will increase the risk of social conflict. Such an approach may also deepen the problems afflicting women because privileging identity claims will embed women even further in self-validating traditions and non-negotiable rules that, by and large, are designed to function for the benefit of men.

TWO WAYS OF CONFRONTING INCOMMENSURABILITY

The rights-based approach

Against these background concerns, normative political theorists suggest two ways to negotiate conflicts that arise between measures to protect sexual equality and those that advance minority autonomy or accommodation while avoiding engagement with identity claims. The first way, the rights-based approach, frames the conflict as a matter of competing rights claims and then tries to distinguish between genuine and merely purported rights. The rights-based approach treats certain claims as fundamental and overriding values. In Ronald Dworkin's words (1977), rights are trumps. They trump the preferences of hostile majorities and the rival non-rights claims of other groups. This does not mean that rights are understood as limitless. Any legal system that takes rights seriously shapes the precise contours of rights. But the language of rights is used to invoke a less flexible set of considerations for generating entitlements than are invoked in the marketplace or in the political sphere where negotiable interests compete for resources. If a particular claim is a genuine right, the expectation is that it should be protected from other claims that threaten it regardless of whom or how many people advance these other claims.

Unsurprisingly, those who ascribe to the rights-based approach are especially sensitive to the incommensurability challenge because, if too many different kinds of claims are viewed as genuine rights, then the chances of conflict between claims will be high and no means will exist to choose amongst them. For instance, under the rights-based approach tensions between cultural, collective, and individual sex equality rights will appear to pose dilemmas between different and non-negotiable values. These dilemmas are difficult to resolve because no uncontroversial way exists to prioritize values that are represented as normatively basic and incommensurable.

Those who employ the rights-based approach in relation to cultural claims are well aware of this problem and often point out that women from cultural minorities face dilemmas in their political activism. For instance, Susan Okin (1998: 680) discusses the choices that some women face in terms of either enjoying cultural community or enjoying sexual equality, both of which are important values. Monique Deveaux characterizes the struggle by Indigenous women to advance sexual equality within their communities as 'a dilemma of reconciling sex equality rights with collective, cultural rights' (2000*a*: 81). Martha Nussbaum discusses the problem in terms of a 'dilemma' between the rights to sexual equality and the rights to cultural autonomy (1999: 81). Chandran Kukathas (2001) structures the clash between feminism and multiculturalism in terms of a dilemma (but unlike others, resolves the dilemma in favour of cultural autonomy). In all of this scholarship, both cultural accommodation and sexual equality are acknowledged as important to women. The question raised is how can these seemingly incommensurable values be reconciled when conflicts between them arise?

Waldron (2000) formulates this problem directly in terms of identity politics and what he refers to as the 'norm of compossibility'. According to Waldron, compossiblity is the idea that two things which are both possible may not be compossible, that is, possible at the same time (p. 159 fn. 5). Waldron's concern is that, if too many claims are put forward as potential rights and thereby non-negotiable entitlements, the norm of compossibility will be strained; the higher the number of non-negotiable claims advanced, the greater the chance that claims will conflict or be incompossible. Identity claims, in particular, appear to strain the norm of compossiblity. Such claims are potentially numerous in diverse societies. They typically involve higher stakes than most other claims due to their highly personal nature and the significance typically vested in them. And they are often opaque and self-validating. Denying an individual's identity claim might appear to involve denying them respect for the person that they are. As Waldron explains it: 'if that respect is demanded in the uncompromising and non-negotiable way in which respect for rights is demanded, the task may become very difficult indeed, particularly in circumstances where different individuals in the same society have formed their identities in different cultures' (p. 160). For this reason, Waldron argues that identity claims should not be advanced as non-negotiable claims if we want to preserve the norm of compossibility, but instead should be recognized by those who advance them as claims which are amenable to compromise. They are claims worthy of respect 'on the basis of reasons rather than on the mere fact of identity' (p. 174). In the context of Waldron's argument, this implies that identity claims are thereby distinct from other rights claims which are appropriately recognized as non-negotiable.

Like Waldron, many of those who adopt the rights-based approach resolve the challenge of incommensurability by disqualifying some claims as rights, usually claims to cultural entitlements. This effectively decreases the number of conflicts that can arise and therefore the strain on public institutions that have to resolve them. Most advocates of the rights-based approach tend to resolve impasses by declaring that one set of claims, usually claims to cultural autonomy or accommodation, are not really rights at all and that hence they are not very important after all.[3] Okin, for example, argues that some women '*may* be much better off, from a liberal point of view, if the culture into which they were born were either gradually to become extinct ... or, preferably, to be encouraged and supported to substantially alter itself ...' (1998: 680). Notwithstanding Okin's careful qualification of this statement, one could *only* conclude that some women would be better off 'if their cultures were gradually to become extinct', *if* one sees the choice between sexual equality and cultural autonomy as a dilemma between incommensurable claims. The dilemma is resolved by demanding that sexist cultures change their ways and this is only possible by arguing, as Okin does, that sexual equality is more fundamental than cultural autonomy because it plays a constant and reliable role in enhancing individual well being. In contrast, 'bending over backward out of respect of cultural diversity does great disservice to many women and girls around the world' (p. 666). In effect, Okin's analysis resolves the dilemma by arguing that, unlike the right to sexual equality, cultural autonomy is a dispensable interest.

Nussbaum also writes about 'the liberal dilemma' and, like Okin, emphasizes that the primacy of certain rights claims comes at the expense of respecting cultural differences. She defends individual rights and dismisses potential rival claims that are group-based or inspired by cultural or religious 'difference' (1999: 38–9). She argues that '[t]he liberal should emphasize this individualistic concept of basic rights and religious liberty' and that '[w]e should not accept the idea that denying any fundamental right of any individual is a legitimate prerogative of a religious group' (p. 107).[4] With reference to cultural groups, and specifically to Indigenous peoples in Canada, Nussbaum notes, 'it is hard to understand how the sad history of a group can provide a philosophical justification for the gross denial of individual rights and liberties to members of the group' (p. 109). Here again, culture is depicted as a minor interest or mere preference that is appropriately trumped by putatively more fundamental rights.

Problems with the rights-based approach

While one can agree with any of these theorists that cultural and religious groups should not deny women sexual equality or violate other individual rights, three problems tend to arise by employing the rights-based approach to reason through conflicts of this nature. First, the rights-based approach exacerbates the perception that claims are incommensurable and thereby gives rise to the risk that important values will be dismissed as minor interests or mere preferences so that other values can enjoy their status as rights. Politics is thus reduced to stark and simplistic dilemmas: either one embraces individual rights or one embraces cultural traditions; either individual rights or collective rights; either sexual equality or cultural autonomy. And once the selection is made, the normative significance of the losing claim is thereby diminished.

This way of framing the issue, as a matter of stark choices, obscures the fact that devising legitimate solutions in any context requires that we pay close attention to the traditions, beliefs, and histories of the groups and individuals involved. The concern upon which much cultural criticism of liberal rights turns is not that liberals interpret rights without implicit reference to context, but rather that they implicitly locate rights within the *wrong* context, usually a context informed by a narrow reading based primarily on Anglo-American culture and history. While this culture is not without its variety, debates, and disagreements about the priority of values and other matters, it is nonetheless a culture dominated by the experiences of a handful of countries. This is not to say that all the values extolled by liberalism are unique or culturally specific. But the way in which different communities give practical expression to abstract values can appropriately vary in response to different historical, social, and cultural factors and controversies. By framing claims in terms of rights, advocates of the rights-based approach risk placing claims within the context dominated by the cultural values of liberal states. Here lies the relevance of the much-repeated criticism that the discourse of rights is an inappropriate tool with which to adjudicate conflicts in Indigenous communities and formerly colonized states. One need not be a cultural relativist or even an unrelenting critic of rights to appreciate that rights are not culturally neutral. Indeed, even those who most champion the internationalization of human rights recognize and seek to overcome the culturally limited mindset that gave birth to rights.[5] Without special efforts to broaden the rights perspective, rights invoke arguments and principles that, while perhaps culturally ubiquitous in some form, are, in the first instance, based on controversies that have shaped Western liberal societies.

A second problem is that individual rights, such as freedom of speech, association, and religion, are often treated as though they are worthy of respect, not on the basis of a set of reasons, but on the basis of the implausible claim that the right, as it is articulated and interpreted by majority or dominant groups, is the ideal rendering of the values it protects and that it is not amendable to change or challenge in light of objections by minority groups to how the right is interpreted. This implausible view ignores how rights come to have meaning through historical processes which are informed by specific ways of doing things, usually formulated by particular ethnic and religious communities in the context of their struggles over a specific historical period. The strain on compossibility that Waldron mentions arises, not merely because of an increase in the number of claims, or because of the deeply personal nature of identity claims, but because many identity claims challenge the way in which specific rights are understood and protected, and contest the factors that ought to be considered relevant today to shaping what counts as a 'non-negotiable' rights-based claim.

The inconsistent acknowledgement of the need to contextualize rights and invite a richer debate about how rights ought to be interpreted characterizes the field of liberal multiculturalism today. For instance, Nussbaum has argued, against a contextualist understanding, that the history of Indigenous communities ought not to count in philosophical arguments about rights violations within these communities (1999: 109). At the same time and without recognizing the inconsistency in her outlook, she emphasizes the importance of context in relation to properly understanding what can be asked of the Catholic Church about who the Church employs to perform various roles. Because individuals have the right to be protected against discrimination on the basis of sexual orientation, Nussbaum argues that the Church may not terminate the employment of a gay or lesbian groundskeeper. And yet, 'it would be wrong to require a religious body to ordain open and practicing homosexuals' (p. 197). To distinguish between when it is and when it is not appropriate to discriminate against people on the basis of sexual orientation, Nussbaum must put aside the discourse of rights and determine what is core or peripheral to the character or identity of the Catholic Church. I am not suggesting that Nussbaum's method in this respect is incorrect. On the contrary, this is precisely the sort of approach that is required of those who want to apply liberal rights fairly to any cultural and religious community. But the approach relies on knowledge that goes well beyond a culturally insensitive understanding of individual rights. The rhetoric of rights is not enough because adjudicating conflicting rights requires that we assess the character or identity of a group and, specifically, the way in which disputed practices sustain or undermine that identity. The religious liberty of the Catholic Church ought to be shaped, in part, by the needs and interests of individuals. But, in large part, it is also shaped by judgments about which practices or traditions are central to the Church's identity and which are not. This is not a matter that the simple invocation of fundamental rights can settle. Nor is it a determination that can be made without considering and weighing the history, traditions, and practices of the Church.[6]

A third problem with adopting the rights-based approach is that institutions, such as courts, which are responsible for adjudicating in conflicts between what are made to appear to be incommensurable values, are often perceived as rendering their decisions in an arbitrary manner that reflects cultural, gender-based, or other political biases. This perception, which is especially common amongst identity sceptics, rests, in part, on the belief that, because there is not a more fundamental value to appeal to in cases where allegedly basic rights conflict, public decision makers simply choose one right over another, based on their own biases. In Canada, for example, the political battles between French and English communities and between Indigenous and settler communities have historically been expressed in terms of a conflict between the different kinds of rights favoured by each culture. The Canadian judiciary and national political leaders are often criticized for imposing, according to their cultural biases, individual rights on communities that favour collective ones (see Eisenberg 1994: 5–8). According to the sceptics, the best way to avoid this perception is to ensure that identity claims are not treated as rights-based entitlements in the first place.

But, for the reasons outlined earlier, diminishing the legal and normative significance of identity claims as a means to meet the challenge of incommensurability is likely to exacerbate cultural divides and unnecessarily exaggerate perceptions of vast cultural differences. To speculate, even hypothetically, about the extinction of a culture or to apply fundamental rights without careful attention to context, history, tradition, and practice, is to take the well trodden path of a profoundly colonial interpretation of liberalism that, understandably, will be swiftly rejected by those whose histories and cultures it seems to ignore. By framing the problem of achieving sexual equality or cultural autonomy in terms of fundamental and irreconcilable values, the rights-based approach poses the choice too starkly. While some women might choose the same values that liberalism endorses, others might not. Rather than lending moral and political strength to the cause of enhancing sexual equality within fragile communities, the rights-based approach may weaken this cause because, unsurprisingly, some women will reject the conclusion that cultural accommodation is a lesser interest and instead put their faith in their cultural community, even helping to define their community in terms that build upon a rejection of the liberal principles foisted on them.[7]

In sum, three problems confront identity sceptics who attempt to avoid identity claims by taking refuge in the fundamentality of rights. First, the rights-based approach emphasizes the incommensurability of values understood to be rights and resolves the impasse between them by showing that some values, often collective and cultural rights, are not as fundamental or important as the more standard individual rights. Second, the approach usually entails advancing an uncritical and insufficiently nuanced view of individual rights as though they provide the ideal rendering of the abstract values at stake rather than a particular, and often highly contentious, interpretation of these values. It thus fails to acknowledge the ways in which the interpretation and meaning of rights are open to change and challenge. And, third, the rights-based approach places damaging pressure on public decision makers such as courts, because in choosing between competing claims, both of which are expressed as rights, their decisions appear to be arbitrary or biased.

Process-based approaches

The process-based approach attempts to resolve tensions between sexual equality and cultural autonomy procedurally. Instead of focusing directly on the substantive values at the heart of conflicts, this approach recommends that we design and implement fair procedures that can generate legitimate outcomes without the need to broach contentious considerations of identity. According to this second approach, conflicts that involve incommensurable claims are best settled by applying community-endorsed processes of decision making. Many different kinds of decision-making processes might be favoured by those who adopt this approach including deliberative processes, democratic and representative processes, or traditional community-based processes. The distinguishing feature of the process-based approach is that substantively acceptable outcomes to conflicts are reached through agreements made under fair conditions and just procedures. Some people who hold this position insist that the value of just procedures outweighs even the outcome of decisions in the sense that the mere fact that fair processes lead to non-liberal outcomes (Deveaux 2006: 209–10) or fail to generate consensus on particular questions (Benhabib 2002: 115) does not count against their legitimacy. Procedural fairness holds that just resolutions are the product of fair processes. Those who frame conflicts using process-based approaches share an optimism that, regardless of outcomes, designing fair and inclusive means to deliberation and decision making is the best way to resolve community disputes, including disputes where claims to sexual equality conflict with claims to cultural autonomy or accommodation.

One of the key strengths of process-based approaches is that they highlight that fair processes will reflect the historical context in which conflicts occur and thereby are more likely to generate decisions that minority communities can embrace as legitimate. Jeff Spinner-Halev (2001) points out that in many concrete cases, the legal and political institutions of the majority historically participated in dominating the minority community and therefore are usually considered to be the wrong institutions to decide whose rights and which values ought to govern these communities. Majority institutions are sometimes to blame for imposing on minorities practices that give rise to conflicts between sexual equality and the autonomy of the minority community. This is particularly true of cases involving restrictive rules of membership, as Song (2007) has shown. In most societies, rules regarding membership, particularly those that restrict women through marriage and divorce, are the key means by which groups distinguish themselves from others and thus retain their identity in light of the pervasive threat posed by the majority of assimilation through intermarriage. Sometimes, the precise form these rules take has origins in majority practices which are either imposed on minorities or borrowed by them.

For instance, the sexist rules of membership in Indigenous communities in Canada[8] were designed not by Indigenous peoples, but by nineteenth century Canadian bureaucrats. Nonetheless, many Indigenous organizations defended the rules when they were challenged in the 1970s by Indigenous women who had lost their membership. Those who defended the rules argued that Indigenous peoples need to have control over demarcating their membership and that changes to these rules should follow solely from Indigenous-initiated and Indigenous-controlled processes. Ironically, critics of the rules made a similar argument: that these sexist rules of membership are reminders that Indigenous people lack control over community membership because the rules were instituted by the Canadian government and are characteristic of the patriarchal traditions of European settler societies, not Indigenous ways of life (see Nahanee 1997; Turpel-Lafond 1997). The histories of colonized peoples present many examples of assimilative policies that lead to internal community conflict of this sort.[9] In light of this history, and the community divisions to which they often gives rise, advocates of the process-based approaches sensibly suggest that conflicts between claims to sexual equality and cultural autonomy ought to be resolved by processes internal to minority communities or by reliable and trusted third-party arbiters such as international tribunals, which are endorsed by the minority community.

A second advantage of the process-based approach, especially a deliberative approach to conflict resolution, is the potential it has to transform rather than entrench social and political divisions amongst groups. Seyla Benhabib favours deliberative procedures to address conflicts involving cultural claims precisely because of their potential to transform citizens by 'opinion and will-formation' and by enhancing their democratic natures through political engagement with each other (2002: ch. 5). Monique Deveaux also favours process-based, deliberative approaches to resolve conflicts between claims to sexual equality and claims to cultural protection partly because she believes that, at the heart of most cultural disputes, are internal power struggles: 'tensions between cultural rights and sex equality protections should be understood as primarily political tensions, rather than as entrenched conflicts over moral values' (2006: 186). The best processes are ones that expose deliberants to the unjust motives or pernicious interests which are a feature of these kinds of community disputes.

In contrast to process-based approaches which often place the onus on communities to resolve internal conflicts, rights-based approaches seem to come up with resolutions to conflicts from 'on high' and impose them on disputing parties regardless of what kinds of solutions communities might come up with themselves. Whereas rights-based approaches offer a means to assess claims independently of community decision-making processes, the promise of the process-based approach is to provide context-sensitive and potentially transformative means to resolve community conflicts.

Problems with process-based approaches

The main problem with process-based approaches in relation to conflicts between sexual equality and cultural autonomy is that they do not (and cannot) do what they seem to promise; they do not replace the need to determine, from a point of view concerned with the justness of decisions, what constitutes the best resolution to conflicts internal to minority communities. This is especially clear when the process-based approach is understood to require that majorities not interfere in the internal politics of minority communities when doing so violates legitimate claims to self-government or autonomy to which the minority has a right. This strong understanding of the process-based approach holds that minority communities, especially those striving for self-determination, ought to make their own decisions according to their own community-based processes.[10] Yet, the problem with this strong understanding is that allowing a community to resolve conflicts, according to its own decision-making procedures, is often not all that different from endorsing the values that dominate the community in the first place. For instance, when the US Supreme Court decided, in *Santa Clara Pueblo v. Julia Martinez* (1978), that the fairest way to resolve disputes within the Santa Clara community is to leave to that community the task of working out solutions according to tribal traditions, the Court seemed to be adopting a process-based approach because its decision favoured whatever decision community-based processes favoured. But, at the same time, it seemed to be endorsing the value of cultural autonomy over other values at stake in the dispute. By respecting the right to cultural autonomy (or self-government), the Court gave authoritative status to particular rules within the minority community, including rules that dictate how subgroups, women, and dissenters ought to be treated within that community (see Shachar 1998: 290).

This points to the general conundrum that affects process-based approaches. If we are willing to accept any solution to a conflict, no matter how inegalitarian or unjust, as long as it is the product of fair processes internal to self-determining groups, then there is little difference in practice between respecting the processes internal to minority groups and making a substantive decision in favour of group autonomy over sexual equality in every case of conflict between them. Those who favour process-based solutions because such solutions respect the right to group autonomy or self-government are, in effect, arguing that group autonomy *is* more important than other potentially conflicting values, such as sexual equality. The argument is no less 'top–down' than arguments used by those who favour a rights-based approach to secure the primacy of sexual equality over cultural autonomy.

Most people who favour the process-based approach do not endorse decision-making processes simply because they are internal to a community, but instead require that they live up to democratic standards or that they be just. Democracy requires that all sides in a dispute be given equal consideration by institutions internal to the community. Therefore, most advocates of this approach argue that legitimate community decision making must display sensitivity to considerations of substantive justice such as equality, inclusion, and accountability. For example, Deveaux (2006) endorses community-based processes not simply because they are internal to a community, but because they are democratic and inclusive. Similarly, Spinner-Halev argues that Muslim minorities in India and Israel ought to have jurisdiction over their own personal laws, but with the qualification that, 'these laws be established by democratically accountable representatives, not just the traditional male religious leaders' (2001: 108). Benhabib insists that the three normative conditions of egalitarian reciprocity, voluntary self-ascription, and freedom of exit and association guide cultural deliberation (2002: 106–8). In all of these accounts, the values that ensure processes are fair and democratic are values that specifically focus on ensuring the equal standing of vulnerable subgroups within communities.

But, once again, this seems to dodge rather than resolve the problem of incommensurability in relation to conflicts between sexual equality and cultural autonomy. Many cases that involve such conflicts also involve complaints that women are not treated as equals in decision-making processes and that their membership status and community standing are more fragile than those of men. In such cases, the problem is precisely that women are not treated as equals within their communities, in the sense that they do not have equal political voice and therefore they cannot participate as equals in discussion or deliberation. All conflicts about sexual discrimination, whether they occur in minority or majority communities, involve, in some way, a denial of women's equal membership, a failure to recognize their equal standing, or a refusal to give their interests equal weight and consideration. Therefore, to require that community processes be democratic, as Deveaux, Spinner-Halev, and Benhabib insist, is to require that women are treated as equals in those processes. But the difference between ensuring that the principles of procedural justice are adhered to and ensuring that sexual equality is respected may be slight. In order to be just, laws must be passed by just procedures. But in order for procedures to be considered just, they must be democratic; allow for all members to participate on an equal basis; and treat all members with equal consideration and respect. These requirements are substantive in informing charters of rights. There is little difference between requiring that processes respect these rights and requiring that sexual equality be guaranteed within all communities. Moreover, one key promise of the process-based approach – that it requires less interference in the affairs of minority communities than do non-process-based approaches – is unsustainable. Approaches that insist on the requirements of procedural justice will interfere significantly in the affairs of communities that fail to have just procedures. Particularly in cases where the view is that women are not treated as equals within their communities, the process-based approach may sanction as much interference in the affairs of a minority community as approaches that sanction imposing substantive values on communities that fail to respect them.

A key virtue of process-based approaches is that they correctly acknowledge that often the only effective way to understand or resolve conflicts within a community is to rely on institutions internal to the community, especially institutions which facilitate deliberation. Internal decision-making processes ensure the legitimacy of decisions. They ensure that decisions are taken in light of relevant historical context. And they potentially provide a means to transform rather than entrench political and social divisions within communities. But to maintain that, in conflicts where claims are incommensurable, fair resolutions are the product of participatory decision-making processes internal to communities begs the question of what is required for processes to be considered fair and may require that communities abandon or alter their own processes in order to protect values, such as sexual equality, whose protection motivates the disputes that internal procedures are supposed to resolve.

Both the rights-based and process-based approaches are means to deal with the incommensurability of claims. But neither approach is satisfactory. By posing claims as incommensurable values, the rights-based approach denies, in effect, that a common currency for adjudicating disputes is available. By posing conflicts as dilemmas and asking those involved to choose sides, it increases the risk that resolutions will fracture communities. Finally, the approach too easily tends to identify, define, and apply rights without consideration of specific historical and cultural factors that can legitimately affect the interpretation of conflicts. A strong tendency exists on the part of those who use this approach to favour claims that fit the historically conventional mold of individual rights.

Process-based approaches fare somewhat better. They are sensitive to contextual considerations and may, in some circumstances, be the best means to mend cleavages within and between communities. But they succeed in these respects only by either dodging direct engagement with the substantive normative criteria that should be invoked in adjudication or by begging the question in favour of one set of values over competing sets. The question to be addressed now is how an approach which focuses on considerations of identity differs from these other approaches and how it satisfies these criteria more adequately than they do.

THE IDENTITY APPROACH

An improved approach to resolving conflicts that involve seemingly incommensurable claims will have the following three dimensions. First, unlike the rights-based approach, it must be context-sensitive and incorporate, from the start, considerations related to the history, traditions, and practices of individuals and groups, the self-understanding that individuals and groups bring to conflicts, and therefore what different groups might consider to be at stake for them within disputes. Second, it will employ a common normative currency for the assessment of claims so as to avoid, at least in the first instance, exacerbating the perception that claims are truly incommensurable or analysing disputes in terms of values that are irreconcilable. In other words, a better approach addresses the challenge of incommensurability by ensuring that claims are comparable along important dimensions and therefore they are not opaque, monolithic, or non-negotiable. Third, a better approach displays some awareness of the political dimensions of most conflicts in the sense that it generates resolutions which bring communities together without dodging the normative issues on which conflicts are sometimes based.

The identity approach meets these criteria by providing a framework in which the strength of conflicting claims is determined on the basis of three conditions: (1) the jeopardy condition; (2) the validation condition; and (3) the safeguard condition. The jeopardy condition requires that claims are assessed in terms of their importance to the identities of those advancing the claim, and in terms of evidence that the practice is seriously jeopardized in the absence of protection in a manner that ensures sensitivity to different kinds of evidence. Given these criteria, the jeopardy condition must tackle concerns related to the putatively opaque and subjective nature of identity claims. These concerns, which are also central to the question raised in the next chapter of how decision makers distinguish between genuine and fraudulent claims, are relevant to the problem of incommensurability because if claims are truly opaque and highly subjective, then decision makers have no non-arbitrary basis upon which to choose amongst them. This is one of Waldron's concerns when he argues that identity claims are 'interpersonally and socially non-negotiable' because they are deeply personal and often based on doctrines or beliefs whose authenticity rests with the rationales they have for those who follow them and not with external institutions (2000: 158). It is also a concern echoed by Barry. On Barry's view, no non-arbitrary and politically legitimate basis exists on which to assess claims about the authenticity of cultural traditions and practices, and we 'cease to engage in moral discourse and switch to the perspective of an anthropologist' once we advance claims based on culture identity (2001: 253).

In practical settings, if contending claims which are central to a dispute are truly opaque and subjective, then it seems that decision makers should either adopt a highly subjective test to assess such claims or they should withdraw from assessing them at all. But, neither of these options poses a satisfactory way to resolve most disputes. While we can acknowledge that identity has opaque facets, it is important also to acknowledge that the facets of identity which are central to many conflicts are usually not as opaque as critics allege. Moreover, it is possible that if decision makers are allowed to, they will treat all aspects of identity as opaque even when they are not, because doing so allows them to avoid making difficult decisions. Treating all identity claims as opaque removes from vulnerable groups a clear way to express and defend their claims, and forces them to seek other possibly more costly and otherwise imperfect means of advancing claims.[11]

In most cases, the jeopardy condition is established on the basis of criteria that render a claim, if not perfectly transparent, then at least sufficiently translucent to allow decision makers to assess the importance and/or threat which groups or individuals claim to confront. For instance, often what matters to claimants is not that decision makers believe the objective truth of their subjective commitments but rather that they understand the importance of these commitments to the believer or the community (see Quong 2002). For example, in most reports regarding the ongoing dispute in North America about the claim of Fundamentalist Latter Day Saints (FLDS) to practice polygamy, the controversy turns on the public belief that polygamy in FLDS communities amounts to the abuse of women and children. That being so, what informs the problem in the first place is the (albeit implicit) public acknowledgement that, for FLDS, the practice plays a central and important role in religious beliefs, in a way of life, and thus in the identity of the FLDS community. According to an approach that assesses polygamy as an identity claim, the strength of the FLDS claim is built on showing that FLDS are not merely people who declare, for example, that they want to marry multiple sex partners. When conflicts involving controversial practices arise, we do not simply accept at face value what individuals or groups tell us is important to them. On the contrary, courts and other public institutions establish something like the jeopardy condition by examining the history and role of a practice; its importance to an individual according to what he or she sincerely believes; and its importance to the group. The sort of considerations that legitimately count as strengthening the jeopardy condition in the case of polygamy in North America include, for example, that the practice of polygamy is part of a group's identity; that it has a history; that efforts have been made to retain the practice in light of opposition to it; and that it contributes to the social fabric of a way of life. Conversely, what counts as a compelling reason to limit or prohibit a practice is not simply because 'we don't do that around here' or because 'we don't like that others do it'. Instead, the claim is weakened in light of evidence which shows that the practice threatens central and important aspects of the identities of other groups or individuals, or that it fails to meet the other conditions because it is forced on members or because it harms them. None of this evidence amounts to accepting claims at face value or, for that matter, assessing their objective truth. Nor does it involve supposing that all facets of a person's or group's identity are fully transparent to public decision makers. There may be highly subjective dimensions of identity that remain opaque to outsiders. However, in many, perhaps most, cases the facets of identity that are relevant to understanding the nature and significance of disputed practices can be examined, and thus claims about how and why identity may be threatened can be reasonably assessed.

The second condition, the validation condition, rests on evidence which shows how controversial practices or rules are validated by those who practice them. The condition will be weakened by evidence that practices are sustained coercively, through indoctrination, or as the result of collective action binds. Unsurprisingly, prohibiting practices like polygamy which are important to religious minorities but are distasteful to dominant groups, is often justified on the basis that the practice is coercively validated. In the case of FLDS polygamy, debates today about how to respond to the practice focus on the claim and accompanying evidence that the practice is validated coercively. Research done on the communities, including the testimonies of those who have left the communities, and examinations of the children who have been apprehended by social services officials, shows or attempts to show that FLDS children are indoctrinated; removed from their homes at young ages; shipped across the border between Canada and the United States, where they are married to older men; that many *de facto* marriages[12] take place between underage girls and older men; and that young men who reject the practice are expelled from the community (see Krakauer 2003; Bramham 2008). To a considerable degree, the decision to prohibit the practice rests on the strength of this evidence which attempts to show that the practice is coercively validated.

Moreover, many of the concerns about FLDS today also implicate the safeguard condition which aims to determine whether adequate safeguards are in place to reduce the risk that practices will harm either those who practice them or others. The challenge presented by this condition is that, while harm is an important standard, what harm consists of is the subject of considerable dispute both within communities as well as between them. Today, establishing this condition in relation to FLDS focuses mainly on the purported abuse of children within the communities and the absence of safeguards, for instance, delivered by social services and public education, given the insularity of these communities. In the past, harm was also central to the reasons given to prohibit the practice. For instance, in *Reynolds v. United States* (1878), the court's reasons for prohibiting polygamy directly refer to the harmful effects of the polygamous sect on the broader community. The court argued that, out of the 'fruits' of the marital contract, 'spring social relations and social obligations and duties, with which government is necessarily required to deal'. The court argued that polygamy corrupts these relations because, amongst other reasons it 'leads to the patriarchal principle... which fetters the people in stationary despotism, while that principle cannot long exist in connection with monogamy' (p. 165).

These nineteenth-century arguments are not convincing today and therefore the strength of the case against the members of FLDS in Texas and Bountiful, BC, rests, in large part, on showing that polygamy is coercively validated; that it is imposed on children; and that communities lack sufficient safeguards to prevent predictable harms that flow from the practice. What makes this a difficult case, according to the identity approach, and what also explains the current reluctance in Canada and the United States to pursue the criminal prosecution of polygamy despite the fact that both countries have criminal laws against the practice, is that, on the one hand, the jeopardy condition seems to be strongly satisfied, but, on the other hand, concerns exist about validation and harm. The matter can be resolved, according to the identity approach, only after assessing whether these concerns are based on evidence which establishes that the practice is coercively imposed and whether safeguards can be established to respond to the potential for abuse. In these ways, the identity approach shows how the case for or against the practice ought to be assessed. If FLDS members can show that the practice is both central and important to their religious identities, that their members validate the practice in a way that avoids coercion and indoctrination, and that safeguards are in place to ensure against harm, then the identity approach suggests that, in the absence of contrary evidence, the practice ought to be allowed.

Applying the identity approach to cases

So far, I have outlined what the identity approach requires in general terms. It remains to be shown how the approach meets the challenge of incommensurability more fully than do the other two approaches and in a way that improves how actual conflicts between claims based on sexual equality and those based on cultural autonomy are understood and resolved. In order to do so, I examine two legal cases that involve a seemingly incommensurable set of claims: *A.-G. Canada v. Lavell* (1974) and *Santa Clara Pueblo v. Julia Martinez* (1978). These cases are similar in some respects. Both involve Indigenous communities struggling to remain distinctive from a settler majority. Both also involve a discriminatory membership rule that revokes the membership status of Indigenous women (and their children), but not men, who marry outside their communities. The rule disadvantages women at the same time as it implicates some interests which are central to the identities of Indigenous communities in that it determines who is a member of the community and who is not, and thus who shares in the community's resources and who does not. Notwithstanding these similarities, the cases have important dissimilarities worth noting. In particular, they arise out of different legal regimes in Canada and the United States to which Indigenous peoples must respond. In the US case, the tribe in question enjoys a limited form of self-government. In the Canadian case, the Indigenous people do not enjoy self-government or at least not when the case in question was decided.[13] Here, I examine these cases as a means to illustrate the contrasting ways in which the three approaches present the conflict between sexual equality and cultural autonomy and the solutions that each approach favours.

In *A.-G. Canada v. Lavell*, two Indigenous women, Jeanette Lavell and Yvonne Bédard, were not allowed to live in their communities after marrying non-Indigenous men. They were not allowed to return to their communities even upon separating from their non-Indigenous husbands. Lavell and Bédard challenged the discriminatory membership rule found in section 12 (1)(b) of the Canadian *Indian Act*. The rule was part of a set of rules that define, in Canadian law, who is a status Indian and who therefore qualifies to live on reserve and to receive other benefits associated with status. When Lavell and Bédard married non-status husbands, they lost their status according to the Act. Lavell and Bédard argued that the rule violated their right to equality before the law and the protection of the law without discrimination by reason of race, national origin, colour, religion, or sex, which was protected at the time by the Canadian Bill of Rights.[14] The Supreme Court of Canada decided the case in 1974 at which time it found against Lavell and Bédard. The Court's reasons reflected, even at the time, its failure to develop a strong interpretation of the right to equality.[15] Beyond the interpretation of equality contained within it, the case illustrates the contrast between employing each of the approaches examined above.

Using the rights-based approach, the case appears, as it did to many of those involved at the time, to pose a clear dilemma between sexual equality rights and cultural autonomy. The right to equality, as guaranteed by a more purposive interpretation of the Bill of Rights, conflicts with the right of Indigenous communities to define their own membership – or at least, the right of Indigenous communities to control changes to how their membership is defined by the *Indian Act*. In 1980, in an effort to emphasize the dilemma posed by these rights, the leader of the National Indian Brotherhood

(NIB) refused to endorse the federal government's plan to amend this disputed section in a way that rendered it less discriminatory until constitutional provisions were in place to guarantee Indigenous peoples the right to self-government (Nahanee 1997: 97–8 fn. 55). The NIB structured the choice confronting Indigenous people, especially Indigenous women, as a dilemma between the right to self-government and the right to sexual equality. The dilemma was resolved by choosing between the rights. The strategy correctly surmised that, if the conflict is posed as a contest between incommensurable rights claims, the right to cultural autonomy is likely to be viewed by Indigenous people as more fundamental than any other claim in light of their circumstances of subjugation in relation to the Canadian state.

The process-based approach correctly points out that one of the key obstacles to resolving this dispute was that, in the eyes of Indigenous peoples, the Canadian state lacks the legitimacy to adjudicate Indigenous membership rules.[16] Yet, after it alerts us to this problem, the process-based approach provides no obvious solutions to it. In the *Lavell* case, the legitimacy of decision-making processes internal to Indigenous communities, including the manner in which Indigenous organizations represented their members' interests, was brought into question by those who favoured changing the membership rules. Internal processes were viewed as unfair because tens of thousands of people whose status was revoked by the membership rule were not allowed to participate in these decision-making processes.[17] The means to ensure the fairness of these processes would have required interfering in the affairs of Indigenous communities perhaps just as much as would have been required by ensuring that membership rules respect sexual equality.

The identity approach requires, first, that identity claims in conflicts are assessed via direct consideration of the ways in which the identity of groups or persons is at stake or jeopardized. In the *Lavell* case, a discussion of identity is found in the dissenting opinion of Justice Laskin. Laskin compares the concerns of each side in terms of the impact they have on the identities of those involved. He argues that the impact of the membership rule on the identities of Indigenous women is profound. On one hand, women who lose status are effectively 'excommunicated' from their society. The membership rule also 'excommunicate[s] the children of a union of an Indian woman and a non-Indian' and creates 'an invidious distinction ... between brothers and sisters who are Indians and who respectively marry non-Indians'. The membership rule is, 'if anything, an additional legal instrument of separation of an Indian woman from her native society and from her kin ...' (*Lavell* 1974: 1366).

The argument to retain the membership rule, presented by the Attorney General of Canada, the Indian bands involved, and Indigenous organizations from across the country, also presented an identity claim. The appellants argued that the purpose of the Act, which is 'to preserve and protect the members of the race', is achieved in part 'by the statutory preference for Indian men' (p. 1386). Laskin responds to this argument by first putting rights aside: 'even without the explicit direction against sexual discrimination found in the Canadian Bill of Rights', he argues, the discriminatory rule cannot be sustained as reasonable because it lacks any historical basis. 'There is no clear historical basis for the position taken by the appellants' that gives preference to Indigenous men over Indigenous women, 'certainly not in relation to Indians in Canada as a whole, and this was in effect conceded during the hearing in this court' (pp. 1387–8). In other words, according to Laskin, this particular membership rule does not play an important role in the identities of Indigenous communities.

Laskin's opinion reflects, at least in part, what an identity approach requires in cases where fundamental values conflict. It requires that the language of abstract and fundamental rights be set aside initially and that claims be reassessed in terms of the role and importance of a practice to identity, how it is validated, and whether it is harmful. Whereas rights-based claims appear to be irreconcilable because they embody values that seem, at least in principle, fundamental, claims that are recast in terms of the conditions associated with the identity approach can be compared to each other. Of the evidence that Laskin considers, he correctly notes that the effect of the membership rule is likely to be profound not only on the women whose status is revoked, but also on their children and their families in general. In contrast, no evidence was offered to convince the court that the patriarchal preference reflected by the rule was a central or important aspect of Indigenous identity. The rule lacked a strong historical connection to Indigenous practices and values. Its history was instead related to colonial imposition. To extrapolate from Laskin's decision, while there may be good reasons, born out of the need to protect community identity, to restrict intermarriage, this protection can be instituted in a variety of ways. The provisions of section 12(1)(b) of the *Indian Act* provide protection in a way that, on the one hand, has damaging effects on the identities of Indigenous women and invidious effects on their families, and, on the other hand, fails to reflect any important feature of Indigenous identity. Once identity matters are actually examined, one discovers that there is no real dilemma here. The identity approach suggests that the case ought to have been decided in favour of Lavell and Bédard based on comparing the effects of the disputed rule on the identities of those involved.

Based on this assessment of the *Lavell* case, one might extrapolate that an approach which assesses conflicting identity claims will always tend to favour sexual equality when it conflicts with claims based on group identity. The survival of a group's identity seldom if ever depends on its adherence to a single practice. A comparison of the impact of discrimination on individual identity and the impact of changing one rule or one tradition on group identity is unlikely to yield results that favour groups. But this observation does not draw the identity approach into question. Instead, it clarifies one reason, according to the approach, why groups must often yield to the interests of their members or other individuals, namely that, groups rarely have as much at stake in such conflicts as individuals do. If it is true that the well being and survival of any distinctive group never hangs upon a single practice and that equality and equal recognition are crucial to the healthy identities of people, then equality *should* never yield to a group's identity claim.

But sometimes group practices are viewed as central aspects of group identity and sometimes groups convince the courts that interests central to their identity are at stake. Consider, for example, the case of *Santa Clara Pueblo v. Julia Martinez.* Martinez and her children brought suit against the Santa Clara Indians because of a tribal ordinance that denied membership to the children of women, not men, who married outside the tribe. Before the case went to the US Supreme Court, the District Court noted in its decision the important ways in which the children affected by this ordinance identified as Santa Clarans; they 'have been brought up on the Pueblo, speak the Tewa language, participate in its life, and are, culturally, for all practical purposes, Santa Clara Indians' (Martinez 1975: 18). It then contrasted the effect on their identities of being denied membership with weighty observations about the tribe's identity: the rules of membership 'reflect traditional values of patriarchy still significant in tribal life . . . [M]embership rules were no more or less than a mechanism of social self-definition', and as such, were basic to the tribe's survival as 'a cultural and economic entity' (p. 15). In the end, the District Court held that 'the balance to be struck between these competing interests was better left to the judgment of the Pueblo' (pp. 18–19).

The Court of Appeal reversed this decision again on grounds that were directly related to identity. The sex-based distinction in the membership rules 'was presumptively invidious and it could be sustained only if justified by a compelling tribal interest' (Martinez 1976 as quoted in Martinez 1978: 113). In relation to establishing such a compelling interest, the Court noted that the membership ordinance is of recent vintage and that it fails to 'rationally identify those persons who were emotionally and culturally Santa Clarans' (p. 113). On these grounds, the Court of Appeal found in favour of Martinez.

The US Supreme Court attempted to interpret the case as primarily about matters of procedural justice and to downplay the considerations related to identity raised in the lower court decisions. The case turned on, first, whether federal courts had jurisdiction to interfere 'with tribal autonomy and self-government' and, second, whether the Indian Civil Rights Act could be used by Indigenous individuals against their own communities.

The majority of the Court found that federal courts lacked jurisdiction (p. 110). But, in rendering its decision, the Court went well beyond the legal rules that established tribal jurisdiction, and instead discussed the connection between respecting this jurisdiction and sustaining the identity of tribal communities. The Court argued that conflicts that involve tribal statutes 'will frequently depend on questions of tribal tradition and custom that tribal forums may be in a better position to evaluate than federal courts' (p. 110). Moreover, federal interference will 'undermine the authority of the tribal court . . . and hence . . . infringe on the right of the Indians to govern themselves' (p. 116). The federal judiciary 'may substantially interfere with the tribe's ability to maintain itself as a culturally and politically distinct entity' if it interferes in this and other conflicts of this sort (pp. 123–4). The Court emphasizes the fact that Indian tribes are different and ought to be allowed to remain different. The tribes are akin to 'foreign states' and have government structures, culture, and sources of sovereignty that are 'in many ways foreign to the constitutional institutions of Federal and State Governments' (p. 123).

In one sense, respecting tribal forums and institutions is appropriately viewed as a matter of procedural justice. But in this decision, the Court explicitly justifies this procedural requirement in terms that are directly linked to sustaining the community's distinct identity. The Court does not simply declare, for instance, that the law prohibits the Court to interfere. Rather, the decision focuses on one of the most crucial claims to protect the identity of any minority group, namely, its ability to maintain itself as a culturally and politically distinct entity by maintaining the legitimacy of its institutions and their capacity to render decisions. This identity claim is the lens through which the Court interprets what tribal jurisdiction entails and why it is important. The message conveyed by the Court's reasoning is that, if the legitimacy of these institutions was not at stake or if these institutions were not responsible for maintaining the cultural and political distinctiveness of the group, then the Court would be more willing to examine the membership ordinance in question. The success of the tribe's claim to retain its rules depends largely on its success at showing that, by overturning the rule, the Court threatens the tribe's political and cultural identity. To understand this conflict in relation to the identity claims at stake suggests that the success of the tribe's claim also depends on comparing the impact of overturning the ordinance on the tribe's identity with the impact of the rule on Martinez's children and others similarly situated. The Supreme Court did not explicitly make this comparison, although if it had, it might not have changed its final decision given its view of what was at stake in this case for this and other Indigenous tribes.

The *Martinez* case differs from the *Lavell* case because in *Lavell* the legitimacy of self-governing institutions and thus their role in sustaining Indigenous identity was not at issue. Had the Santa Clara Indians not convinced the Supreme Court of the importance of their institutions to sustaining their identity, then the Court might have considered more carefully other factors such as, for example, the recent vintage of the membership ordinance and whether cultural survival can be secured without recourse to sexist classifications.[18] Either way, the case is a difficult one. Yet, the difficulties of this case are obscured by conceptualizing the problem as a contest between abstract and fundamental rights such as the right to cultural autonomy and the right to sexual equality. These rights must first be translated into values associated with protecting group and individual identity in order to understand what was at stake in the conflict. Nor would the difficulties be resolved using the process-based approach because this approach begs the key question raised by the case as to whether internal processes *ought* to be used to resolve the conflict. According to the identity approach, the difficulties of this case arise from, on the one hand, comparing the effects of the discriminatory rule on the identities of those who lost status with, on the other hand, the effects on the identity claim of the Santa Clara and other similar tribes if the US Court overturned a decision made by the institutions of a self-governing tribe. Had the Court fully compared the identity claims at stake on each side, it might have still decided in favour of the Santa Clara tribe if it was convinced, as it was, that overturning the membership ordinance jeopardized the identities of all Indian tribes.

CONCLUSION

The challenge of incommensurability rests on the idea that no politically accessible or coherent basis exists upon which to evaluate conflicting views about how identity matters or about how matters putatively fundamental to identity can be weighed against each other in any given conflict. This challenge applies to many different approaches, including ones that employ rights. In some cases, assessing claims as claims to protect something important about identity renders conflicts more transparent and solutions more obvious.

So while incommensurability is a problem, it is not a problem that should lead us, in particular, to abandon assessments of identity claims. The challenge to understanding and resolving conflicts that involve values that seem incommensurable, such as those found in *Lavell* and *Martinez*, is to construct a method of assessment that reveals the ways in which matters of profound importance to the identities of those involved are at stake in these struggles. When rights are used to express the fundamental importance of particular interests and values, they can end up obscuring the way that claims impact on identity and they can create impasses which are only resolved by declaring one right (usually the conventional understanding of an individual right) to be more important than the other. These declarations can appear arbitrary and biased to those who have been historically excluded from shaping the conventional understandings. The process-based approach resolves the impasse by deferring to the authority of process and thereby dodging the substantive normative matters that arise in such conflicts.

Rather than replacing rights or negating the importance of fair processes, an approach which assesses the identity claims at stake in these conflicts offers the best terms upon which a solution can be reached when rights conflict and processes fail. According to such an approach, conflicts, such as those that involve sexual equality and cultural autonomy, often involve contending identity claims. These competing claims can often be compared once they are translated into the specific values and interests related to identity at stake in the conflict and assessed in terms of their role and centrality, how they are validated, and whether they cause harm. The identity claims at stake are assessed in the contexts in which they arise. Solutions are based on values that are considered crucial in these contexts. In these ways, the aim of the identity approach is not to yield easy results in all difficult cases. But in most cases, it meets the challenge of incommensurability and thereby narrows the cases that are considered to be truly difficult.

5

Religious Identity and the Problem of Authenticity

The right to freedom of religion is one of the most important and well-established rights protected in Western constitutions. While the abstract principle of freedom of religion receives broad and strong support in Western societies, people tend to disagree about how the abstract principle applies in particular cases, specifically who it ought to protect, and what sort of practices it ought to protect as a result of its fair application. Many of these disagreements implicate identity claims in that they involve religious groups making claims that something which is important to their religious identity requires that they receive an entitlement, additional resources, different opportunities, or more power. These claims are sometimes assessed by public decision makers in ways that involve determining whether beliefs or practices important to the identity of a group are genuinely at stake.

I have argued that claims of this nature ought to be assessed according to an approach with three dimensions: (1) the jeopardy condition which looks at the extent to which a practice for which protection is sought is crucial to a claimant's identity; (2) the validation condition which examines how the practice or a restriction placed on it has been validated; and (3) the safeguard condition which involves assessing whether the practice predictably threatens serious harm and what the costs of avoiding harm are. These conditions provide the reasons why claims ought to be considered either strong or weak. Generally speaking, claims are strong and ought to be accepted where evidence shows that jeopardy is high, validation is fair, and risk of harm is low. Claims are weak and may be legitimately rejected where jeopardy is low, validation is coercive or otherwise unfair, and risk of harm is high and difficult or costly to lower. At the same time, these conditions are designed to promote institutional humility, to treat people from diverse backgrounds with respect, and, pragmatically, to address the large number of claims in contemporary politics that expressly appeal to identity considerations. The identity approach also provides a way of addressing identity claims without translating these claims into other idioms, like rights or mere interests, which can distort their meaning and importance to those making the claims.

The previous chapter examined one kind of reservation about this project, namely that identity as an idiom encourages the proliferation of incommensurable claims. This chapter takes up a different challenge which I shall call the challenge of authenticity. The challenge of authenticity presses the concern that it is impossible to distinguish reliably between claims that are genuine or 'authentic' for the people who make them and those which are made fraudulently in order to garner particular entitlements. Authenticity is a problem in relation to all claims about what constitutes one's identity, but it is especially well illustrated in cases about freedom of religion because the truth or falsity of religious or spiritual claims is generally viewed as highly subjective and appropriately treated as personal and private. Generally speaking, public decision makers ought not to be involved in determining the authenticity of a religious belief. Yet, at the same time, the worry is that claimants will manipulate identity in order to secure benefits, such as an exemption from military service or to escape criminal prosecution for possessing or ingesting prohibited narcotics. Unless the authenticity of identity claims can be ascertained, and the sceptics claim it cannot, identity can be used as a smokescreen to gain access to benefits that are not properly justified. Therefore, decision makers seek ways to ensure against the success of fraudulent claims (Greenawalt 2006: 8).

In order to decide whether a group is entitled to what appears to be a privileged exception to an otherwise generally applicable law, decision makers develop approaches that can help them determine whether claimants genuinely adhere to a religious identity. In the absence of such assessments, courts must accept at face value the subjective importance of claims, as expressed by claimants, and thereby forego the possibility of ensuring against fraudulent claims. Therefore, the need to ensure authenticity and to ensure against successful fraud stand in tension with each other in the sense that the more decision makers try to identify fraudulent claims the more they call into question the authenticity of claims (and the integrity of claimants).

This chapter explores the challenge authenticity poses to according identity claims a legitimate role in legal decision making by examining two ways in which courts deal with this problem. The first way arises in the US case of *Employment Division, Human Resources of Oregon v. Smith* (1990) which involves the claim by members of a religious minority to ingest a prohibited narcotic for religious reasons. In his opinion, written for the majority on the US Supreme Court, Justice Scalia suggests that decisions about such controversial religious practices are best left to legislatures rather than to courts, and he couches his reasons in terms of respecting the authenticity of religious beliefs. Ironically, the case shows how the invocation of the importance of acknowledging authenticity easily becomes a way for public decision makers

to justify withholding entitlements from religious minorities. Unde
of respecting the idiosyncratic and highly personal dimension of
convictions, courts refuse to recognize and assess accessible evidenc
the importance of a practice to religious belief. Instead, they sometimes
that courts should not and indeed *cannot* scrutinize the significanc
religious practices to identity, and therefore they cannot entertain claims
resources or opportunities that are predicated on such evidence. As a resu
religious groups are sometimes treated disrespectfully and are unfairly denied
important resources and opportunities. This first response avoids the danger
of fraudulent identity claims, but it does so at a high price.

A second way in which courts try to negotiate the challenge of authenticity is by focusing on the sincerity of claimants rather than on the truth or falsity of their beliefs according to religious dogma or conventional community practices. The sincerity approach receives broad expression today in the freedom of religion jurisprudence in Canada and is clearly reflected in the recent case of *Syndicat Northcrest v. Amselem* (2004), which involves the claim of an observant Jew to build a '*succah*' on his balcony in contravention of a tenancy code agreement. Judging sincerity tends to be viewed as a good means of respecting the authenticity of beliefs and protecting against successful fraud. But *Amselem* shows that sincerity is rarely sufficient as a means to assess the genuine value of a religious practice and courts lack transparency in decision making when they claim to base their decisions primarily on sincerity. After examining these two cases, I turn to ways in which the tension between authenticity and fraud is better addressed using an approach which focuses directly on assessing identity claims.

THE PROBLEMS OF AUTHENTICITY

The authenticity of a belief is often taken to depend wholly on the subjective attitudes held by believers. Thus, if someone believes that a practice is important to their identity, then it is, or at least no one else is in a good position to challenge this belief. Charles Taylor describes the modern ideal of authenticity as 'a new form of inwardness' which arose with the subjective turn in modern culture in the eighteenth century. '[W]e come to think of ourselves as beings with inner depths' whose lives ought to be modelled on standards and beliefs which are internal to us as individuals (1991: 28). Authenticity relies on a process of self-discovery and self-affirmation. On this account, assertions people make about what is important to their identity may be false – because people can misrepresent what they truly believe – but, due to the alleged subjectivity of authenticity, such assertions cannot be reliably challenged or interrogated by outsiders.

Since, on a wholly subjectivist construal of authenticity, external decision makers are in no position to interrogate or challenge what a believer says is important to his or her identity, it might seem that the best way to acknowledge the importance of authenticity is simply to avoid direct engagement with what people say they believe about their identity. So, especially in disputes over the accommodation of religious practices, one response to the problem of authenticity is for public decision makers not to assess the authenticity of religious beliefs at all. This is, in effect, the response of the Court in the case of *Oregon v. Smith.*

A second response to the problem of authenticity is to employ criteria that focus on the character of a person's beliefs about identity. The hope is that genuine claims can be distinguished from fraudulent claims while nevertheless respecting the highly subjective nature of a person's convictions about their identity. Instead of considering the actual plausibility of assertions people make about the importance of a practice to their identity, the second response focuses on ascertaining whether their convictions about such matters are sincerely held.

To see what lies behind this response, it is worth briefly considering a bit more fully some of the ways in which fraud can be an issue in identity claiming. Fraudulent claims might be ones that have genuine religious importance for some persons or groups but not for the claimant making the claim. The possibility of this type of fraud raises puzzles about how to determine who counts as a genuine member of the religious group or spiritual community. For instance, the practice of taking drugs like *peyote* or marijuana might credibly be viewed as a genuinely religious or spiritual practice for some minorities. Yet the concern is that some people might exploit this fact and represent themselves as members or perhaps would-be members of a community primarily in order to be exempt from generally applicable laws which prohibit taking or trading in these drugs. Fraudulent claims might also be those that falsely represent a belief as religious or spiritual in order to advance a non-religious interest. For instance, the claim by some Ngarrindjeri women in Australia that Hindmarsh island is the site of 'secret women's business' of a spiritual nature was found by a Royal Commission established to investigate the matter to be fraudulent in this sense. The suggestion is that the claim was advanced strategically in order to stop a causeway from being constructed.[1] Sometimes fraudulent claims are those where religious claimants use genuine religious doctrine to advance mere personal preferences. For instance, the Danish Cartoon Affair involved the charge that some Muslims were making embellished claims about Islamic standards of blasphemy because, although they were merely offended by the cartoons, they sought a stronger public response to the cartoons than mere offence could justify. Representing the cartoons as an affront to Muslim spiritual identity would seem to add force to their complaints about the cartoons (see Laegaard 2007; Levey and Modood 2008).

The challenge in all these types of cases is for public decision makers to identify fraud while respecting the subjective and deeply personal nature of beliefs advanced by claimants. Against this background, one seemingly attractive response is simply to assess the sincerity of claimants. On this response, an identity claim has force to the degree it is predicated on the sincerely held convictions of a person, whether or not the convictions are idiosyncratic or implausible. This, in effect, is the response of the courts in the case of *Amselem* where the courts claim to assess the importance of Amselem's religious claim by assessing how sincerely he believes the practice of having his own *succah* on his balcony is important to the proper celebration of a Jewish holiday and therefore to his religious identity.

A third response, and the one I favour, is to rely on criteria which go beyond mere sincerity. Authenticity can be appropriately acknowledged in the course of assessing the credibility of assertions made by claimants about their identity by considering relevant cultural, social, and historical evidence. To use more onerous criteria to assess religious identity claims may seem to exacerbate the peril of authenticity by creating perverse incentives for groups to distort their practices and misrepresent their beliefs in order to meet the objective criteria used to assess their claims. In some contexts, the worry is that groups will deliberately distort their identity so as to meet the expectations of decision makers. This concern is raised by Elizabeth Povinelli who argues that minorities 'perform' their identity in order to fit into the majority's distorted and essentialist conception of the minority's culture. She has traced such performances in the presentation of Aboriginal land claims in Australia which involve advocates and anthropologists making calculated decisions about, for example, who to put forward as a 'traditional Aboriginal owner', how to present history and cultural change, and whether to argue that Christian belief alienated Aboriginal people from their traditional beliefs (1998: 599). These decisions are designed, on the one hand, to build a successful legal case, but, on the other hand, they effectively strip out all nuances about the nature of communities and their identities, and thereby distort identity in order to fulfil the expectations of the decision makers. The risk is high for any litigant that courts will reject claims that fail to meet their expectations about minority identity and authenticity. Therefore, minorities participate in ensuring that judges will have no difficulty making sense of their claims even if this means distorting the authenticity of minority practices.[2]

Religious groups often realize the importance to their case of emphasizing easy to grasp (for the majority) sets of practices. But to comply with majority expectations raises a second problem because it increases the risk that minorities will not be able to convince majorities of their claims where minorities are 'performing', to use Povinelli's term; the risk arises that their performances will sometimes fail to be convincing either because they contradict majority expectation or because they exaggerate and distort what is found by other means to be genuinely important to the minority. The majority will therefore appear to be justified in designing processes capable of detecting fraud. Cases where courts find that people are not really 'pacifists' or where they have been 'brainwashed' by their religious communities are especially significant in justifying the need for fraud detection.

This third response suggests that grappling with authenticity can create an incentive for claimants to distort their identities and this, in turn, provides an impetus for decision makers to develop more detailed and onerous criteria for detecting fraud and thereby managing minorities. But a strong tendency in decision making, revealed by the first two responses, points in the opposite direction, namely that decision makers will avoid direct consideration and assessment of identity claims if they can, and that such avoidance has detrimental consequences for religious minorities. In order to meet the complex challenge of authenticity, we need to determine how decision makers distinguish between authentic and fraudulent claims without simply perpetuating the need to guard against successful fraud, and thereby create more perverse incentives for groups to distort their identities to meet the criteria necessary to make successful claims. I will turn to this task later in the chapter. First, I want to explain in greater detail why the first two responses to authenticity, epitomized in the cases of *Smith* and *Amselem* respectively, are inadequate.

PAYING LIP SERVICE TO AUTHENTICITY: THE CASE OF *OREGON V. SMITH*

In the case of *Oregon v. Smith* (1990),[3] a majority of five judges on the US Supreme Court refused to assess the claim made by Smith that ingesting small amounts of *peyote* is integral to his religious beliefs and therefore protected under the Free Exercise Clause of the US Constitution. Smith was denied unemployment insurance benefits after he was dismissed from his job at a drug rehabilitation centre for ingesting *peyote*. Peyote is a hallucinogenic drug, prohibited as a narcotic under Oregon law. It is used for sacramental purposes by members of the Native American Church, of which Smith was a member, and is legal for this purpose in several American states.[4]

The majority in the Court rejected Smith's claim to a constitutional entitlement to use *peyote.* What is interesting for our purposes is that they claimed that the case placed them in an impossible position of either accepting Smith's claim at face value or interrogating his religious identity, neither of which they were willing to do. To accept the claim at face value was immediately dismissed for potentially leading to social chaos by elevating religious precepts to the stature of law and allowing 'each conscience to be a law unto itself' (p. 890). Alternatively, to assess Smith's religious identity was also dismissed partly because, according to Scalia who wrote the majority decision, it required the Court to assess (and perhaps challenge) the authenticity of Smith's religious beliefs: 'What principle of law or logic can be brought to bear to contradict a believer's assertion that a particular act is "central" to his personal faith? Judging the centrality of different religious practices is akin to the unacceptable "business of evaluating the relative merits of differing religious claims"' (p. 887). It is inappropriate for judges to determine the centrality of religious beliefs: 'It is no more appropriate for judges to determine the "centrality" of religious beliefs . . . than it would be for them to determine the "importance" of ideas . . . in the free speech field' (p. 887). The court is in no position to 'contradict a believer's assertion that a particular act is central to his personal faith'. To decide otherwise is to invite a 'parade of horribles' where judges become the arbiters of religious doctrine – from assessing the religious status of the Quaker belief against paying taxes, to evaluating the spiritual significance of the Amish belief against military service. In the view of the majority, it seemed prudent to manifest respect for the subjectivity of religious conviction by leaving the doctrinal commitments of Smith unexamined and unchallenged but also irrelevant to the resolution of the case. This, I suggest, only pays lip service to authenticity.

The concern that Scalia expresses for respecting the personal faith of religious believers is laudable in one sense. But, the evidence in this case about whether *peyote* use was an authentic practice in Smith's religious community was not especially difficult to assess. The anthropological evidence, for instance, clearly established a rich history of 'peyotism' going back to 1560 in Mexico and then spreading to the United States and Canada. *Peyote* rituals were shown to be 'similar to bread and wine in certain Christian churches', but considered even more important than merely a sacrament because '*peyote* constitutes in itself an object of worship; prayers are directed to it much as prayers are devoted to the Holy Ghost . . .'. Evidence showed that *peyote* is connected to community values such as inducing feelings of brotherhood, and enabling participants to experience Deity. *Peyote* is also used as a 'protector' akin to how Catholics wear medallions: 'an Indian GI often wears around his neck a beautifully beaded pouch containing one large *peyote* button' (*Employment Division, Human Resources of Oregon v. Smith* 1988: 668–9).

Moreover, the consequence of failing to address the evidence concerning the spiritual significance of *peyote* and thereby treating Smith's religious identity as opaque seemed more likely to deny Smith and his community respect than to display respect for them. The Native American Church is, after all, a small, poor, religious, and largely Indigenous minority in Oregon. It sought a legal exemption for its members to ingest a drug which is treated in the United States as a 'prohibited narcotic'. Such an exemption would permit its members to observe faith-based rituals without being criminalized or, as in this case, fired from their jobs and rendered unable to collect unemployment insurance. Given the general legal status of *peyote* as a banned narcotic, Smith was well aware that his claims raised the suspicion that he was using his faith as a mere pretext to justify recreational drug use. So his legal team presented evidence to establish the integrity of members of the Church and the plausibility of viewing *peyote* use as central to the religion. Besides tracing the historical origins of the *peyote* ritual, they explained that the Church preaches a package of personal commitments to its members which require fidelity to family, self-reliance, abstinence from alcohol, and that reconnect members to their historical rituals which centrally involve ingesting *peyote*. These rituals are generally viewed as sources of esteem for those who partake in them. Anthropological evidence was also presented in Court to show that the rituals are 'ego-strengthening' and help members see themselves 'not as people whose place and way in the world is gone, but as people whose way can be strong enough to change and meet new challenges' (*Employment Division, Human Resources of Oregon v. Smith* 1990: 915).

Smith also introduced evidence drawn from addiction research which showed that peyotism plays a positive role in combating alcoholism amongst American Indians. This kind of evidence was probably introduced in an attempt to establish that the ritual does not amount to what many members of the American public might otherwise suppose, namely irresponsible drug taking. As noted in the dissent of Justice Blackmum, much of the evidence aimed to fight prejudice: 'The carefully circumscribed ritual context in which respondents used *peyote* is far removed from the irresponsible and unrestricted recreational use of unlawful drugs' (p. 914). Similarly, the evidence showed that, unlike other narcotics, *peyote* plays little if any role in the illegal drug trade, a fact again noted in Blackmum's dissent. 'The Federal Government and half the states make an exemption for the ceremonial use of *peyote* without inviting a flood of claims from other religions, and the government provides no evidence that sacramental *peyote* has ever harmed anyone' or that *peyote* plays a role in the illegal drug trade (pp. 911–12). The state of Oregon, in particular, fails to present a credible case that it has a compelling interest, partly because it made no effort to prosecute users of sacramental *peyote* or to prosecute Smith.

The majority's decision in Smith's case could have rested on arguments which showed that peyotism was not as central to the religious identity of Church members as Smith claimed it was, although this would have been a difficult conclusion to reach in light of the overwhelming evidence presented to the contrary. The Court could have also rejected Smith's claims on the basis that to allow Church members the right to ingest a prohibited narcotic would predictably lead to harm or abuse or would cause a slippery slope to such abuse.[5] But in light of the evidence discussed by Blackmum, this argument was also weak and unconvincing. Finally, the court could have had good reasons to doubt whether Smith and his co-claimant, Black, were actually ingesting *peyote* for religious as opposed to recreational purposes. The men were members of the Church, but they were on a lunch break from their job at a drug rehabilitation centre when they were caught taking *peyote*. But again, this suspicion, if it existed, could have been verified on the basis of accessible evidence about how the ritual is conventionally practiced. Or evidence might have been presented which showed that the conventional practice admits variations which predictably cause harm. But no evidence of this sort was discussed in the ruling. In my view, unless Smith's practices were highly idiosyncratic or predictably harmful, the suspicion that he sometimes takes *peyote* for recreational purposes is irrelevant to establishing the entitlement. To treat it as relevant invites the worst kind of overbearing state scrutiny of individual motivation and behaviour for no legitimate purpose.

In the end, the majority in *Smith* refused to assess the claim based on challenges associated with authenticity, which it claimed were too great even though the evidence in this case was neither highly subjective nor difficult to comprehend. To treat this evidence as inscrutable or opaque, under the guise of respecting authenticity, is a perverse example of how respecting the authenticity of identity can be used by dominant groups to deny minorities protection for important religious practices.

But the challenges presented by the case go further than noting how easy it is for public decision makers to pay lip service to authenticity in order to avoid making difficult decisions about minority entitlements. In *Oregon v. Smith*, the majority did not simply argue that the matter could not be decided, but rather it argued that the court was the wrong institution to make such decisions. So a second aspect of this case, and a second kind of argument made by the majority, is that legislatures are better contexts than courts to make decisions of this sort. Legislatures may also base their decisions on whether they believe the religious practice is genuine as opposed to fraudulent and therefore offer no assurances that the 'unacceptable business of judging the centrality of different religious practices' will be avoided. However, one argument in favour of legislative solutions is that cases like *Smith* are difficult cases that involve weighing different kinds of interests and potential harms. Some people reasonably argue that legislatures are better equipped to determine whether sometimes it makes sense to bend a rule or admit an exception.[6] So *Smith* raises an important question of whether difficult decisions about the accommodation of minorities are best left to legislatures.

There are several different good reasons to think that legislatures are better equipped than courts to deal with such contentious matters. But first it is worth looking at an unconvincing rendition of this position which is advanced by Brian Barry specifically with reference to *Oregon v. Smith.* Barry's position illustrates an important mistake often made in the context of debates about minority accommodation and equality. He suggests that exceptions, like the one sought by the Native American Church, should be considered on a 'pragmatic' rather than a 'principled' basis and decided only by legislatures. This position is indicative of Barry's general argument on minority accommodation, which is that laws should either stand because their aim is so compelling that no imaginable exceptions ought to be made to them, or there should be no law whatsoever, because the argument for exemptions is sufficiently powerful. But in between universal constraint and laissez-faire, 'a great deal of finagling is needed', and, according to Barry, this finagling ought to be left to legislatures (2001: 51). Barry's argument regarding *Smith* gives rise to the question of how to distinguish between disputes that invoke constitutional entitlements and those that require 'finagling' and thereby only raise pragmatic concerns. As Barry explains it, most disputes about religious practices involve both pragmatic and principled dimensions and sometimes more harm than good is done by sticking to ideal principle rather than being pragmatic by 'bending the rules' or admitting small exceptions in order to avoid a greater harm. Yet, in illustrating this position, Barry unintentionally reveals just how morally arbitrary such distinctions often are. For instance, Barry argues that the Catholic Church ought to be able to choose its own priests even if it chooses on the basis of criteria that deny sexual equality. He points to the historical struggles surrounding the Reformation and specifically the struggles between the Catholic Church and Henry the Eighth in order to make the point that requiring of the Catholic Church fidelity to the principle of sexual equality may do more harm than good in the sense that it may drive discrimination underground or create a rift between the Church and the State. In this vein, he predicts that secular courts today are unlikely to 'reproduce the work of the Reformation in the guise of enforcing a law against employment discrimination' (p. 176). The stakes are just too high. To be pragmatic requires allowing the Church to discriminate.

But rather than clarify the matter, the illustration reveals the way in which principles, like freedom of religion, are shaped and structured in morally arbitrary ways by interpretations that are primarily focused on responding to the interests of some dominant religious groups and ignoring the interests of others. The history, which Barry invokes in this example, points to the reasons, in the first place, why the rights to freedom of religion and association in Western societies encompass the right of churches to choose their own religious leaders without state restriction. The meaning of the principle of freedom of association is itself not only invoked by the history of the Reformation, but also to a considerable degree, it is created by this history as well. Ordination is central to the Church's identity partly because of its historical struggles with Henry the Eighth. Religious freedom and freedom of association entail the right to choose one's own religious leaders for every religious community in the West largely because of a history, considered important in the West, which involved the struggle between one particular religious group and the State. So although he does not acknowledge it, there is a principled, and not merely an ad hoc, pragmatic basis on which to determine whether exemptions are appropriate or whether the principle has been defined too narrowly in the first place. But to understand this principled basis requires an approach in which evidence concerning the relation between principles and identities is confronted directly and openly. Moreover, the identities of minority groups, not merely dominant groups, must have salience in establishing the meaning and scope of the entitlement.

The problem then with relying on the distinction between what is pragmatic and principled in a case like *Oregon v. Smith* is that the particular interpretation of the principle (i.e. freedom of religion) is shaped by a history of pragmatic considerations about appeasing certain religious groups. So invoking the distinction as a means to separate the 'exception from the rule' amounts to nothing more than noting the difference between the exception a minority wants today and the exceptions that dominant groups have succeeded in securing in the past. Barry's more general argument, that laws should be designed so that they minimize the need for exemptions and thereby treat minorities and majorities equally, seems far more sensible a guide for a case like *Oregon v. Smith.* In a secular society, the moral principle of treating people of different faiths as equals and regardless of whether their religious community has been historically dominant cannot rest on imposing the norms created by majority experience on minorities (also see Greenawalt

2006: 81–2). The distinction between what counts as pragmatic and what counts as principled in this case rests on this mistake.

A more convincing rationale for relying on legislatures rather than courts in cases that involve religious freedom is located in the fact that decisions often involve high administrative costs or the development of complicated procedures which might impose overwhelming burdens on public institutions. Courts may reasonably leave it up to legislatures to decide whether to take on these kinds of burdens (p. 82). In relation to the *Smith* decision, for instance, Congress amended the *American Indian Religious Freedom Act* in 1994 to allow 'traditional use of *peyote* by Indians for religious purposes, and for other purposes'. The amendment requires that enforcement of the rule distinguish between Native members of the Native American Church who use *peyote* and non-Native members. It also means that drug enforcement agencies distinguish between *peyote* and other drugs such as marijuana and alcohol that are also used for religious reasons. All of these distinctions potentially cause enforcement problems or impose on the State the need to administer laws in ways that it may not be effectively able or willing to do.

But even these considerations are often insufficient to excuse decision makers from the important task of reshaping public understandings of how entitlements such as freedom of religion ought to be interpreted. While courts should not blithely impose on public institutions onerous enforcement and administrative costs, decisions over whether such costs are worth bearing involve questions which courts are often in a good position to assess. Decisions overweighing the costs in this case directly involve assessing the importance of the practice to a religious claimant and then comparing the strength of this claim to the costs of protecting that practice or the 'compelling interests' of the State in restricting the practice. The compelling interest test, which has some broad parallels with the identity approach, was a conventional part of American jurisprudence on freedom of religion until *Smith*. The majority in *Smith* rejected the test because it required the court to assess the authenticity of Smith's claim that *peyote* was central to his religious identity, which they were unwilling to do.[7] Following this decision, in 1993, Congress reinstituted a version of the test through the *Religious Freedom Restoration Act*.

The conclusion here is not that courts are necessarily better or worse than legislatures at sorting out some conflicts that involve minority practices. But as Justice O'Connor argues in her separate but concurring opinion in *Smith*, '. . . the First Amendment was enacted precisely to protect the rights of those whose religious practices are not shared by the majority and may be viewed with hostility'.[8] The problems of authenticity easily become exaggerated and can be used as an excuse by decision makers not to recognize accessible and compelling evidence about the importance of a practice to the religious identity of a group, as in the Court's decision in *Smith*. If religious identity is treated as fully and completely subjective, then public decision makers have good reason to refuse to assess whether minority practices ought to shape our understanding of the principle of freedom of religion. But, as we have seen, the nature and significance of the subjective (and hence inscrutable) dimension of religious identity can be grossly exaggerated. When this occurs, minority claims can be denied a fair hearing under the guise of recognizing authenticity. The risk of this occurring is especially high where hostility and suspicion are directed against a minority in the first place. The Court's refusal to assess Smith's evidence is a case in point. The refusal denies to members of the Native American Church the chance to fight against broadly held, hostile suspicions about the character of their religious practices and the motives of their members. This means, moreover, that they cannot effectively call into question both the standards by which majorities assess the practices of religious minorities and the meaning they attribute to the constitutional protection of religious freedom. In this way, the hubris of dominant institutions can go unchecked, the opportunity to achieve some institutional humility is lost, and the background conditions remain unfairly biased against minorities.

DISTORTING AUTHENTICITY: SINCERITY IN *SYNDICAT NORTHCREST V. AMSELEM*

A second way to respond to the problems of authenticity is to distinguish between genuine and fraudulent claims by using criteria that expressly embrace the subjective, variable, changing, and deeply personal nature of religious beliefs and practices while avoiding any consideration of the doctrinal plausibility of assertions made by claimants about their religious identity. Approaches that seek to adjudicate identity claims by focusing and trying to ascertain the mere sincerity of claimants' religious beliefs are examples of this second response. On this approach, what principally matters in determining whether a religious practice which violates existing rules merits protection is an assessment of the sincerity of a claimant's beliefs. Specifically, the key question is whether a disputed practice is an important part of an individual's subjective understanding of their religious faith and not whether the practice can be credibly represented as particularly important to the tenets of his or her religious faith. Here, the focus on subjective understanding displays sensitivity to the sometimes idiosyncratic ways in which people understand their religious identity and therefore this might seem like a good way of dealing with authenticity. But the problem with this second response is that, in most contexts, courts cannot actually rely entirely on mere tests of individual sincerity. Moreover, to claim to do so often comes at the expense of offering transparent and credible reasons for the decisions courts actually reach. The sincerity approach initially seems like a simple and effective way of negotiating the challenge of authenticity but, as we will see, the apparent simplicity of the approach is illusory. Many disputes cannot even be analysed coherently through the lens of sincerity, and attempts to do so result in misidentification or distortion of how authenticity functions in many contexts.

The virtues and drawbacks of using sincerity to assess religious identity claims are well illustrated in *Syndicat Northcrest v. Amselem* (2004), a case in which the Canadian Supreme Court developed a sincerity approach to assess claims regarding the accommodation of allegedly important religious practices. The dispute in *Amselem* arose between an orthodox Jewish man and the collective of owners at a condominium in Montreal where Amselem and other orthodox Jews lived. Amselem was prevented from building a *succah* on his balcony.[9] The dispute was over whether Amselem could be prevented from building his own private *succah.* The bylaws of co-ownership to which Amselem agreed when buying his condominium and which establish the rights of the owners as a collective to enjoy their property in conformity with the contract established between them prohibited structures being built on balconies unless they were approved by the collective of owners. Syndicat Northcrest offered to build him and other Jewish residents a communal *succah* in the gardens of the complex. But Amselem argued that this would be inconvenient and distressful, and that his personal celebration of the holiday required that he have access to his own *succah* on his own balcony.

The authenticity of Amselem's belief about the need for a private *succah* was drawn into question when the lower courts discovered that, according to some rabbinical interpretations, Judaism does not require believers to construct their own private *succahs* and that often Jews use communal *succahs* constructed by their synagogue or community centres. This was discovered by consulting two rabbis as 'expert witnesses' who verified that a communal *succah* is sufficient to allow residents to fulfil their religious obligations.

The Supreme Court reversed the lower court's decision and argued that the lower court failed to respect the deeply personal and variable nature of religious belief. 'Religious fulfillment', it argued, 'is by its very nature subjective and personal' (para. 72). Convictions need not be consistent with religious dogma or even with the past practices of individuals: 'Because of the vacillating nature of religious belief, a court's inquiry into sincerity, if anything, should focus not on past practice or past belief but on a person's belief at the time...' (para. 53). The Court strongly criticized all attempts to establish the centrality or obligatory nature of the practice by consulting religious experts or religious leaders (see para. 66); 'Requiring proof of the established practices of a religion to gauge the sincerity of belief diminishes the very freedom we seek to protect' (para. 54). The Court affirms instead that religious belief is 'profoundly personal' (para. 41), 'freely and deeply held' (para. 39), 'integrally linked to one's self-definition and fulfillment' (para. 39), and 'a function of personal autonomy and choice' (para. 42). In the words of the majority, 'although a court is not qualified to judicially interpret and determine the content of a subjective understanding of a religious requirement, it is qualified to inquire into the sincerity of the claimant'. On the basis of this criterion, the Court decided that Amselem has a sincerely held personal belief with a nexus in religion that outweighs the other considerations at stake. The option of using a communal *succah*, they conclude, will diminish Amselem's joy associated with celebrating the religious holiday (para. 75) and, by comparison, the aims of the tenancy agreement which prohibits temporary structures such as *succahs* are 'nominal' and aesthetic (para. 86).

The problem with this decision is less the result the court reaches than the manner in which it claims to be deciding the case. It claims to base its decision on individual sincerity. On closer inspection, we can see that the approach has three parts. First and most importantly, claimants must show that their claim is based on a sincerely held personal belief that the practice is required by their religious faith. The criteria that establish sincerity are supposed to provide decision makers with multiple ways to assess the credibility or honesty of individual claims without examining religious doctrine. These criteria include assessing the individual's demeanor while testifying their previous religious experience, and the relation between this previous experience and the current belief in question. It could also involve examining the relation between the belief and conceptions of a divine being or morality, the directness of the connection between the religion and the disputed practice, and the extent to which the religious belief is applied in practice.[10] Although some of these considerations clearly take the court beyond assessing individual sincerity, the general idea is that sincere beliefs are ones consistent with the individual's other current religious practices, and possibly consistent with the practices and beliefs of other adherents to the faith. Evidence about sincerity is 'intended only to ensure that a presently asserted religious belief is in good faith, neither fictitious nor capricious, and that it is not an artifice' (para. 52). The objective is to avoid requiring that individuals establish the validity of their religious practice by verifying that the practice has a central role in the claimant's understanding of religious dogma.

The second part of the approach requires evidence that the sincerely held belief has a connection or 'nexus' in religion. This criterion is potentially far more controversial because, unless interpreted very generally, it could undermine the very objective of privileging sincerity by instead requiring that claimants show that their religion endorses the practice. But the Court is clear that this second requirement aims only to establish that the disputed practice is 'religious' and therefore that it is the sort of practice which derives protection from the constitutional right to freedom of religion as opposed to freedom of conscience or thought.

The third part of the approach requires that the Court assesses whether the law restricting the practice imposes a 'reasonable limit' on freedom of religion. Again, much depends on how this part is interpreted. In Canadian jurisprudence, the question about 'reasonable limits' arises once courts have established that a right is violated.[11] In *Amselem*, the Court would inquire into whether the tenancy agreement imposed a reasonable limit on Amselem's religious freedom by weighing the proportional importance of the tenancy agreement against the importance of violating Amselem's right to freedom of religion by denying him a private *succah* on his balcony. If the Court is consistent, then the standard used to assess the importance of the private *succah* depends on what Amselem sincerely believes to be important.

The sincerity approach takes seriously the problems of authenticity by establishing the authenticity of a practice on the basis of evidence that can be reliably assessed but which steers clear of contentious consideration of doctrinal requirements of a religion. Sincerity indirectly indicates that a practice has genuine value rather than objectively establishing its genuine value. Sincerity is based upon a subjective understanding of what is valuable and means treating believers, like Amselem, as the authorities of whether their practices are important to their religious identities. Believers are thereby not asked to put aside the good reasons why they really engage in their practices and instead offer up reasons that will be congenial to the needs of outsiders to understand them. They are only asked to offer evidence that they are generally honest rather than manipulative, and consistent in their practices rather than capricious. The test depends on establishing a quality of belief which, one assumes, is absent in cases where claimants are acting in manipulative ways. Moreover, because the test depends on establishing a quality of belief, it potentially broadens the scope of beliefs that courts are willing to protect under freedom of religion. For instance, John Borrows (2008) argues that one benefit of Canada's sincerity approach is that it potentially broadens the scope of the kinds of spiritual beliefs or notions of the sacred that the court is willing to recognize, and therefore is an effective way to challenge the historical exclusion of spiritual practices of some religious minorities and Indigenous peoples.

Whether the presence or absence of sincerity can be reliably detected by a public institution is a good question. But the test is at least designed to distinguish between genuine and fraudulent claims in a manner that avoids privileging the established tenets of religious faith according to religious elites; that takes seriously the relation between identity assessments and the subjective nature of religious belief; and that potentially broadens the scope of religious freedom so that it is more inclusive of religious minorities.

These virtues notwithstanding, the problem with the sincerity test is that individual sincerity rarely provides an adequate basis upon which to resolve disputes which involve religious identity claims. The first reason to suspect that sincerity is not enough is based on the observation that, in actual legal practice, few if any claimants ever fail this test because all the cases that make their way to court, and certainly all that end up being heard by appeal courts, are those that involve sincere claimants. In other words, insincere claims are not usually heard in the first place by the courts which have designed and apply the test.

The second reason to suspect that sincerity is not enough is owing to the nature of many religious claims. The 'religious' nature of some claims and the reason why some religious claims are important (or not) often rest on how they connect individuals to a community with an established and recognized set of beliefs that aim at spiritual enlightenment. Individuals may have their own subjective interpretation of religious doctrine, and courts may want to recognize and affirm the importance of this subjective aspect of religious identity. But in doing so, courts sometimes choose amongst different aspects of what is important about any particular religious identity.[12] In the context of some religious belief systems, the court's choice to privilege individual sincerity and thereby to privilege the individual's subjective and perhaps idiosyncratic understanding of how to express his or her religious identity may well ignore what a particular religious community or tradition views as important about a practice. In some cases, conflicts may even be more difficult to resolve because what is valuable about a practice is lost when individual sincerity is chosen as the decisive determinant of the value of a religious practice.

Consider, for instance, the importance of understanding the other kinds of religious values at stake in potential disputes that arise around the Jewish practice of keeping *kosher*. In part, the practice of keeping *kosher* is important because individuals sincerely believe it to be important and it has a 'nexus' or connection to what Jews believe is commanded by the Torah. But it also functions to establish a set of shared practices that keep communities together by requiring that members eat only from kitchens which are *kosher* (and therefore not eat their meals with those who do not keep *kosher*), that they shop at businesses which sell *kosher* food, and buy products that are labeled *kosher.* When conflicts arise, as they often do, about whether a particular brand of food (e.g. a soft drink or potato chips) can be labeled '*kosher*' or not, these conflicts cannot be adequately resolved by relying on what individuals sincerely believe to be *kosher.* Relying on individual sincerity neglects the communal function of the practice. But nor does it seem especially satisfactory for a religious elite to dictate what should receive the *kosher* label because this potentially places too much power, over a large and pluralistic community with a good deal of consumer power in some regions, in the hands of a small group of people. In Canada and the United States, conflicts over what counts as a *kosher* food are resolved through a system of patented symbols whereby a manufacturer of a product may apply to use a particular patented symbol on its packaging and be granted use of the symbol if the product meets the *kosher* requirements specified by those holding the right to use the symbol. Different symbols exist, each of which designates different interpretations or standards of *kushrüte.*[13] Communities and individuals decide on which foods to buy based on the standards of *kushrüte* to which they adhere where standards are represented by the different symbols found on food packaging. The method is effective largely because it is sensitive to the importance of individual choice in religious practice while recognizing the communal dimension of how the practice functions and how it has value in relation to Jewish collective identity.

Because religious identity often has this collective dimension, it is nearly impossible for courts to avoid assessing the tenets of religious faith or to base their decisions entirely on individual sincerity, despite their eagerness to avoid scrutiny of religious doctrine and traditions. Even in a case like *Amselem,* the Canadian court relies far more heavily on assumptions and assessments about religious dogma than would be necessary if sincerity is the real basis of the decision. For instance, after criticizing the lower court for relying on rabbinical experts, the Supreme Court reiterates the testimony of rabbinical experts who argue that the private *succah* is conventional practice amongst observant Jews in Canada and that, in any case, personal joy, which is potentially experienced best by celebrating holidays as one chooses, is essential to the holiday's 'proper celebration'.[14] On the one hand, this evidence seems to suggest that the subjective standard of sincerity is appropriate because how people experience 'personal joy' is subjective. But, on the other hand, the standard is appropriate only because, in Judaism (and many other religions), some matters are left up to individuals to interpret and decide for themselves, but other matters are not. It is one thing for Amselem to argue that he needs his own private *succah* to celebrate a recognized Jewish religious holiday which is celebrated around the world much as he claims it is, and quite another for him to claim, for instance, that he should be allowed to take sacramental *peyote* to celebrate the holiday properly. The first claim might be the subject of dispute within the Jewish community, but it is within the realm of being a recognized and reasonable position to take within that community, even if ultimately it is unsubstantiated directly by religious dogma. The second claim is idiosyncratic, though, in principle, it could be based on a sincerely held personal and religious belief which the believer has a long history of practicing. Even if a Jewish claimant sincerely believes that *peyote* brings him closer to God, sincerity will not satisfy the court and will not likely be viewed as a legitimate means to ensure 'personal joy' in celebrating Succot. Rather, what counts, at least to some degree, is that the individual acts as part of a religious community where the belief and practice in question is considered important or within the realm of what is deemed subjectively important. This shows that considerations of sincerity themselves operate within the confines of considerations that cannot be couched in terms of mere sincerity. Instead, one needs to consider evidence about the general character of a religion, the practices it plausibly includes, and the role and importance of these practices to the religion. Any attempt to reduce such matters to sincerity is a pretence that distorts what is really at issue.

The insufficiency of the sincerity approach is further illustrated when courts assess what constitutes a 'reasonable limit' to religious freedom. To weigh the reasonableness of a law that limits or prohibits a religious practice in order to determine whether that law is proportional in its importance to the importance of the practice it limits, depends on having a good sense of how important the religious practice is that the law limits. The sincerity approach suggests that the importance of the religious practice should be assessed on the basis of whether individuals sincerely believe it to be important. But herein lies the problem which was noted in the majority decision in *Oregon v. Smith.* If religious practices which violate laws are assessed entirely on the basis of whether individual practitioners sincerely believe their practices to be important, then this test could conceivably amount to accepting, as a potential limit on public policy, any individual interpretation of what religious doctrine, divinity, or sacredness requires of individuals in practice, as long as they sincerely hold their beliefs.

An alternative to the sincerity approach is one that assesses the importance of a religious practice by considering features of religious identity other than those which are accessible by establishing individual sincerity. According to the identity approach, part of the burden that governments assume when they protect an entitlement like freedom of religion is the burden of treating religious identity with respect and ensuring that institutions are not unfairly biased against different religious traditions. The identity approach holds that the importance of religious practices ought to be assessed in relation to both what is centrally important to individual identity and what is centrally important to the identity of a religious community. Individual sincerity is an important feature of assessing religious identity claims because sincerity can be a means to ensure that communities are not imposing practices on unwilling members (such evidence would weaken claims considerably) and because protecting an individual's self-understanding is, in large part, what it means to protect religious identity in the first place. But to assess the importance of a religious identity claim requires exploring beyond what individuals sincerely believe and beyond establishing a simple 'nexus' between religion and a sincere individual belief. What makes a religious claim strong includes evidence that something central to a religious way of life is threatened. Despite surface rhetoric to the contrary, this kind of assessment often occurs in legal decision making anyway, as the analysis of *Amselem* suggests. It occurs because sincerity provides only partial information about what is important to religious identity. The aim of the identity approach is to ensure that such assessments occur transparently and are part of a structured approach that relies on accessible evidence.

In current practice, what the sincerity approach illustrates, ironically, is that sincerity is not enough both in the sense that individual sincerity is only one aspect of what is important to both believers and their communities about religious identity and in the sense that attempts to base decisions only on sincerity are likely to be disingenuous. While individual sincerity is helpful in meeting some problems related to authenticity, the approach, as applied by Canadian courts, entails covert assessments of religious identity and lacks transparency in this respect. Some religious believers might benefit from a test which claims to adhere to a highly subjective standard while implicitly locating a practice within religious dogma. But, in general, these kinds of implicit assessments will disadvantage groups whose practices are unfamiliar, viewed with hostility, or considered potentially dangerous by decision makers.

In sum, the problems of authenticity raise the question of how to assess claims made about religious identity while respecting the subjective and deeply personal nature of claims important to religious identity. What the cases and approaches discussed so far show is that stereotypes about minority practices are entrenched not only when decision makers assess identity claims, but also when they refuse to assess evidence that challenges existing stereotypes, as they did in *Smith*. Evidence that is accessible and readily evaluated is sometimes treated as inscrutable by public institutions. When institutions refuse to contemplate evidence about identity, they merely pay lip service to the problem of authenticity. And authenticity functions as a rationale for avoiding difficult decisions that might call into question institutional biases based on dominant interests that religious minorities often face. Highly subjective tests are also not the answer to the problem of authenticity. Religious dogma shapes the parameters within which a believer's personal interpretation of religious dogma is located and these parameters are often considered implicitly by methods that claim to focus only on sincerity of personal belief. Moreover, sincerity of belief sometimes reveals an incomplete set of the valuable features of a religious practice or a tradition. For courts to emphasize the subjective dimensions of sincere individual religious belief above all other features of religious identity, some of which are equally if not more important to a religious community, has the effect of distorting the authenticity of religious beliefs and does so, ironically, under the guise of meeting the challenge of authenticity.

REASONING ABOUT RELIGIOUS IDENTITY

Identity sceptics urge decision makers to avoid direct engagement with identity. Although the challenge of authenticity provides some motivation for identity avoidance, avoidance strategies are fraught with difficulties. With this in mind, we can now briefly consider how the identity approach can grapple with identity while avoiding and even addressing the problems of authenticity. Recall that the identity approach requires that decision makers directly assess identity claims which groups make via three criteria: (1) the jeopardy condition; (2) the validation condition; and (3) the safeguard condition. In setting out these conditions, the approach responds to the concern that, without fair and transparent guidelines, public decision makers will avoid decision making which requires the assessment of minority identity claims, and they will pass decisions on to other institutions, or make decisions on bases, like individual sincerity, that are deceptively minimal and lack transparency. Moreover, the more decision makers are reluctant to assess the identity claims of religious minorities, the more the success of minority claims will depend on the extent to which a minority's practices are viewed as similar to practices that have already shaped the dominant understanding of entitlements rather than those which challenge that dominant understanding. In this sense, the incentive to 'perform' identity is high where minorities have little or no choice but to translate their identity claims into those that fit dominant stereotypes or dominant understandings of what entitlements mean. In contrast, the identity approach rests on the observation that sometimes unjust circumstances are best contested and transformed by groups that are able to draw on the social experience, history, traditions, and the sense of community embodied by their identity to mobilize themselves and argue that the public sphere is unjustly exclusive or unfairly intrusive.[15]

The first condition, the jeopardy condition, gauges the strength of a claim in terms of its importance to the identities of those advancing it, including its importance to individual believers and its importance to religious communities. To establish that a religious practice, which is important to a claimant's identity, is jeopardized requires both an assessment of its importance according to what individual claimants sincerely believe to be important and a broader analysis of how the practice functions in the context of the religious community. The objective in this regard is not to value the individual's experience over that of the community or vice versa, but to recognize that both sets of values can be at stake and that often far more is at stake for one actor than for another. In cases like *Smith* and *Amselem*, the approach therefore requires both evidence of communal practices, including the sort of evidence offered by the Native American Church, and evidence that individuals are sincere in their beliefs, much along the lines that the Canadian Court has specified in *Amselem.* Since religious beliefs and dissent have important subjective and deeply personal features, the question of whether a practice is important to individual identity is answered, in part, by determining whether or not the individual is sincere in his or her beliefs. Similarly, since communal values and traditions are sometimes also at stake, an assessment of whether something important to a community's identity is jeopardized requires decision makers to assess the practices and beliefs of religious communities and could include, for instance, assessing evidence about religious dogma, variation in the practice, debates about the sanctity of the practice, and how the practice functions in relation to broader religious values, such as preserving a sense of community or cultivating a 'joy in celebration'.

In some cases, such as *Amselem* and *Smith*, one overall effect of locating beliefs in the context of communal traditions is that doing so will lend meaning and force to individual sincerity of belief in ways that are transparent and explicit. A second effect is associated with institutional humility because to locate beliefs in the context of communal traditions allows marginalized communities to explain how something important to their religious identity is at stake and thereby to challenge what might be morally arbitrary ways in which the entitlement has been defined thus far. A third effect of examining what is at stake for religious communities (as opposed to individuals) is that doing so shows that sometimes very little if anything is at stake for communities and that therefore the conflict rests entirely on showing that something important to an individual's religious identity is seriously jeopardized. A fourth effect is that assessing the collective identity dimension places a limit on the need to detect fraud and thereby arrests the tendency of public institutions to become overly suspicious of the possibility that fraudulent claims are being made under the guise of religious freedom. Beyond assessing evidence which shows that something important about a community's religious identity is jeopardized or that something important about an individual's religious identity is jeopardized, suspicions of fraud are irrelevant to public decision making about religious freedom.

The validation condition contributes to gauging the strength of a claim by investigating the processes through which practices are identified as important by communities. The aims of this condition include ensuring that individuals are not coerced into complying with group practices and that groups are not bound to particular practices because of a collective action problem. The validation condition will be weak where evidence exists that individuals are directly prevented from religious dissent in ways that have distorting and disabling effects on their ability to be the authors of their own lives and, similarly, where groups cannot relinquish practices even if they wanted to. In addition, the validation condition asks public decision makers to be sensitive to different ways in which practices are validated by community members, including the extent to which members have discretion about how they follow doctrine or celebrate holidays. As *Amselem* revealed, some religious traditions require that individuals make religious practices their own so that they can better experience 'joy in celebration'. The parameters of individual discretion are also relevant to the validation condition both in assessing whether something important about the distinctive identity of a group is jeopardized by a restrictive law and in the sense of assessing whether religious dissent is restricted by communities in ways that distort the identities of their members.

It may appear at first that the identity approach attempts to skirt some of the most difficult issues that arise in relation to religious practices because it gauges the strength of claims by valuing both what individuals sincerely believe and what religious traditions and communities claim to be important features of their religious identity. Specifically in relation to religion, what individuals value and what communities value can conflict because individuals 'live' their religion in ways that sometimes depart substantially from religious dogma, yet they nevertheless view themselves as members of the community to which the dogma is central. For instance, the identity approach could be read as suggesting that Catholics who live out of wedlock or Jews who refuse to circumcise their sons may well have weak claims as Catholics or Jews, should public conflicts about these practices arise. Yet, indeed, rather than avoiding the issue, the weakness of some individual claims is precisely what the identity approach aims to uncover, and for good reason. Generally speaking, the State should not be in the business of reshaping religious traditions or requiring that communities accept members who reject their practices.[16] But when public conflicts arise that engage matters of religious identity, public institutions should take seriously the identity claims of both communities and individual dissenters. Although much depends on precisely what is at stake for individuals (and, as I have argued in Chapter 4, the stakes for individuals tend to be much higher than they are for communities in such conflicts), sometimes it is reasonable for decisions to favour communities, especially if challenges threaten to destroy communities by undermining practices that are generally supported and legitimately validated by other community members. Individual sincerity and dissent are important within the identity approach, but they are not the only considerations to be weighed in resolving conflicts. Sometimes the best solution is for decision makers to find ways that individuals can dissent from community practices without undermining, for the rest of the community, important practices which are legitimately validated and unharmful. Sometimes communities should be required to change their practices, but sometimes the identity approach will suggest that communities should be protected and that individual dissenters ought to leave the community without penalty.[17]

Finally, the safeguard condition gauges the strength of a claim in terms of whether it significantly harms practitioners or places anyone at risk of substantial harm. In some cases, concerns about harm introduce a nest of difficult questions which are centrally important to the entitlements of religious minorities. The practices of some religious minorities challenge mainstream regulations (and sensibilities) regarding the treatment of children, medical treatment, and risky practices for the purpose of avoiding spiritual harm. Neither *Amselem* nor *Smith* involve especially difficult questions about harm, and therefore this is not a good place to introduce or attempt to answer these complex questions. However, what can be said more generally is that the identity approach requires that in cases where harm is at issue, decision makers focus on assessing risks of harm and safeguards to decrease this risk. The aim of doing this is to change the terms of how putatively harmful practices are discussed from terms which emphasize a contest between practices which harm and those which do not harm, to terms which emphasize the different degrees and different kinds of risks that communities take in relation to harm. When the discussion is restructured in this way, the likelihood is greater that the practices of dominant groups will also be viewed in terms of risk and thus be open to scrutiny as well.

The cases of *Amselem* and *Smith* have been discussed above in order to highlight two problems which arise when decision makers attempt to display some sensitivity about the authenticity of religious beliefs. The first problem is that decision makers will use authenticity to avoid decision making and that, consequently, assessments of the importance and the harmfulness of religious practices will occur by default and according to the stereotypes and biases that inform public attitudes and perceptions. In response to this problem, the identity approach rejects the majority's arguments in *Smith* that public decision makers cannot assess the identity claims of religious minorities and that such claims are best left to legislators. Had the Court used the identity approach in *Smith*, it would have assessed the case on the basis of evidence which showed that the *peyote* ritual is a central and important practice to members of the Native American Church, that it is central to Smith's religious identity in the sense that he sincerely believes in the importance of the practice, and that he was engaging in the practice, generally, in the manner in which members of the Church engage in it. The Court would also have assessed evidence about whether the practice causes harm, for instance, whether it contributes significantly to an illegal trade in dangerous narcotics, or whether the manner in which Smith engaged in the ritual (while at work) placed people at risk of harm, and if so, how these risks might be diminished. Some, though not all, of these considerations were discussed in the decision. On the basis of the evidence that was discussed in the dissenting, concurring, and majority opinions, Smith had a strong identity claim.

The second problem is that decision makers will engage in decision making that lacks transparency as in the case of *Amselem*. Had the Canadian Courts used the identity approach to decide the case of *Amselem*, they would not have come to a different decision but rather would have based their decision on more transparent reasons. Amselem's claim established that his personal way of celebrating Succot, which was consistent with conventional practice in his community though perhaps not required by religious dogma, was jeopardized by a tenancy ordinance that restricted temporary structures on balconies. Evidence for Amselem's claim that something important about his religious identity was at stake was established by his sincerity. Evidence for the claim that many Jews erect private *succahs* was established by religious experts who also verified the importance in Judaism of allowing some personal discretion regarding how religious holidays are celebrated. These considerations would have been established by the jeopardy and validation conditions. But the conditions are not especially strong because, after all, Amselem was not being denied the right to celebrate the holiday and because, as the experts discussed, many observant Jews use communal *succahs* to observe it. In some cases though, even a weak jeopardy and validation condition help a religious claim if very little is at stake in terms of any harm or risk of harm associated with the practice.[18] In this case, the decision reflects that the stakes for those opposed to Amselem's *succah* were low. The *succah* was temporary. No safeguards were necessary. At most, the structures would temporarily affect the aesthetic appearance of the building and thereby cause Amselem's neighbors some annoyance for eight days a year. When viewed on these terms, Amselem's claim is the stronger one.

CONCLUSION

The concerns and problems raised by cases about religious identity go well beyond those discussed in this chapter. My aim here has been limited to explaining what kinds of problems are raised by authenticity, what kinds of responses to these problems exist, and why an approach which examines claims in relation to their importance to the identity of a group or individual provides reasonable and fair responses.

The challenge of authenticity is to develop an approach capable of distinguishing between genuine and fraudulent claims in a reliable and meaningful manner without creating perverse incentives for minority claimants to distort or oversimplify the rationales for their practices in order to meet what they perceive are the expectations which dominant groups have about them. One final question, then, is, how does the identity approach respond to the perverse incentive minorities might have to distort or inauthentically 'perform' their identities in order to meet the criteria set out by majorities for what constitutes a successful claim.

The conditions set out in the identity approach, which include jeopardy, validation, and harm, impose specific, evidence-based requirements on groups which wish to advance a claim to protect some aspect of their religious identity. In part, the aim of these requirements is to acknowledge that the biases of public decision making and the stereotypes that sometimes inform public understandings of minorities can only be weakened when decision makers question stereotypes and confront bias. Decision makers sometimes retreat from the task of making difficult decisions which require that they confront institutional biases. They engage in a form of hypocrisy when they claim that their decisions strictly avoid identity assessment because usually such assessments occur by default and in the absence of decision making.

The burden on groups may be less onerous when claims are assessed using the identity approach, in part because the approach attempts to ensure that groups do not have to translate claims which are related to something profoundly important about their religious way of life, into an idiom that is distant from and potentially distorting of what they view as centrally

important about the claim. The identity approach aims to provide religious groups with a basis to challenge and transform unjust circumstances by legitimately drawing on the social experiences, history, traditions, and sense of community embodied by their identity to argue, before public institutions which are open to assessing these claims fairly, that public laws or political practices are unjustly exclusive or unfairly intrusive.

This may not provide a full and definitive answer to scholars who have observed that freedom of religion jurisprudence has been shaped to a significant degree by unsubstantiated distinctions between the religious and the superstitious, or between normal and abnormal religious beliefs. These distinctions legitimize the power and naturalize the beliefs of dominant groups while marginalizing and excluding minorities. But what follows from observations of this kind is crucial. Here I have argued that in a context where these kinds of distinctions operate, methods of public decision making which avoid assessing the disputed practices of religious minorities may, in fact, reaffirm the meaning that majorities impart on these practices and thereby reinforce the disesteem and disrespect that the majority has towards these practices and those who practice them. Public institutions that refuse to assess identity claims may, in effect, help to shield the status quo from being drawn into question. This is not to suggest that decision makers successfully avoid imperiling the integrity of claimants in every case where they publicly assess a person's deeply held and personal spiritual life. But the question of how best to avoid imperiling the integrity of claimants and the authenticity of their deeply held beliefs while nonetheless resolving disputes fairly rests on assessing the identity claims at hand and not on avoiding the assessment of identity overall, either by passing off conflict resolution to other institutions or by claiming to focus only on whether individuals appear to be sincere.

6

Indigenous Identity Claims: The Perils of Essentialism and Domestication

The basic legal and political entitlements of Indigenous peoples found in national constitutions, treaties, and international conventions are often framed in broad and general terms. As a consequence, there is often a gap between the abstract commitments found in legal and political documents and the specific, often quite practical, regulations over land use, fisheries, taxation, child welfare, education, and so on, that are supposed to flow from these general commitments. This gap is bridged, at least in part, when decision makers interpret abstract statements of legal principle in light of what specific groups claim is important and distinctive about their identity.

There are good reasons to be suspicious of this feature of decision making, perhaps especially in relation to communities that have been colonized. But the failure or unwillingness of public decision makers to engage in evaluating identity claims also raises serious problems. As I have shown in previous chapters, often the wisest course in decision making is not to give in to the problems associated with identity claiming, but rather to adopt a more defensible guide to assess such claims. Such a guide, I have argued, is informed by two normative principles. First, it must display respect for people whose identity claim is under consideration. This depends on taking seriously what people claim is important to their identities while nonetheless interpreting identity to be a product of lived experience and shaped by social context. Second, it must ensure institutional humility in the sense that it must proceed on the basis that institutions are unlikely to be neutral towards the identities of different groups. In addition to these principles, a satisfactory method of public decision making must be sensitive to whether identity claims point to serious jeopardy or mere inconvenience, whether claims are based on matters legitimately validated by the communities concerned, and whether claims are intended to protect benign or harmful practices.

Those who are sceptical about identity politics often point to cases about Indigenous rights as exemplary of the problems with it. Two problems are emphasized. The first is that identity claiming inevitably leads to an objectionable form of essentialism. Essentialism is viewed as a problem endemic to all identity claiming, but its dangers are especially well illustrated in relation to the claims of Indigenous peoples. The concern often expressed is that any attempt to interpret rights by reference to what is important to a community's identity has the effect of arbitrarily 'freezing' an aspect of that identity by elevating particular historical practices as core to the community and, at the same time, ignoring other features of the community. Cultures are thereby treated as one-dimensional and static rather than multidimensional and dynamic. In normative political theory, essentialism is probably the most common criticism of identity politics and cultural rights. It arises when peoples are understood in terms of one or two distinctive characteristics or when they are narrowly understood in terms of some of their particular practices. For instance, some allege that when cultural rights are reduced to 'rights to practices', as many Indigenous rights often are, they lose their power as the means by which minorities can effectively respond to current and changing circumstances.[1] Sometimes, the concern is expressed that cultural practices should not be valued *a priori*, as constitutive of identity and therefore as if they are beyond critical reflection.[2] Instead, identities and cultural practices ought to be viewed as responses to historical circumstances, deeply contextual and thereby 'contingent products of strategic political processes' (Johnson 2000).[3] The concern repeatedly expressed in the scholarship is that identity claiming seems to fixate uncritically on traditional practices and treats them as essential to culture.[4] Therefore, by directly broaching identity claims and highlighting their centrality in the interpretation of entitlements, the risk is that public decision makers will encourage a reductive, static, and ultimately disempowering view of identity. Although no one disagrees that this variety of essentialism should be avoided, the critics claim that it is part and parcel of identity politics.

A second and growing problem associated with Indigenous identity claiming is what I call 'domestication'. The basic concern here is that identity politics diverts attention from the way in which disputes involving Indigenous people are, in the first instance, disputes about the questionable basis of Western State sovereignty over Indigenous lands and resources. Instead of understanding disputes as ones which arise between self-determining political communities, they are understood as domestic disputes about the suitable accommodation of difference within one sovereign state. Identity claiming is viewed as contributing to this type of domestication because it focuses attention narrowly on whether a particular practice ought to be accommodated by the existing laws of the State and thereby draws political energy and resources away from efforts to advance Indigenous self-determination. It implicitly relies on the continuation of colonial authority because it treats as unproblematic a governance system in which the courts of former colonizers have power to make decisions about what is central to Indigenous identity. By making identity claims before courts and legislatures, Indigenous communities may, in effect, legitimize decision-making processes which are external to their communities and often controlled by the State(s) responsible for dominating their communities in the first place. In these ways, the concern about domestication has special resonance in the context of Indigenous politics in light of the colonial history epitomized by the denial of the right to self-determination and self-government. Together, the challenges of essentialism and domestication strongly counsel Indigenous communities against identity claiming and, if sound, raise suspicions regarding any approach which facilitates the public assessment of Indigenous claims in terms of Indigenous identity.

In this chapter, I develop a qualified and cautiously optimistic endorsement of identity assessments in the case of Indigenous identity claims. I do not want to suggest that the public assessment of Indigenous identity has been successful or that essentialism and domestication do not pose risks and challenges. On the contrary, this chapter begins by illustrating the challenges they pose in the context of examining what is perhaps the most systematic and explicit approach to the assessment of Indigenous identity claims used by any public institution in the world. It is also one widely considered to be disastrous. The 'distinctive culture test' (DCT) has been developed by the Canadian Supreme Court to interpret the constitutional rights of Indigenous peoples.[5] The DCT displays the problems identified by critics as endemic to public assessments of Indigenous identity claims. But the larger and, to my mind, more significant problem with it is that few if any countries or communities in the world have developed a defensible and systematic alternative to it. Some governing bodies (especially at the international level) have interesting ideas about how Indigenous identity claims ought to be interpreted. But, to my knowledge, no public institution has developed a set of normatively defensible and transparent criteria by which to assess the identity claims of Indigenous people. Perhaps, in part, because of the challenges posed by the critics, little incentive exists, either in State governments or in Indigenous communities, to develop and refine a more defensible guide to assess Indigenous identity claims. So the question is, if such an approach was developed, what would it look like? This chapter looks at some answers to this question with the aim of showing that the problems of essentialism and domestication are not as solid as they seem to be. Moreover, the problems can be avoided without abandoning decision-making processes that assess identity claims.

CANADA'S DISTINCTIVE CULTURE TEST

Indigenous peoples have launched numerous legal cases in Canada, which appeal to the constitutional protection of Indigenous rights, in order to secure recognition of the entitlements to specific resources or to establish exemptions from laws that threaten the distinctive practices to which different Indigenous communities adhere. For example, Canadian courts have been called upon to determine whether the protection for Indigenous rights found in Canada's Constitution entitle the Sto:lo people to sell salmon without a licence, whether the Maliseet and Mi'kmaq First Nations can cut timber from Crown land without State permission to do so, or whether the Mohawk people of Akwesasne can import goods duty-free across the international border between Canada and the United States which divides their territory.

In order to address questions about the practical meaning of the constitutional guarantees for Indigenous rights, the Courts developed the DCT in 1996.[6] The DCT requires litigants who seek to establish a specific legal entitlement to explain how something distinctive and central to their Aboriginal identity is jeopardized in the absence of granting the entitlement. It requires, first, that claimants define the practice they wish to protect precisely and show that it is jeopardized by specific state regulations (*Van der Peet* 1996: paras. 51–4).[7] Second, claimants have to show that the practice which is jeopardized is 'central and integral' to the Indigenous culture of their community (para. 55). Third, the practice must be 'distinctive' specifically to their community in the sense of being 'a defining characteristic' of their culture (para. 56), or one that 'makes the community what it was' (para. 55). The fourth and most controversial criterion is that the practice must have 'pre-contact' origins which means that (in its original form) it was central to the distinctive Indigenous culture of the community before Europeans arrived and made contact with the community (paras. 60–1). The idea behind the 'pre-contact' criterion is that only practices that were central to the community *before* Indigenous–European contact, and remain central today, count as eligible for protection under the constitutional provisions.

The DCT was first formally applied in *R. v. Van der Peet* (1996). Van der Peet, a member of the Sto:lo First Nation, appealed her conviction under the British Columbia fishery regulations for selling ten salmon without a licence to do so. She argued that her right to trade in salmon is derived from her membership in the Sto:lo First Nation, a nation whose cultural identity is intimately tied to salmon fishing. At trial, Van der Peet presented detailed historical evidence which traced Sto:lo traditions that involve fishing for food and ceremonial purposes, and which established their importance to Sto:lo identity. Trade in salmon, she argued, has been part of the Sto:lo way of life since pre-contact times. The Sto:lo have caught and dried their salmon in a distinctive way since time immemorial. They have traded fish upstream occasionally. No one but they themselves controlled their catch and, once European settlers arrived in 1827, and established the Hudson's Bay Company at Fort Langley, the Sto:lo immediately began trading salmon with the Fort for other goods. Within seven years, the trade had grown immensely: 'the amount of salmon cured at the fort was 605 barrels, as well as quantities of half-barrels, tierces, and hogsheads. In 1837, 450 barrels of salmon caught and traded by the Sto:lo were shipped by traders at Fort Langley to Hawaii, and the amounts increased thereafter' (Lambert 1998: 250).[8]

Van der Peet initially lost her case at the provincial level because the judge decided that trade between Sto:lo and Europeans was 'opportunistic and casual' rather than an exercise of an Indigenous right.[9] Then, on the initial appeal, Van der Peet won her case.[10] The British Columbia Supreme Court found that, once the salmon were caught, the Sto:lo had the right to do anything they wanted with the salmon: 'eat it, cure it, throw it back, give it away, worship it, or trade it'. On appeal again, the BC Court of Appeal was split 3:2 against Van der Peet, although all five judges agreed that 'aboriginal rights were rooted in those customs, traditions, and practices that were integral to the distinctive culture of the particular aboriginal people' (pp. 250–1). At the Supreme Court of Canada, Van der Peet finally lost her case. The majority on the Court argued, after applying the criteria of the DCT, that Sto:lo commercial trade in salmon (as opposed to fishing and consuming salmon) was occasional, not central, to pre-contact Sto:lo identity and therefore could not count as a constitutionally protected Indigenous right.

Legal scholars generally agree that the DCT is misguided and, in particular, that the pre-contact criterion is a poor way to determine which Indigenous practices ought to be viewed as protected under the ambit of constitutionally recognized Indigenous rights. The Canadian Court defends the pre-contact criterion on the basis that it provides a legally sound way of reconciling pre-existing Indigenous rights with the assertion of Crown sovereignty (*Van der Peet* 1996: paras. 40–3). The idea invoked by the courts is that because Indigenous peoples were the first occupants of the land, had formed distinctive ways of life, authoritative traditions, and institutions of governance before settlers arrived, the Constitution must be interpreted to reconcile their right to these pre-contact traditions with the rule of law as it took shape after contact.

However, from a broader perspective, concerned with Indigenous entitlement, equal respect, and fairness, the pre-contact criterion is arbitrary, unduly confining, and in some cases, plainly absurd.[11] One set of problems stems from what counts as 'pre-contact', which is not at all easy to establish. Given that over 500 distinctive First Nations communities live in Canada today, some in remote locations with little if any contact until recently with outsiders, it is impossible to attach a date to 'contact' for the purposes of defining a constitutional right.[12] A second set of problems arises because the requirement effectively eliminates the possibility of protecting a practice which arose as the result of relations between Indigenous and settler communities, even if the practice was and continues to be central to the distinctive cultures of the communities. Economic practices, in particular, are virtually eliminated from consideration because, by their nature, such practices tend to be opportunistic, and opportunities changed once settlers arrived. As the Court observed about salmon trade in *Van der Peet* and about Mohawk trade routes in *Mitchell*,[13] economic activities tend to change depending on the trading partners, goods, technology, etc., available. Unsurprisingly, the arrival of Europeans and European goods significantly changed the opportunities available to Indigenous communities in ways that altered their practices, potentially including, practices that became central to their identity.

The role played by economic activities, in sustaining distinctive identities, gives rise to especially challenging questions for public decision makers. On the one hand, some distinctive communities are reasonably described as primarily, if not entirely, economic associations. For example, family farming communities, which are today threatened to near extinction by agri-business, are economic communities as well as communities with distinctive identities, with a distinctive way of life and distinctive practices. To protect family farming communities from market forces may be economically and politically unsustainable. Nonetheless, the distinctive nature of these communities and their way of life give rise to identity claims which ought to be considered by decision makers when faced with legislative or legal disputes which threaten them. The question is often not whether reasons related to identity are relevant, but how they ought to be weighed in relation to other factors. An *a priori* refusal by decision makers to recognize economic activities as potentially integral to identity generates arbitrary decisions, because for many peoples, social, political, spiritual, and 'economic' practices are interconnected to such a degree that trying to distinguish a cultural practice from an economic one is futile.

For example, in *R v. Sappier* (2006), the Mi'kmaq and Maliseet communities in Nova Scotia claimed the right to cut timber on Crown land for domestic use without State permission to do so. Anticipating that the Court would refuse to protect economic activities as cultural entitlements, the claimants were careful to frame their claim as being restricted to 'domestic use', in other words, not for sale or barter. But the evidence they provided built a compelling case that their communities have always used the timber on their lands to survive, as a source of shelter, transportation, tools, and fuel (para. 24) since pre-contact times. Using the DCT, the Court granted the right and agreed that using wood from these lands had always been key to their survival. But it reasoned that survival for the Mi'kmaq and Maliseet communities today ought to be interpreted according to standards similar to those which existed pre-contact. Thereby, the Indigenous right covers harvesting wood only for domestic uses and excludes harvesting for barter or commercial sale. The incoherence of the distinction between domestic use and commercial sale is immediately apparent in this decision, as a separate (though concurring) opinion in this case suggests.[14] If the value of an Indigenous practice is that it was integral to how a community survived, on what basis then can the Court limit the definition of the practice so as to distinguish between cultural and economic survival? The Court appears to be guided by criteria other than those found in its own (rather restrictive) test.

Essentialism and domestication in the distinctive culture test

Decisions like *Van der Peet* and *Sappier* illustrate how the DCT essentializes Indigenous identities in two general senses. First, there is a historical dimension to how identity is essentialized. Even though the court acknowledges that protected practices can be those that have changed over time, the DCT holds that rights attach only to those practices which have historical importance and pre-contact origins. All discussion of Indigenous identity and entitlement in these cases and all the evidence submitted by claimants aim at establishing the historical centrality of their current practices. Borrows describes the court's perspective as treating 'Indigenous' as retrospective: 'It is about what was, "once upon a time," central to the survival of a community, not necessarily about what is central, significant and distinctive to the survival of these communities today. . . .' (1997–8: 43). Practices which are symbolic today yet had important functions 150 years ago are more likely to pass the test than practices which are crucial to a community's way of life today but arose mainly as means to help communities survive in the midst of colonization. So, according to the DCT, what matters above all else in establishing an entitlement is a demonstration of the ways that practices and identities have not changed and peoples have not adapted (or not very much) to their changing circumstances. Thus, the type of identity that appears salient to winning recognition of rights is static and located at an arbitrary point in a people's history.

Second, the critics point out that, with or without the pre-contact criterion, the DCT essentializes Indigenous identities by reducing 'cultures' to particular practices and then holding out the promise to protect only practices which are deemed to be central and integral to a culture. The concern is that by focusing on practices, the test artificially reduces culture to a set of practices (see Barsh and Henderson 1997; Borrows 1997–8; Christie 1998). The DCT conceptualizes culture as a static, ordered system of somewhat discreet practices and meanings, wherein each practice can be assessed to determine both its centrality to the culture as a whole (which implies that a whole can be delimited), and whether the practice alone distinguishes the culture from other cultures. This ignores the fact that seemingly insignificant practices are often crucial in sustaining 'larger and more central' practices, and falsely supposes that the centrality of any cultural practice is not likely to vary depending on circumstances (Barsh and Henderson 1997: 1000–3). The critics also argue that cultural essentialism is exacerbated by the DCT's first criterion, which requires that a disputed practice be specifically defined for the court so as to avoid 'excessive generality'. Although this criterion seems innocuous enough, it poses a dilemma for claimants which highlights the test's essentialist nature: if they define their claim too generally and in a manner that incorporates the adaptability and fluidity of a practice, the chances are greater that it will fail to pass the rest of the test, especially the pre-contact requirement; if they describe it too specifically, statically, and discreetly, and it passes the test, it may be too narrow to be of real value to them.[15] As a result, the DCT has been criticized for being too risky from a litigator's point of view to be a helpful means of establishing Indigenous rights using the Constitution (Ross 2005: 16).

Decisions in which the DCT is employed can also be used to trace the problem of domestication at work. The problem of domestication is that efforts to justify rights in relation to identity divert public attention and community resources away from appropriate recognition of the self-determination of Indigenous communities and implicitly concede that the state exercises legitimate political authority over Indigenous communities. Inviting courts to assess the identity claims of Indigenous peoples ignores the fact that Western states have illegitimately imposed their rule on self-governing Indigenous communities and territories. The obfuscation of Indigenous self-determination is especially manifested in the courts' insistence using the DCT that claimants avoid 'excessive generality' in specifying their identity claims. This stipulation, according to Borrows, serves to discourage claimants from arguing that hunting, fishing, or trading practices are central and integral to the broader 'pre-contact' 'cultural' tradition of self-government and self-determination (1997–8: 47). When viewed through the lens of identity, at least on the DCT interpretation, the constitutional guarantees of Indigenous rights seem to offer Indigenous peoples public accommodation for some discrete Indigenous practices, which is little more than religious or cultural minorities can expect from the government. This, of course, is a far cry from substantive recognition of real Indigenous entitlement. The DCT may also complicate the kinds of arguments that claimants have to make, and place such a heavy onus on the availability of evidence (some of which must speak to how peoples lived 'pre-contact' and therefore before written records were kept) that, in effect, the test could proliferate disputes and drain communities of resources. Russell Barsh and James Youngblood Henderson describe the predictable outcome of the DCT in the following way:

> ... First Nations will bear even greater uncertainty as to the extent of their resources, and the scope of their political authority. More community resources will be devoted to defensive litigation, and the volatility and unpredictability of First Nations' rights and jurisdiction will deter investment on reserves. Reserves may turn to higher-risk investments, including those on the edge of legality such as casino gambling, simply because they generate sufficiently large profits to pay the costs of defending the right to pursue them. (1997: 1006)

Drawing from these observations, the problem of domestication then is not only that, at best, identity claiming secures for minorities minor adjustments to state policies, but that it also disempowers vulnerable, at-risk, communities by encouraging them to adopt high risk strategies that drain their resources and predictably make little difference to their political status and well being.

The tide of criticism against the DCT in legal scholarship is overwhelming. Nearly all of the critical material points to two chief flaws in the test: essentialism and domestication. By reducing cultures to pre-contact practices, the DCT freezes Indigenous cultures to a particular point in history and undervalues cultural change and adaptability. More generally, the test reduces ways of life to practices, and it places at the centre of constitutional entitlement the task of figuring out how best to protect discrete cultural practices rather than how best to enhance the agency and self-determination of Indigenous peoples in Canada.

ALTERNATIVE APPROACHES

Very few if any systematic alternatives exist to Canada's DCT, even though the sort of identity assessments for which the DCT is a guide are those that are likely to occur any time the abstract provisions of an international convention or national constitution are translated into specific policies about land, resources, or governance that give real substance to the entitlements for a particular Indigenous community. One example of this translation occurring at the international level, though in a manner that is far less systematic than found in Canada, can be found in the decisions of the United Nations Human Rights Committee (HRC) in their interpretation of the International Covenant on Civil and Political Rights (ICCPR). Article 27 of the ICCPR establishes the rights of persons who belong to 'ethnic, linguistic or religious minorities ... in community with other members of their group, to enjoy their own culture, to profess and practice their own religion [and] to use their own language'. The Article has been used in several cases by Indigenous communities to argue that their cultural rights are violated by the activities of states. In the course of translating the abstract principles of Article 27 into more substantive decisions, most of which refer to specific disputes over land use, the HRC has developed four standards by which to assess Indigenous identity.

First, in Article 27 decisions, cultural identity is broadly conceived to include the protection of practices that are central to community life such as the use of the community's language, the practice of their own religion, and, 'in general... all those characteristics necessary for the preservation of their own cultural identity'.[16] Decisions have specifically favoured economic activities as cultural practices, as well as protections for resources necessary for carrying out these activities.

For example, in *Ominayak, Chief of the Lubicon Lake Band v. Canada* (1984), the HRC concluded, using Article 27, that the Lubicon community's cultural identity was in jeopardy as a result of a provincial law which expropriated Lubicon land in order to allow oil and gas exploration to take place on it.[17] The argument before the HRC was based on evidence of the community's profound dependence on having access to the land and its historical importance. Given its remote location, the Lubicon had little contact with non-Indigenous society, a fact reflected in its social institutions. Community members primarily speak Cree and many do not speak, read, or write English. Evidence showed that the Lubicon's hunting and fishing activities were essential to maintaining the subsistence economy underpinning its distinctive culture, spirituality, and language. The HRC agreed that the Lubicon could no longer survive as a people without access to their lands. It reached its decision against Canada after weighing the impact of the development projects on the Lubicon's identity claims. It agreed with the Lubicon that the survival of their community was imperiled by the oil and gas exploration, and recognized that economic, not merely social or religious, activities were protected cultural rights under Article 27.[18]

Second, the HRC decisions often reflect a distinction between laws that disrupt community practices and those that destroy these practices. On the one hand, this means that groups might have to absorb some disruption to their way of life. For example, in *Länsman et al. v. Finland* (1992), a group of Sami reindeer herders contested a quarry development on a mountainside where they kept pens and a network of fences which they used in their breeding and herding activities. They argued that their culture 'has traditionally been and remains essentially based on reindeer husbandry', a claim the HRC accepted, and that the quarry disturbed their husbandry activities. But, after assessing the impact of the quarrying to date, the HRC disagreed with the Sami that the quarrying activity was sufficiently disruptive. It argued that not 'every measure, even a minor one, which obstructs or impairs reindeer husbandry must be interpreted as prohibited by the Covenant'. On the other hand, the HRC recognized that cultural practices can be adapted over time and still be eligible for protection. What seems crucial in distinguishing disruption (as in *Länsman et al.*) from destruction (as in *Ominayak*) involves understanding the role and importance of an activity or practice to the identity of a group, including its relation to a particular place, and to the community's sustainability.[19]

Third, Article 27 decisions interpret the right for culture to be sustainable and future-oriented. Public policies and regulations which cut off a community from the means to sustain crucial aspects of its identity in the long-term will violate this standard. Some HRC decisions incorporate an awareness, which is lost by the DCT because of the pre-contact requirement, that practices which ensure intergenerational continuity, and secure the long-term well being of communities, are especially important to protection as cultural rights. For example, in *Hopu and Tepoaitu Bessert v. France* (1993), a case which involved a land-use dispute between Indigenous Polynesians and French Polynesian authorities in Tahiti, the issue was whether an ancient burial site, slated for development, contained the 'family members' of the Indigenous community there. The case turned on what constitutes 'family' and whether access to the burial sites of their ancestors constituted a practice central to cultural identity. In a ruling which favoured the Indigenous people, the HRC decided that the term 'family' must 'include all those comprising the family as understood in the society in question' (para. 10.3) and moreover that the claim was important because 'the relationship to their ancestors [is] an essential element of their identity' (para. 10.3).[20] Even if no evidence existed that the survival of the community was in jeopardy, the HRC recognized that the value of family relationships and intergenerational continuity was deeply important to cultural identity and that the costs imposed by the development project exceeded what was reasonable to impose on the community.

And, finally, the fourth standard is that states must consult with the groups with whom they have conflict (Scheinin 2000). The 'right to meaningful consultation' has been invoked in three Article 27 cases all having to do with competing land-use disputes and the cultural rights of Indigenous people. On the one hand, the requirement may be interpreted as mainly a means to ensure that parties have exhausted alternative remedies before the cases reach the HRC. On the other hand, failing to consult a community can be a powerful strategy if it indicates the unwillingness of one community to recognize the existence of another as distinctive. A 'duty to consult' is a means of recognizing that a community deserves respect and recognition in relation to decisions that have an impact on its collective way of life. Conversely, the failure to consult could amount to the position that no such obligation exists because no distinctive community exists that requires consultation.

Article 27 provides a set of nascent standards for the assessment of Indigenous identity claims that views cultural activities in a broad sense which includes economic activities; that aims at being sensitive to cultural change and adaptability; that highlights the importance of practices which are sustainable and future-oriented; and that requires states to consult and thereby recognize distinctive communities in their midst. It is viewed by some Indigenous rights scholars as reflecting a 'norm of cultural integrity' which, according to Anaya, 'upholds the right of Indigenous groups to maintain and freely develop their cultural identities in co-existence with other sectors of humanity' (1996: 98). However, to date, these standards are not fully articulated as an approach by the HRC or other international bodies and do not consistently show up in every decision.[21] Moreover, little incentive exists to develop these standards into a more complete approach, at least under Article 27. For one thing, the HRC has been criticized for following a different and far narrower set of standards when hearing cases that involve the rights of non-Indigenous cultural minorities.[22] At the same time, the ICCPR is not specifically designed to protect Indigenous people and its generic nature in this regard has provided impetus for a more targeted approach, such as the one taken in the Draft Declaration on the Rights of Indigenous Peoples.[23]

The more general and seemingly serious problems, which the HRC approach cannot address, are what I call the problems of essentialism and domestication. With respect to essentialism, the HRC approach, despite its virtues, nevertheless bases entitlements on practices that are found to be central rather than contingent to identity and that are historically enduring rather than recent responses to current circumstances. Therefore, in terms of essentialism, the HRC could be criticized for essentializing Indigenous culture through its decisions which recognize, for example, that a subsistence economy is central to the Lubicon's distinctive culture, or that reindeer husbandry is so closely connected to the Sami culture that it 'must be considered part of the Sami culture itself' (*Kitok v. Sweden* 1985).

The problem of domestication also persists in the HRC approach. The HRC has explicitly refused to hear claims made under Article 27 which directly implicate the right to self-determination.[24] It thereby appears to offer groups little more than the DCT might offer, namely accommodation within a regime that ultimately upholds the State system and thereby one which is indirectly responsible for colonial rule in the first place.

The conclusion to which these problems point is that any approach that attempts to protect cultural identity by assessing what is important to that identity will essentialize and domesticate cultural groups. Any approach, no matter how sensitive, accurate, inclusive, or reasonable, which considers matters crucial to the identities of Indigenous peoples as possible grounds for entitlement decisions, appears to invite the perils of essentialism and domestication.

Yet, as I see it, the problem with this conclusion is that it rests on such an abstract understanding of how entitlements are translated through decision making into substantive policies that it is nearly useless, either in distinguishing between better and worse approaches or in comprehending the manner in which groups can effectively protect their distinctive ways of life or advance their entitlement to self-determination or self-government. Therefore, it is worth briefly re-evaluating the problems of essentialism and domestication in order to determine, in light of the specific nature of the challenges faced by Indigenous peoples, whether or how decision makers might avoid static, reductive, and assimilationist interpretations of these claims.

ESSENTIALISM REVISITED

The problem of essentialism arises, in part, when groups are 'frozen' in time to a retrospective and nostalgic understanding of their identity. But a distinction can be drawn between approaches, like the Canadian DCT, which encourage a narrow and blinkered use of historical argument, and the more general usage of history by many groups, not only those that are Indigenous, to point out the connection between the longevity of their practices and the sustained importance of the practice to their identity. It is worthwhile drawing this distinction because many groups consider the meaning of their identities and view their practices as meaningful in relation to particular histories. For instance, how a community understands itself in relation to other groups often implicates historical struggles; how it ensures intergenerational continuity is often revealed by investigating the history of its practices; the significance it invests in particular places, again, implicates its historical relationship to a place. But using history to trace what is important about practices is distinct from assuming that historical longevity *is* what is important about practices. It is possible that practices which were crucial to a community's identity were abandoned long ago and replaced by new ones that do not resemble the old practice but perform the same role. It is also possible that because of disruptions to the community's way of life, new practices were never adopted and traditional ones were lost, resulting in community dislocation and dysfunction.

For example, consider a community like the Makah in what is now Washington State. The Makah have recently argued for the right to hunt whales, a practice that they traditionally engaged in but were forced to abandon because of international and national laws against the whale hunt. While conservation and animal cruelty might count as weighty reasons to deny the Makah the right to hunt whales today, the reasons that count in their favour are not simply that the Makah engaged in whale hunting before European settlers arrived, but rather that hunting whales is woven into the social, political, and familial organization of the community in such a way that, once the practice was disallowed, the community became dysfunctional in some ways. One of the interesting questions posed today, in light of many years without the whale hunt, is whether reinstituting the hunt is a means to reclaiming community functioning. Many members of the Makah community claim that it is. Whether their argument is sound or not, its strength partly depends on establishing the connection between whaling practices and the identity-related values the practices serve, including the values they served historically, and also the values that they will plausibly serve or could serve today.

To replace this sort of inquiry with the question that would be asked using the DCT, of whether whale hunting was central to Makah identity pre-contact, does not merely narrow the inquiry's focus inappropriately, but amounts to supposing that, historically speaking, the 'tail wags the dog' insofar as the longevity and continuity of the practice are mistaken for its meaningfulness and the important role it fulfils in actualizing particular values related to the community's identity and way of life. The fair assessment of identity claims requires reasoning that connects disputed practices to the values they serve. This must include the way in which they connect communities to a meaningful past and present, and to a sustainable future.

The mistake that decision makers make is not that they consider the historical origins and significance of a practice to be important, but rather that they fail to consider how history informs and stands in relation to challenges that communities face today. The problem with the DCT is that its historical focus on 'pre-contact' origins creates a great incentive for claimants to provide evidence about the historical importance of their practices. But it provides them and the courts with little if any incentive to examine the ways in which identity claims, which are crucial to healthy communities, can effectively fulfil important roles today. The history of a practice dominates the DCT approach to the point of distracting claimants and decision makers from the main point of the enterprise, namely, to discover whether the distinctive culture of an Indigenous community is in jeopardy, and whether protecting a practice or access to a resource can overcome that jeopardy.

Essentialism also arises when particular group practices are chosen by public decision makers as being more central or important than others. But once again, this problem loses some bite when examined more closely. First, usually groups seek legal recognition for their distinctive practices because denying legal recognition also shapes cultural practices and influences their importance in a minority community in ways that many within the community consider undesirable. In other words, some forms of essentialism are imposed on groups whether or not identity claims are assessed by public institutions. Culture is indeed largely relational and not a 'natural or essential' sort of thing. But rather than resolve the matter, this merely raises the question of whether relations ought to be those of restriction or accommodation, and how communities ought to decide. In many cases, the alternative to naming practices and protecting them is just another form of interference.[25] What is often presented in Canada, in scholarship and public policy, as the alternative to recognizing exemptions for Indigenous practices as protected entitlements are approaches that favour the assimilation of Indigenous peoples into mainstream Canadian society where no group is entitled to exemptions and where laws are constructed by democratic majorities to reflect mainly their own values and way of life. (see, e.g., Flanagan 2000). A similar observation can be made about the political circumstances in which many national minorities find themselves today. Moreover, even where the intention behind denying an Indigenous identity claim is not to impose on Indigenous peoples a homogeneous *national* identity, often the aim is to empower market mechanisms which have their own homogenizing effects. For instance, one alternative to protecting Sami reindeer husbandry from quarry development in Finland is instead to favour regional development schemes which treat all group interests as appropriately vetted through competitive market forces.

Groups often advance identity claims because they think that certain threatened practices are good ways in which to protect particular values or to sustain ways of life that are important to their identities generally or in their present social circumstances. The questions raised in legal cases about cultural practices are not only, as the critics suggest, whether a practice is 'definitive' of a culture, but also whether a practice is both a meaningful and a good strategy by which a community can secure its way of life. For example, the argument made by the Makah, to reinstitute the whale hunt, attempts to trace the connection between whale hunting and traditional practices surrounding leadership and governance. Meaningful leadership, according to this argument, emerges from those who are whale hunters. Therefore, reinstituting the hunt is possibly an effective way to begin to reclaim governance practices that are viewed as meaningful by the community (see Van Ginkel 2004).

Similarly, when the Sami argue to protect reindeer herding from quarry developments, they are presumably doing so because reindeer herding is meaningful to all or some of them.[26] Yet, they are also attempting to ensure greater control over an economic activity that is valued by the community today because it ties the community to its history, to its geography, because it informs its central social, familial, and religious activities, and because protecting the practice is a way of ensuring that the community does not dissolve as its members are forced to seek jobs elsewhere. Reindeer husbandry is important to Sami identity both historically and also because of the way the practice is connected to other values important to sustaining community today. Its meaning and importance derive partly from its relation to Sami history, partly because it generates a particular political economy within the community, and partly because it gives the Sami some control over land use. The same is true in the case of the Sto:lo. The Sto:lo attempt to secure for themselves an Indigenous right to trade in salmon through Canada's Constitution is a means to defend or deepen the relation between the Sto:lo and a resource which connects the community to its history and geography, its social structure, and spiritual beliefs. In none of these cases does the argument to protect a distinctive practice bind communities to a static identity. Rather, the identity claim is an expression of group agency and possibly a means to develop strategies which effectively respond to historical circumstances.

DOMESTICATION REVISITED

Many critics would argue that these reassurances miss the broader and unavoidable peril of domestication, namely that identity claiming diverts the energy and resources of Indigenous communities away from venues or campaigns which could secure or advance self-determination and requires that Indigenous communities advance their claims in contexts ultimately controlled by the State or dominated by interests of the State system. But this criticism loses sight of what abstract ideals like 'self-determination' entail in practice and, at the same time, takes an exceedingly narrow view of what any given case or legal strategy might effectively accomplish.

For one thing, sometimes Indigenous groups advance identity claims in the course of seeking interim protections for resources which the community considers crucial to secure in the course of its struggles for self-determination. For example, Indigenous ways of life, throughout the world, are often threatened by commercial ventures that destroy lands, deplete resources, and pollute the environment in ways that directly threaten the cultural security of a community. Interim legal measures can effectively contribute to securing Indigenous rights given the nature of the resources upon which Indigenous communities throughout the world tend to rely. Many Indigenous peoples seek protection for pristine land areas, such as Clayquot Sound on the west coast of Canada, the Amazon Basin, and Sarawak in Borneo, which are intimately connected to their history, their practices, and way of life. While the recognition of the right to self-government or self-determination might conceivably protect these resources at some time in the future, many of these resources will be gone long before self-government agreements can be reached.

Second, identity claims can contribute to capacity building in Indigenous communities which is an important component of self-government. One consequence of the destructive effects of colonial rule is that, today, some Indigenous communities have to rebuild capacities of governance, including the capacity to protect their distinctive culture, to manage the use of their land and resources, and their governing orders. Building these capacities is important to Indigenous self-determination which requires building institutions and governing practices by which ongoing self-government is possible (Anaya 1996: 82).[27] Identity claiming arises all the time in this context because, in building institutions of governance, many communities, understandably, want to reinvigorate traditional practices to serve contemporary capacity-related needs, and some of these practices are controversial both within the community and in relation to the laws and values of the dominant community. For instance, inter- and intra-community controversy surrounds the Makah efforts to reinstitute the whale hunt, the efforts of many Indigenous communities in North America to establish casinos on their reserves, and to reclaim traditional and sometimes sexist practices as part of traditional political order. Obviously, what is crucial in all of these cases is that the means established to fulfil capacity building are adequate to the task. It is important that traditions are good strategies to fulfil contemporary needs including the need to build contemporary functional institutions. But part of what also determines their adequacy is the extent to which communities view practices as their own. That is, it involves the recognition of practices by the community as reflecting their self-understanding, their way of life, and thus giving expression to values important to their identities. Distinctive values and practices, which are related to identity, provide a guide which helps communities (or other decision makers) to decide how best to reconstitute and reclaim Indigenous traditions of law and governance to build suitable institutions today (see Alfred 1995; Borrows 2002).

Third, identity has proven to be effective at framing issues and conflicts for the purpose of mobilizing Indigenous peoples. Evidence over the last thirty years has shown that identity claiming mobilizes Indigenous communities in a manner that fighting economic injustice in an earlier era failed to do (see Postero and Zamosc 2004; Yashar 2005; Van Cott 2006). Specifically in Latin America, Indigenous communities have effectively mobilized to defend their practices, including practices that are connected to broader entitlements to control their land, to access resources, and to address community poverty. This strategic use of identity perhaps points to its fleeting and limited importance in relation to more enduring issues like self-determination (see Jung 2008). Nonetheless, it might also show that identity claiming is a necessary condition to advance claims for self-determination.

In sum, claims which are framed in terms of identity are used to establish interim protections for land, wildlife and habitat, and other resources, which are often the fragile subjects of self-government agreements between Indigenous peoples and settler societies. Identity also provides some of the values and reasons for building or rebuilding Indigenous institutions that provide communities with the capacity to be self-determining in meaningful ways. On these bases, it is a mistake to conclude that identity claiming, in general, diverts the energy and resources of Indigenous groups away from advancing self-determination.

CONCLUSION: WHAT DOES A BETTER APPROACH LOOK LIKE?

No magical fix exists to working out fair relations in diverse societies. An approach that guides public decision makers regarding how they should assess identity claims is not intended as a cure-all for conflicts between minorities and majorities, or between Indigenous peoples and settler states. Sometimes the claims of Indigenous peoples are not best expressed in terms of their identity. Rather, such an approach is intended to fill a gap that exists between the mandates and entitlements which communities develop to govern their relations together and the substantive decisions by which these mandates are translated into concrete regulations or decisions.

A defensible approach to the public assessment of identity claims would allow for a broad and purposive interpretation of the sorts of activities and practices that might be considered identity claims, including economic activities. It would proceed to assess the strength of an identity claim on the basis of the three conditions previously outlined.

First, the jeopardy condition would require that claimants like Van der Peet show that something important to her community's distinctive cultural identity is jeopardized in the absence of an entitlement. The strength of the jeopardy condition is gauged by assessing the centrality of the practice to the claimant's identity and the extent to which it is jeopardized as opposed to merely inconvenienced. The condition would not rely on a preconceived idea of how many years a practice must be important in order to be viewed as part of a group's identity. Instead, the strength of an identity claim depends in part on its historical meaning and importance for a group (which may be established using historical evidence) and its effectiveness at sustaining that meaning and value within contemporary contexts. In this respect, the strength of Van der Peet's claim rests partly in the importance of salmon trading to the Sto:lo way of life, but also on whether trade in salmon is a meaningful and effective way of sustaining that way of life today and into the future. Van der Peet's claim would be weakened by evidence that the salmon fishery is unsustainable or that, apart from a few people like her, the community no longer is interested in trading salmon or views the practice as especially meaningful.

Second, the public assessment of identity contains a validation condition which requires that the strength of an identity claim be assessed in terms of whether it has been appropriately validated. Validation is meant both to ensure that practices are not foisted on community members (or some members) and to bring into the assessment process internal disputes about what are considered controversial practices. For some Indigenous communities, the prospect of resuscitating historical traditions is understandably fraught with intra-group disputes because communities disagree about which traditions ought to be resuscitated and what their significance should be. The validation condition considers these disputes relevant to assessing the strength of the claim, but it does not treat the mere existence of disagreement as evidence that the important role or value of a practice is entirely indeterminate. Rather, the validation condition gauges the strength of the claim in terms of the efforts communities are able to make to resolve such disputes.

The validation condition would also be sensitive to the way in which dominant groups have validated their decisions to interfere in the practices of minorities. It could incorporate, for instance, the 'duty to consult' as found in the HRC approach, which would mean that, in the absence of evidence of consultation, for example, between Canada and the Sto:lo to establish a licensing regime, the claim of Canada to regulate the fishery in light of Sto:lo opposition is weaker than it would be had adequate consultation taken place.

Finally, the approach includes a safeguard condition which would measure the strength of a claim in terms of whether it harms practitioners or places anyone at risk of harm. The cases here do not obviously implicate the issue of safeguards, but in cases where this is an issue, the identity approach gauges the strength of claims in terms of the absence of harm or the costs of avoiding predictable harm.

Admittedly, these are broad and general conditions whose virtues depend on how they handle the details of any given case. Nonetheless, they stake out a position which requires that institutions are designed with the capacity to assess the identity claims of minorities, including Indigenous peoples. They are not simple requirements to meet. But the point here is that these requirements speak more directly to the values which are important to sustaining communities; to securing ways of life; and to ensuring fair and transparent decisions. They are grounded in a position that fair relations are often secured by engaging, not abandoning or ignoring discussions about group identity, and by promoting understanding among people who share an attachment to their ways of life, but have different ways of life, in which different practices are meaningful to them.

7

Conclusion: Reasons of Identity

One of the animating ideas of this book is that there are politically salient reasons of identity. In order to explore this idea, I have articulated an approach whereby claims people make on the basis of something distinctive and important about their identities can be assessed in a transparent and fair manner. A principled and context-sensitive method through which reasons of identity are assessed by public institutions is a necessary feature of good and legitimate decision making in diverse societies. Moreover, in the absence of an articulated method for assessing reasons of identity, multiculturalism is incomplete and will appear to be dangerous.

The identity approach is not meant to replace the need for inclusive democratic deliberation or attentiveness to human rights. However, even within well established democracies, it is not enough to require that legislators, social workers, teachers, and the public become more involved in deliberating about cultural or religious conflicts or to insist that their decisions must be consistent with human rights and other abstract facets of justice. Good decision making depends on more than answering the question, 'Who decides?' As I noted, in relation to the religious arbitration debates in Canada, even discussions that appear to be fair and inclusive can become so abstract that the issues which are deeply important to real people in real communities are effectively ignored. And sometimes the abstract ideals, like those embodied in human rights, are understood in different ways by different communities and thereby provide insufficient guidance in resolving specific conflicts. Good public decision making in diverse societies requires a set of guidelines through which identity claims can be assessed fairly and through which the practical meaning of abstract ideals like equality, rights, and multiculturalism, which arise in relation to identity, can be determined.

As the title of this book suggests, reasons of identity are discernable reasons that are amenable to public examination and assessment. But they are neither the only kind of reason nor, in all cases, the most important reason, to justify a group's entitlement to a resource or opportunity, or to compel a decision maker to resolve a conflict one way rather than another. The argument in this book is that institutions must have the capacity to assess identity claims, not that all cases about minority conflicts are about identity or that all approaches which avoid identity claims are fatally flawed. Sometimes, indirect strategies that bypass direct consideration of identity and focus only on individual rights (as conventionally understood) or other considerations not obviously related to distinctive identities are effective and appropriate ways of capturing the importance of a minority's claim. However, in some settings, these indirect methods distort conflicts, bias procedures, generate dilemmas, or otherwise pose inadequate ways of debating or resolving the problem.

None of this suggests that the identity approach can adequately resolve all ethnic or religious conflict. To the contrary, as discussed in relation to Indigenous claims, identity claims sometimes contribute only in a modest (albeit important) way to helping vulnerable groups argue for self-determination. However, as I have shown, one reason why identity claims have normative value is that treating people with respect requires that public decision makers take seriously these claims as possible reasons why entitlements ought to be recognized. A second reason that addressing identity directly matters is that the assessment of identity claims is a prerequisite to ensuring that institutions have the capacity to reflect on their own biases or on the possibility that unfair criteria related to how identities are understood have shaped the way in which decisions have been made in the past. This is what I called the capacity of institutional humility. The point here builds on an observation that Charles Taylor once made that understanding another people's language of self-understanding can protect us against our own ethnocentrism (Taylor 1985: 126). The wisdom of Taylor's observation is well illustrated in some of the conflicts examined in this book. They have shown that when identity is not addressed in a principled and direct manner, it ends up being addressed implicitly and haphazardly. In most, if not all, existing societies today, implicit assessments of minority identities give rise to the risk that conflicts will be understood in light of false stereotypes about minority groups and false assumptions about the neutrality and fairness of dominant practices and procedures. In the absence of institutional humility made possible via direct, open, structured, and fair assessments of identity claims, institutional hubris flourishes. Where false understandings and racism prevail and remain unchallenged, unequal power relations amongst groups become entrenched.

This book has examined many different kinds of conflicts and cases involving religious, cultural, and indigenous minorities, in order to show that identity claims are not opaque or difficult to assess, at least, not any more difficult than other questions which publics and public decision makers confront all the time. Four central concerns about such claims have generated a large scholarship that is deeply skeptical about the wisdom of according identity claims a role in democratic politics. Part of my objective has been to confront and refute different varieties of identity scepticism. Thus, I have tackled (1) problems relating to the incommensurability of multiple identity claims; (2) doubts about the possibility of establishing the authenticity of identity; (3) the worry that identity claims have potential to essentialize persons and groups; and (4) the danger that trading in identity fosters the domestication or assimilation of minorities. I have tried to show that none of these concerns provides sufficient reason to conclude that identity claims are generally opaque, or that public decision makers are unable to treat these claims as reasons for action which can be assessed in a transparent and fair manner.

There are, of course, other reservations about assessing identity claims besides the four main ones I have analysed in the foregoing chapters. One common complaint is that approaches to diversity such as the one defended here appear to embrace a conservative or 'traditionalist' form of multiculturalism rather than a progressive liberal one. The traditionalist view of identity is one that emphasizes the importance of particular, quite narrowly construed, practices to people's identities. It is conservative because, by seeking to preserve cultural practices, the traditionalist position risks rewarding conservative elites while threatening the capacity of communities to debate the need for changing their traditional ways. Kymlicka, for instance, has argued that multiculturalism must be given a liberal interpretation in order to avoid these problems and, moreover, that a liberal interpretation of multiculturalism challenges traditionalism: 'the liberal view of multiculturalism is inevitably, intentionally, and unapologetically transformational of people's cultural traditions' (2007: 97–108).

While the charge of myopic traditionalism may apply to some accounts of identity, it does not apply to the approach I have developed. To begin with, as many of the cases and conflicts examined in this book show, posing a stark dichotomy between traditionalist and liberal forms of multiculturalism is misleading. It fails to capture many of the complicated reasons why people argue for the protection of their practices or many of the legitimate reasons why certain practices ought to be protected. Sensitivity to identity does not always mean simply preserving old ways but, by the same token, at least when they are properly understood, traditional practices are not in all cases inherently illiberal. There is no predetermined and clear distinction between traditional practices and liberal values. Second, I have also argued that the preservation of authentic traditions per se is a misguided and even dangerous political pursuit. Along with conservative elites and policy makers focused on developing the means to detect fraud amongst claimants, theorists of multiculturalism share the blame for encouraging the mistaken belief that the 'authenticity' of a group's traditions or cultural practices is something to be explored or discovered.[1] The value of distinctive practices and traditions to identity is not to be simplistically located in a misleading and illusive notion of authenticity. More to the point, groups can argue for the protection of traditional practices for reasons that are conservative in some ways and transformative in others. Probably the clearest example of this is found in the claims of Indigenous peoples who seek protection for traditional practices partly so that they can meaningfully develop good governance practices which can help their communities survive into the future. In such instances, traditions function in the service of political transformation. There does not seem to me to be any point in deciding whether this kind of project is more conservative or liberal. Our focus should instead be devoted to establishing fair criteria by which to assess the credibility of the claim that a practice is meaningful to a community's identity, that it is validated in a legitimate manner, and that it is not harmful.

To be clear, I have no doubt that conservative political forces sometimes attempt to harness identity claiming as a way of resisting progressive change.[2] But, as I have argued in this book, conservative political forces are also often at work amongst those who argue that identity claims are opaque and beyond critical assessment. In this context, it is important to remember that scepticism and criticism of identity claims have enormous resonance in public decision making. The mistaken belief that identity claims cannot be the subject of reasoned debate has become an excuse for decision makers to avoid making difficult and controversial decisions that challenge the status quo. The problem democratic publics confront today is not only how to control overzealous and 'activist' courts or legislatures, but also how to compel these institutions to make difficult decisions and to live up to principled commitments. Part of the difficulty that public institutions face in relation to identity claims is that they have received little, if any, guidance as to how to translate vague mandates about protecting diversity into decisions which apply fairly to specific groups in specific contexts.

While I believe that the assessment of identity claims in an open, direct, and structured manner is feasible and important, I do not want to suggest that all identity claims are easily assessed. A principled approach to the assessment of identity claims, such as the one developed in this book, cannot provide an algorithm for decision makers. Rather, the approach identifies three broadly defined conditions – jeopardy, validation, and safeguard conditions – which, when fulfilled, illuminate the reasons why some identity claims are stronger than others and why some resolutions to conflicts are more fair and reasonable than others. The main message here is that an identity claim should be accepted roughly if (1) evidence shows that failure to protect a practice places the identity of a person or group in serious jeopardy; (2) the processes through which a group has come to accord a practice importance are suitably fair and inclusive; and (3) protection of the practice does not threaten serious harm to anyone. By contrast, there is less reason to protect a practice (and claimants will have a weaker case) when identity is not jeopardized; the processes of validation are not inclusive, fair, or otherwise legitimate; and a threat of serious harm predictably follows if the practice is protected.

Some readers might think that the chances are nonetheless slim that public decision makers will actually adopt the sort of guidelines that I have suggested and defended in this book. I cannot, of course, predict that my approach will be embraced, but it is worth noting that despite massive scepticism from political theorists, public officials already broach identity issues directly. The approach developed in this book builds on this fact and attempts to provide guidelines for the assessment of identity claims that distinguish between good and bad practices.

The significance of the fact that public decision makers already assess identity claims should not be underestimated. Public institutions have a wealth of experience in addressing identity claims directly. The guidelines suggested here organize the most important questions and concerns which are often already addressed by courts and legislatures and, in this sense, enhance and complement the resources available to public institutions to assess identity claims. I have tried to underline the need to be more explicit and direct about these assessments because most institutions fail to approach such assessments in a systematic manner and therefore decision makers often fail to consider all the relevant conditions of identity assessment, or to be critically aware of challenges that some of the conditions present and how these challenges can be met.

Even with these guidelines, some conflicts will still present 'hard cases'. This is partly because the guidelines are broad and open to interpretation, and partly because it is not always obvious how the different conditions ought to be weighed in cases where some are strong and others weak. For instance, one question I have not tackled is how to resolve conflicts where the jeopardy condition is strong but the validation and safeguard conditions are weak. These might appear to be important omissions and limitations. But they are not addressed here because I do not believe that one best way exists to make such decisions in the abstract. Too much depends on the context and, in any case, the point of developing these guidelines is not to strip out disagreement from decision making about cultural or religious entitlements. Using an identity approach will not eliminate hard cases entirely. But it will decrease the number of cases which will be considered truly difficult ones and refocus debate and disagreement on matters where people might indeed disagree rather than on matters where it seems that people are talking past each other, avoiding the key issues entirely, or effectively silencing each other. In our diverse political communities, reasonable political discourse about identity is both possible and necessary. We need to abandon the idea that identity is somehow beyond reason and we need to grapple openly and honestly with reasons of identity. I hope this book makes a contribution to this pressing task.

Notes

CHAPTER 1

1. The amendments were proposed as part of the preamble to the Charlottetown Accord (1992) which, in the end, failed to be ratified because it did not receive an adequate level of endorsement through a series of provincial referendums.
2. This was eventually the course adopted for Indigenous peoples by the Royal Commission on Aboriginal Peoples (1996).
3. For a nuanced assessment of these debates in relation to several European countries, see Phillips and Saharso (2008).
4. Tariq Modood describes this especially well in the British context and with respect to religious values as 'points of symbolic, institutional, policy and fiscal linkages between the state and aspects of Christianity' (2005: 142). On this basis, he argues that states court disaster when they respond to the demands for religious accommodation by insisting upon strict fidelity to conventional doctrines such as the distinctions between public and private, Church and State, or the secular and the religious. Policies which reaffirm the public/private divide, for instance, end up strengthening 'the privileged position of historically integrated [religious] cultures at the expense of historically subordinated or newly migrated folk' (p. 134).

CHAPTER 2

1. The Charter's preamble outlines the commitment of members to common values while respecting 'the diversity of the cultures and traditions of the peoples of Europe as well as the national identities of the Member States . . .'.
2. The Draft Declaration establishes protection for Indigenous peoples through recognizing 'collective and individual rights to maintain and develop their distinctive identities and characteristics . . .' See UN DocE/CN.4/Sub:2/1994/2/Add.1 (1994).
3. The general aims of the Convention Concerning Indigenous and Tribal Peoples include 'Recognising the aspirations of these peoples to exercise control over their own institutions, ways of life and economic development and to maintain and develop their identities, languages, and religions, within the framework of the States in which they live . . .'. In addition, Article 2(b) requires governments to promote 'the full realization of the social, economic and culture rights of these peoples with respect for their social and cultural identity, their customs and traditions and their institutions'.
4. Article 8.2 of the Convention states 'Where a child is illegally deprived of some or all of the elements of his or her identity, States Parties shall provide appropriate assistance and protection, with a view to re-establishing speedily his or her identity'.

5. Article 1 states, 'States shall protect the existence and the national or ethnic, cultural, religious and linguistic identity of minorities within their respective territories and shall encourage conditions for the promotion of that identity'.
6. Explicit mention of 'identity', or articles that directly address cultural rights or 'Indigenous identity', can be found in the constitutions of Argentina, Belize, Bolivia, Brazil, Bulgaria, Croatia, Ecuador, Guatemala, Kosovo, Mexico, Nicaragua, Panama, Paraguay, Peru, Poland, Romania, Slovakia, Slovenia, Venezuela, as well as statutes passed by regions in Italy, Spain (Cataluña), and Germany (Lander). In most cases, these provisions have been entrenched in the last thirty years. Thank you to Ilenia Ruggiu for sharing her research on these trends.
7. Similar efforts with respect to wild rice are discussed in Carlson (2002).
8. Amongst the most well known cases (many of which are probably familiar to readers), are *Mhd. Ahmed Khan v. Shah Bano Begum* (1985) where the Supreme Court of India decided how to interpret Muslim personal law and religious arbitration in disputes about divorce; *People v. Moua* (1985) where the defendant, charged with rape and kidnapping, convinced the judge that he thought he was engaging in the practice of bride capture; *Santa Clara Pueblo v. Julia Martinez* (1978) and *A.-G. Canada v. Lavell – Isaac v. Bédard* (1974) about the sexist membership rules adhered to by Indigenous communities in the United States and Canada.
9. Renteln (2004) is an important exception to this trend. Her study offers a comprehensive survey of US cases that employ the 'cultural defence' and a cautious endorsement of the need for courts to accept these defences under some circumstances, unless they involve irreparable harm.
10. See Fontes (2005) for an analysis of the mistakes made by social services in cases that involve child protection and cultural minorities. With respect to police enforcement, see Janet Chan's (1997) study of policing in Australia. Chan argues that biases endemic to 'policing cultures' often escape formal scrutiny and accountability mechanisms (p. 225) and will be difficult to detect unless specific, targeted efforts are made to identify and assess them.
11. Also see Christine Korsgaard's discussion of 'practical identity' which, as she describes it, provides the grounds for the reasons a person possesses to act: 'a view of what you ought to do is a view of who you are' (1996: 117).
12. See Dauvergne (2005: ch. 3) for a discussion of the tendency in legal analysis to use but not define the term. See the study by Vallance (2006) of the inconsistent use of culture in Supreme Court of Canada decisions.
13. Amy Gutmann offers a similar definition: 'the defining feature of an identity group is the mutual identification of individuals with one another around shared social markers...' (2003: 13). See Festenstein (2005: ch. 1) for a discussion of several different approaches to cultural identification and a comprehensive consideration of the reasons why a trait might be viewed as important to identity.
14. A similar observation animates the argument at the centre of Iris Young's work (1990) on a politics of difference.

15. Along similar lines, some critics of identity politics point to the ways in which identity can be used as a 'low-cost strategy' to immunize a particular interest from compromise (see Johnson 2000: 412; Weinstock 2006: 23).
16. See Young's discussion (1990) in chapter 2. For an excellent critical assessment of the role of choice in liberalism and thereby the failure of liberalism to address many challenges related to sexual inequality, see Chambers (2007).
17. Sociological accounts of identity often point out that a person's identity is only apparent to them when they are aware of their 'difference' or aware of being excluded (see, in particular, Connolly 1991; Hall 1996).
18. Virginia Tilley (2002) looks at the way in which non-Mayan Indigenous groups in El Salvador try to present themselves as Mayan in order to meet the expectations of international funding and human rights organizations because these organizations recognize the Mayan people of Guatemala as the standard for what counts as an 'Indigenous' community.
19. I discuss the perverse incentives for minorities to 'perform' their identities in Chapter 5.
20. As Carlson shows, the Sto:lo social and political system implicates salmon fishing in several ways. For instance, more politically powerful families have designated camps at places on the Fraser River which are more advantageous to catching fish. The more fish they catch, the more prosperous the family becomes. The system is distinctive yet at the same time very similar to how economic and social systems of privilege are interconnected in most societies.
21. Oral histories were accepted as evidence of Indigenous land occupation in *Delgamuukw v. British Columbia* (1997). But, according to some scholars, the extent to which the Court thereby should be viewed as more open to different kinds of evidence is questionable. The credibility of oral history is neither stronger nor weaker than the credibility of some of the written records accepted by courts. Indeed, many people believe that the acceptance of oral histories in Indigenous cases does not display an openness of courts to different kinds of evidence at all since oral histories have been used in courts for a long time, for instance, to prosecute war criminals decades after the crimes were committed (see Portelli 1998).
22. I discuss the sincerity test in Chapter 5.
23. The role played by the duty to consult in cases involving Indigenous identity claims is discussed in Chapter 6.
24. FMC is sustained by myths ranging from the relation between the practice and fertility to the way in which the practice protects people from HIV and other diseases. Sources that are generally considered credible to community members tend to be local or African-based.
25. See especially, Beaman's study (2008) of the standard of harm used to delineate freedom of religion in Canada.
26. My thanks to Megan Purcell for impressing this point upon me.

CHAPTER 3

1. The distinction between *multiculturalism* and *multinationalism* is often used in normative political theory to recognize that the claims of national minorities, such as Indigenous peoples and the Québéçois, are different from those of other cultural and religious minorities especially in the sense that *national* minorities are inappropriately subjected to 'accommodation' processes which typically involve the mainstream courts of one nation determining the legitimacy of the practices of a minority group. For minority nations, the main issue, in many cases, is securing jurisdiction to make these kinds of decisions autonomously within their own territory. Nonetheless, the 'normative commitments of multiculturalism' could apply to accommodation processes between national minorities and majorities where minority nations have jurisdiction over a given territory, yet conflicts arise about accommodating disputed practices within this territory or coordinating policies with other groups in nearby jurisdictions. In this respect, the principles of normative multiculturalism, which provide some of the reasons to protect cultural, linguistic, and religious distinctiveness, apply in any context where there is a need to decide to resolve such conflicts.
2. The *Arbitration Act, 1991* SO 1991, c17, allows anyone in the province to designate a third party as an arbitrator to resolve their civil disputes including commercial disputes, construction disputes, rental disputes, intellectual property issues, and, in the area of family law, matters arising as the result of marriage breakup such as spousal support and the division of matrimonial property. The Act does not allow private arbitration over any matter that would affect the civil status of an individual nor does it include any matter that falls within criminal law. The Act stipulates that consent is a necessary condition for establishing binding arbitration: an '"arbitration agreement" means an agreement by which two or more persons agree to submit to arbitration a dispute that has arisen or may arise between them' (*Arbitration Act, 1991* SO 1991 c17, s1).
3. For discussion of the general movement in Western democracies towards alternative dispute resolution, see Barrett and Barrett (2004). For a discussion of the movement in Canada, see Canadian Bar Association (1989).
4. Amongst the most important reforms, the Report recommended that arbitrators keep records of their past decisions and make these available to clients, the public, and the Ministry of the Attorney General; that arbitrators and mediators receive standardized training in legal procedures; that arbitrators screen all clients separately using standardized processes for 'issues of power imbalance and domestic violence' (Boyd 2004: 136); that independent legal advice be offered and waived or accepted in writing with a signature and witness; that the principles, rights, and duties of the religious law used in arbitration be explained as well as set out in writing; and that the potential consequences be understood. For a concise description of the proposed reforms, see Boyd (2005).
5. In surveying most of the public debate on this issue, I found only two critics who challenged the general framework of the debate. First, one vocal member of the

Canadian Council of Muslim Women argued that conservative Muslims were misusing the term 'multiculturalism' (Wente 2004). However, her comment was not the subject of the general commentary. Second, the Boyd Report directly responded to Mumtaz Ali's claim that because multiculturalism allows Indigenous people special rights, it ought to allow Muslims such rights as well. Boyd argued that comparisons between the autonomy afforded to Canada's First Nations and the Muslim community were misleading: 'From my perspective', Boyd claimed, 'comparisons in this direction are erroneous at best' (2004: 87–88).

6. For a more illuminating view of legal pluralism applied to the controversy over religious arbitration in Canada, see Macdonald (2005).
7. Some people suggested that the legislation, though presented by the government as a 'ban on religious arbitration' (see 'Ontario bill bans faith-based tribunals' 2005), does nothing of the sort. Private parties are still free under the Ontario law to exempt themselves from the provisions of the Act and govern their relationship contractually by incorporating any norms they choose, including religious ones (Ontario 2005). Moreover, the government could have characterized the amendments to the Act as being built on the recommendations of the Boyd Report, which proposed similar conditions, and laid out the conditions and constraints that family law arbitration awards must meet to be enforceable by the courts. Instead, it chose to frame its legislation and intent in terms of a 'ban' on religious arbitration.
8. Later in the debate, Mumtaz Ali's characterization of Muslim arbitration practices contradicted the impression left by his initial statement: '*shari'a*', he argued, 'has elasticity to adjust itself' and 'I draw the line where the Canadian law asks me to do certain things. I have to obey Canadian law' (Krauss 2004). Again, his characterization was not questioned.
9. See Macklin (2006) for a comparison of the practices of religious arbitration and the rules surrounding prenuptial arrangements in Canada in terms of which better meets the aims of sexual equality. Macklin cites the case of *Hartshorne v. Hartshorne*, where a prenuptial agreement, which was ultimately upheld by the Supreme Court of Canada, had been prepared and presented by a man to his future wife on their wedding day and signed by her despite her protests and despite the independent legal advice she received that the agreement was unfair in comparison to what default entitlements would allow her. The couple already had one child and, unbeknownst to either spouse, the woman was pregnant with their second child. The Supreme Court upheld the agreement largely on the basis of the women's voluntary consent to it.
10. One concern often expressed about identity politics is that, as Brubaker and Cooper (2000) show, identity 'groups' are more often than not identity 'organizations' in the sense that they are organized interest groups whose leaders present themselves as the leaders of the community at large. The problem the authors then identify is that government will often consult with these interest group leaders as though they are the official and legitimate spokespeople for the community. But what the Ontario debates suggest is that even where consultation

is more pluralistic, as it was through the Boyd commission, and debate is more democratic in the sense of involving more public deliberation, the very way in which key concerns structure public debate leads to particular people becoming self-appointed spokespeople for communities. They assume such positions, not because of any official role they have, but just because they are willing to engage in debate where others in the community are silent. These leaders are no more authentic than those who are spokespeople for ethnic or religious interest groups.

11. Anne Phillips (2007: 172–6) discusses the way in which religious arbitration in the Muslim community in Britain has proven to be helpful and empowering to British Muslim women. Much seems to depend on how these services are set up to function, which is a matter over which the State can exercise some influence but only if religious arbitration in some guises is viewed as legitimate rather than illegal.
12. '... Rawls's view is in fact common within the liberal tradition ... The freedom that liberals demand for individuals is not primarily the freedom to go beyond one's language and history, but rather the freedom to move around within one's societal culture, to distance oneself from particular cultural roles, to choose which features of the culture are most worth developing, and which are without value' (Kymlicka 1995: 90–1). Kymlicka's insistence on the individual's capacity to revise her attachments is highlighted in his criticisms of the position taken by Rawls (1985) in 'Justice Political, not Metaphysical', that some religious commitments are neither revisable nor autonomously affirmed (see Kymlicka 1995: 158–63).
13. Several scholars have argued that Kymlicka's distinction between national cultures, which receive strong protections according to his approach, and voluntary immigrant groups, which receive more modest protections, is too stark and possibly even incoherent (see, e.g., Carens 1997: 44; Young 1997*b*; Benhabib 2002: 66; Modood 2007: 33–4).
14. Linguistic minorities might be an example of relatively uncontroversial cases of this sort. See Kymlicka and Patten (2003) for a discussion of the connection between linguistic communities and a multicultural approach which is built around the idea of protecting a range of options and societal cultures.
15. My thanks to Jakeet Singh from whom I borrow this way of phrasing the objection.
16. See especially Benhabib (2002: ch. 3) and Phillips (2007). For a counter-argument, see Modood (1998, 2007: 97–8).

CHAPTER 4

1. Prins and Saharso (2008) explain that women are often seen as cultural brokers who bring the norms of the majority to their communities. Therefore how they are treated within their communities tends to be a focal concern.

2. The titles of two works on this subject illustrate this conundrum well: *Is Multiculturalism Bad for Women*? (Cohen, Howard and Nussbaum 1999) and 'Is feminism bad for multiculturalism?' (Kukathas 2001).
3. Kukathas (2001, 2003) is one of the only advocates of the rights-based approach who argues that dilemmas between sexual equality and cultural autonomy ought to be resolved in favour of cultural autonomy.
4. Nussbaum's more recent work on the subject argues that a better approach to conflicts between sexual equality and religious autonomy is one that 'acknowledges the weight of the values on both sides' (see Nussbaum 2000: 187–212).
5. This is one of the driving motivations behind capabilities theory (see, in particular, Sen 1999; Nussbaum 2000).
6. The correct conclusion to draw here may not be that the Catholic Church ought to be allowed to discriminate against gays and lesbians. The identity claim of the Church has to be assessed and weighted against the claims of those individuals who are subject to its discrimination. As I explain below, in many cases of this sort, what is at stake for the identities of those who are subjected to discrimination is usually considered greater than what is stake for a community which adheres to discriminatory practices.
7. For example, Turpel-Lafond (1997: 68), herself an Indigenous woman, argues that sexual equality is not an authentic organizing political principle of many Indigenous communities. See also Deveaux's description of the traditionalist perspective amongst women in Indigenous communities (2000*b*: 533). Also see Narayan (1997) who discusses a similar tendency which poses obstacles to feminism in India.
8. Under these rules, Indigenous women lost their Indian status upon marrying outside their community whereas Indigenous men kept their status and passed it on to their non-Indigenous wives. The rules were revised in 1981 and the revisions were implemented in 1985.
9. See Narayan (1997: 396) and Spinner-Halev (2001: 95–6). Frantz Fanon's *The Wretched of the Earth* is a brilliant discussion of the phenomena. For a recent development of these ideas specifically in relation to Indigenous peoples in Canada, see Coultard (2007).
10. A weaker understanding of the approach might hold that majorities should not interfere in minority decision-making processes when doing so will predictably backfire or taint the legitimacy of decisions for the communities which have to abide by them. This weaker understanding does not avoid the need to determine, independently of minority decision-making processes, how best to resolve conflicts. Rather, it suggests that community-based procedures are sometimes the best way to reach solutions whose adequacy can be determined independently of the procedures in question. This constitutes a weak understanding of the process-based approach because, according to it, community decision making merely performs strategic and legitimating (albeit important) functions, while the substantive moral work of deciding which claim ought to prevail in cases of incommensurable conflicts is accomplished in some other way.

11. The next chapter explains why these two options are often attractive to decision makers and shows that they are often chosen in actual settings even when evidence that a claim is important to a group's identity is clear and accessible, and even when it is clear that treating the claim as opaque is detrimental to a marginalized minority.
12. These are called 'celestial marriages' according to FLDS doctrine.
13. Several comprehensive land claims and treaties have been signed in the last ten years and more are likely to follow. However, most Indigenous communities in Canada do not enjoy a recognized right to govern their own communities free of the controlling dimensions of Canada's *Indian Act.*
14. In 1982, the *Canadian Charter of Rights Freedoms*, which includes more comprehensive protection for equality rights, was entrenched in the Canadian Constitution. The *Charter* has constitutional power over the *Canadian Bill of Rights*, which is merely a federal statute.
15. The majority of the Court found against Lavell and Bédard on the grounds that equality before the law meant only the 'equal subjection of all classes to the ordinary law of the land as administered by the ordinary courts' (*Lavell* 1974: 1366). In other words, the equality provisions were not violated as long as a law, meant only to apply to Indigenous women, was applied equally to all Indigenous women (see Whyte 1974 for an analysis of the court's convoluted interpretation of equality).
16. The problem of legitimacy which I raise here is primarily political rather than legal. It turns on whether the community in question views the state's processes as the best processes by which a decision ought to be made. It does not draw into question the *de jure* power of the Canadian government to change its own legislation – namely the Canadian *Indian Act.*
17. Approximately 70,000 people were expected to have their status as Indians reinstated in 1974 had the Court decided in favour of Lavell and Bédard (see Nahanee 1997: 95).
18. These considerations are raised by Mackinnon (1987: 68).

CHAPTER 5

1. For critical assessments of the conflict, see Bourke (1997) and Simons (2003).
2. Povinelli and others who study similar 'performances' often note that courts have difficulty accepting representations of identity which are inconsistent with their entrenched expectations. For instance, Lori Beaman (2008) conducts an extensive analysis along these lines of the case of Bethany Hughes, a 17 year old who refused a blood transfusion for religious reasons. When Hughes argued before the Court that she did not want a transfusion but also did not want to die, her claims, taken together, were treated as evidence that she was immature, brainwashed, and therefore incapable of withholding consent or reasoning through her situation despite strong evidence to the contrary. Beaman assesses the evidence and concludes that Hughes was neither immature nor brainwashed. She argues that

the Court's conclusion has more to do with its entrenched belief that people must be committed to their health in a particular way and that they must treat science and medicine as valid even when treatments have poor rates of success.

3. The case is well known for temporarily changing the direction of American jurisprudence on religious accommodation. As Justices Blackmun, Brennan, and Marshall state in the dissenting opinion: '[The majority] effectuates a wholesale overturning of settled law concerning the Religion Clauses of our Constitution. One hopes that the Court is aware of the consequences and that its result is not a product of overreaction to the serious problems the country's drug crisis has generated' (*Oregon v. Smith* 1990: 908). Whereas before *Smith*, the Court required that the State show a 'compelling interest' before restricting a religious practice, the majority in *Smith* dismisses the compelling interest test and argues that Oregon has the right to restrict religious practices as long as the aim of doing so is not evidently discriminatory. In 1993, Congress was convinced to pass the *Religious Freedom Restoration Act* which reinstates the compelling interest test that was rejected by the majority in *Smith*.
4. *Peyote* is legal for sacramental purposes in California, Arizona, New Mexico, and Colorado.
5. Justice Sandra Day O'Connor based her separate, concurring opinion on these concerns.
6. In addition to Barry (2001), discussed here, see also Sullivan (2005) who argues, on different grounds, for legislative solutions to conflicts involving religion.
7. In rejecting the test, the majority in *Smith* argued that the only way to assess whether a law fulfils a 'compelling government interest' is by weighing just how compelling that interest is against just how central or important the disputed practice is to the religion of a claimant. In other words, the test required courts to assess both the importance of the 'compelling government interest' and the importance and thereby authenticity of a religious identity claim. To consider only the compelling nature of the State's interest, and leave aside the assessment of the centrality of a religious practice is 'utterly unworkable' as Scalia correctly noted. Doing so would be akin to supposing that the same degree of 'compelling state interest' would be required

   > to impede the practice of throwing rice at church weddings as to impede the practice of getting married in church... There is no way out of the difficulty that, if general laws are to be subjected to a 'religious practice' exception, both the importance of the law at issue and the centrality of the practice at issue must reasonably be considered. (p. 890)

   On the basis of these concerns, Scalia argues that decisions to make exceptions to generally sound laws are best left to legislatures and the political process.
8. O'Connor goes on to state that

   > The history of our free exercise doctrine amply demonstrates the harsh impact majoritarian rule has had on unpopular or emerging religious groups such as the Jehovah's Witnesses and the Amish. Indeed, the words of Justice Jackson in *West Virginia State Bd. of Ed. v.*

> *Barnette* (overruling *Minersville School Dist. v. Gobitis,* 310 U.S. 586 (1940)) are apt: 'The very purpose of a Bill of Rights was to withdraw certain subjects from the vicissitudes of political controversy, to place them beyond the reach of majorities and officials and to establish them as legal principles to be applied by the courts. One's right to life, liberty, and property, to free speech, a free press, freedom of worship and assembly, and other fundamental rights may not be submitted to vote; they depend on the outcome of no elections'. (*Oregon v. Smith* 1990: 902–3)

9. A *succah* is a temporary, open-roofed structure, made of different kinds of spare materials, which is erected for eight days during Succot (one of the holiest holidays in Judaism) to symbolize the temporary shelters erected by the Jews in the desert during their exodus from Egypt. Some observant Jews live and eat their meals (or some meals) in the *succah* during these eight days.
10. *Re Civil Service Association of Ontario (Inc.) and Anderson* (1976 9 OR (2nd) 341 at 343) quoted in Woehrling (1998: 394).
11. Section 1 of the *Constitution Act, 1982* states that: 'The *Canadian Charter of Rights and Freedoms* guarantees the rights and freedoms set out in it subject only to such reasonable limits prescribed by law as can be demonstrably justified in a free and democratic society'.
12. Ben Berger (2007) describes the manner in which the Court makes such choices as 'cultural'. He argues that the Canadian courts interpret freedom of religious so as to ensure that individuals can exercise autonomy and choice with respect to their religious beliefs. This has both the effect of privileging an individual autonomy-based view of religious freedom, as reflected in the sincerity test, and of ignoring the many dimensions of religion that depend on community.
13. The standards represented by the symbols sometimes reflect innovative and progressive political goals, like organic and sustainable farming techniques used to produce the food, or just working conditions in food production, which some Jewish congregations view as religiously important (see Shapiro 2008).
14. If... they sincerely believed that they must build a succah of their own because the alternatives... will... impermissibly detract from the joyous celebration of the holiday, the joy of which, as intimated by their witness Rabbi Ohana, is essential to its proper celebration, then they must prove that these alternatives would result in more than trivial or insubstantial interferences and non-trivial distress. In my opinion, this has been successfully proven. (*Amselem* 2004, paras. 75–6)
15. My thanks to Steffen Neumann for impressing this point upon me.
16. This is true for many reasons, including that, as Kukathas (1998) argues, public involvement often only worsens the conflict.
17. Ayelet Shachar (2001) has written about how this balance, between individuals who wish to transform their communities and communities which resist transformation, is secured in relation to religious rules over marriage and divorce. Shachar develops an approach which takes seriously the need for solutions that recognize the importance of both individual dissent and community identity.

18. The decision might have gone differently had Amselem's way of celebrating the holiday placed others at risk of harm, for instance, if the *succah* had to be placed in a manner that unavoidably blocked a fire exit.

CHAPTER 6

1. This concern is developed in agency-based approaches to cultural protection (see, in particular, Phillips 2007).
2. See Malloy (2005: 168). Many accounts in political theory focus on this *a priori* feature of essentialist understandings of groups. For instance, according to Fuss, essentialism refers to the idea that a person, thing, or group has an 'essence' which is irreducible, unchanging, and therefore constitutive of the person, thing, or group (1989: 2). Barry characterizes the views of several multiculturalists as essentialist in the sense of entailing 'a naturalized conception of groups as internally homogeneous, clearly bounded, mutually exclusive and maintaining specific determinate interests' (2001: 11).
3. Festenstein provides a thoughtful account of identity which is sensitive to its historical and strategic nature, but he does not conclude that identity or recognition politics are thereby problematically essentialist (see especially Festenstein 2005: 27–8).
4. Modood has responded to this charge in his studies of public policies and debates about multiculturalism in Britain. He shows that essentialism arises mainly in critiques of multiculturalism in which critics attribute to multiculturalists a view of cultures as centered around a fixed cultural essence and as 'discrete, frozen in time, impervious to external influences, homogeneous and without internal dissent' (2007: 89). As Modood shows, the view is manifestly absurd and largely acts as a straw man in debates about cultural accommodation (also see Modood 1998).
5. In Canada, Indigenous rights are protected in Section 35 of the *Constitution Act, 1982* which states

    1. The existing aboriginal and treaty rights of the aboriginal peoples of Canada are hereby recognized and affirmed.
    2. In this Act, 'aboriginal peoples of Canada' includes the Indian, Inuit and Métis peoples of Canada.
    3. For greater certainty, in subsection (1) 'treaty rights' includes rights that now exist by way of land claims agreements or may be so acquired.
    4. Notwithstanding any other provision of this Act, the aboriginal and treaty rights referred to in subsection (1) are guaranteed equally to male and female persons.

6. The test was developed in the context of the case *R. v. Van der Peet* which I discuss later.
7. For a more extensive analysis of the factors considered by the court relevant to fulfilling the test, see Borrows (1997–8).

8. Justice Lambert heard the case at the British Columbia Court of Appeal.
9. *R v. Van der Peet* (1996) 3 CNLR 155 (BC Prov. Ct).
10. *R v. Van der Peet* (1996) 58 BCLR (2d) 392 (SC).
11. The absurdity of the DCT is evident in cases that involve the Indigenous rights of the Métis people, which are also protected in the Canadian constitution. The Métis people, whose lineage is traced back to unions between French explorers and Indigenous women, did not exist *pre*-'contact'. In *R. v. Powley* (2003 SCR 207), a case about whether a member of the Métis community could hunt moose without a state-issued hunting licence, the Court was forced to confront this absurdity and did so by deciding that, despite its putative constitutional importance, the pre-contact requirement did not apply to the Métis.
12. Similar concerns were raised in two dissenting opinions on the Supreme Court. As Justice L'Hereux-Dubé argued

    Is it the very first European contacts with native societies, at the time of the Cabot, Verrazzano and Cartier voyages? Is it at a later date, when permanent European settlements were founded in the early seventeenth century? In British Columbia, did sovereignty occur in 1846 – the year in which the *Oregon Boundary Treaty, 1846* was concluded – as held by the Court of Appeal for the purposes of this litigation? No matter how the deciding date is agreed upon, it will not be consistent with the aboriginal view regarding the effect of the coming of Europeans. (*Van der Peet* 1996: para. 167)

    Also see Chief Justice Beverly McLachlin's dissent (starting at para. 224) and *Lambert* (1998: 251–2).
13. *Mitchell v. M.N.R.* (2001) 1 SCR 911. At issue in *Mitchell* is whether the Mohawk people have the right to cross the Canada–US border without paying duty for goods they bring across the border. Grand Chief Michael Mitchell, a member of the Akwesasne Mohawk community, was charged duty on a number of consumer products which he purposely carried into Canada from New York State, with much publicity and notice to the Canadian government. He refused to pay the duty, claiming that he and all members of his community had an Indigenous right to import goods duty free from the United States for personal use, for trade with other Indigenous groups, across the international border that now divides the territory of the Mohawk people. The existing Indigenous reservation and the historical territory of Akwasasne lay partly in the provinces of Ontario and Quebec and partly in New York State. Mitchell submitted evidence on behalf of his community from historians, archeologists, and oral histories relayed by elders who confirmed that, previous to contact with Europeans, the Mohawks travelled north to trade and that trade was a distinguishing feature of their way of life. In applying the DCT, the Supreme Court denied Mitchell's claim largely on the basis that the evidence did not show an ancestral practice of trading *north* of the St. Lawrence River – the practice was not a 'defining feature of the Mohawk culture' (para. 54) nor 'vital to the Mohawk's collective identity' (para. 60) in pre-contact times. Instead, most of the trade routes were east–west.
14. Justice Binnie recognized the implausibility of distinguishing between an economic and cultural activity in this case and argued that the right should extend to

bartering or selling items made out of the wood within the community: 'A division of labour existed in aboriginal communities, pre-contact. Barter (and, its modern equivalent, sale) within the reserve or other local aboriginal community would reflect a more efficient use of human resources than requiring all members of the community to do everything for themselves.'

15. The Court will redescribe claims if they think that disputed practices have been defined opportunistically or in an overly cautious manner in order to meet the DCT's criteria.
16. From a 1985 decision of the Inter-American Commission on Human Rights in favour of the Yanomami peoples whose ancestral lands were threatened by land-use development projects in Brazil. See Case No. 7615 (Brazil), Inter-American Commission Res. No. 12/85 (5 March 1985), *Annual Report of the Inter-American Commission on Human Rights, 1984–5*, O.A.S. Doc. OEA/Ser.L/V/II.66, doc. 10, rev. 1, at 24, 31 (1985) (quoted from Anaya 1996: 100). James Anaya points out that the Inter-American Commission on Human Rights of the Organization of American States has also used the norms of Article 27 in decisions favouring the rights of Indigenous peoples to survive as distinct cultures where 'culture' is understood to include economic and political institutions, land-use patterns, language, and religious practices.
17. The Lubicon alleged that Canada violated the community's right to self-determination as protected under Article 1 of the ICCPR because it allowed a provincial government to expropriate its land for oil and gas exploration and development. The Lubicon had a recognized treaty (Treaty No. 8 of 1899) with Canada which entitled members to hunt, trap, and fish on its traditional lands which they claimed was violated by the expropriation and which the Canadian government denied. The HRC refused to consider the case in relation to the right to self-determination and Article 1, and instead decided it in relation to the protection of cultural rights in Article 27.
18. The HRC has rejected claims where they find that communities are constituted solely by sharing an economic way of life. In *Diergaardt et al. v. Namibia*, the Rehoboth Basters community in Namibia, which is a community of farmers whose lineage is traced back to unions between male Dutch settlers and African women, argued that because the State confiscated its lands and property, it endangered the traditional existence of the community as a collective of cattle-raising farmers. The HRC rejected the Rehoboth claim under Article 27 because the community failed to demonstrate that it possessed a distinctive culture or how the distinctive properties of the community were based on their way of raising cattle. An individual and concurring opinion written on the case suggests that economic activities are central to a culture only when other elements are also present as they are in the case of Indigenous communities. These issues are more readily resolved in regard to Indigenous communities which can very often show that their particular way of life or culture is, and has for long been, closely bound up with particular lands with regard to both economic and other cultural and spiritual activities, to the extent that the deprivation or denial of access to the

land denies them the right to enjoy their own culture in all its aspects. In contrast, the claim of the Rehoboth 'is, essentially, an economic rather than a cultural claim and does not draw the protection of article 27' (Individual Opinion by Elizabeth Evatt and Cecilia Medina Quiroga [concurring], in *Diergaardt et al. v. Namibia* 1997: 157).

19. Article 27 may be violated where individuals 'are not allocated the land and control of resource development necessary to pursue economic activities of central importance to their culture' (Kingsbury 1992: 490; see also Macklem 2001).
20. Because France has made a reservation to Article 27, the Article was not the grounds for the decision in this case. Instead, the HRC relied on Articles 17(1) and 23(1) both of which recognize the importance of family. For commentary, see Scheinin (2000); see also Macklem (2008).
21. The success of Article 27 at establishing a norm of cultural integrity depends partly on the manner in which these standards are applied across many decisions made about Indigenous claims in national and international forums. For an assessment of the application of these norms, see Knop (2000). In addition, see Anaya's analysis (1996: 98–104), which traces the application of these norms in decisions of the Inter-American Commission, in Convention 169 of the International Labor Organization, and in the Draft Declaration of the Rights of Indigenous Peoples.
22. Kymlicka (2007: 35) points out that the Article was originally drafted to secure a commitment to the rights of individuals and, in its application, adopts an 'anti-discrimination' approach to cultural rights in all cases other than those involving Indigenous peoples. For a more optimistic view about the Article's capacity to address the rights of cultural minorities, see Thornberry (1991).
23. See Kymlicka (2007) for a general defense of a more targeted approach.
24. In *Ominayak*, the HRC reframed the Lubicon's claim, which was initially presented by claimants as a violation of the right of peoples to self-determination under Article 1, into a claim about cultural rights under Article 27. In a General Comment (Human Rights Committee, 'General Comment 23, The Rights of Minorities (Article 27)', 8 April 1994. Report of the Human Rights Committee, Vol. 1 GAOR, 49th Session, Supplement No. 40 (A/49/40): 107–10), the HRC states that the 'right to enjoy one's culture' excludes consideration of claims of self-determination.
25. Nikolas Kompridis explains that the problem of essentialism, as it is usually presented by critics of cultural claims, tends to do more work than the critics intend. Kompridis explains that the putative antidote to essentialism is often an 'anti-essentialist' view of cultural identity, which succeeds in presenting a view of culture as 'porous, fluid, hybrid and renegotiable' but at the expense of explaining how anyone could be attached or even care about cultural continuity when culture is experienced in this way. He cautions that critics have 'normativized hybridity', and thereby make it difficult to understand why political claims made on behalf of culture (or, I would add, any other identity) are considered important by those who make them (2005: 320).

26. The related question of whether every Sami person engages in reindeer husbandry (or wishes to) or views husbandry as valuable in an authentic manner to them personally is irrelevant to decisions about whether reindeer husbandry ought to be a protected activity because it is important to Sami identity. Even those who do not partake in the practice may want to protect it because it is an effective means to give communities control over their ways of life.
27. For a discussion of capacity building, see Anaya (1996: 80–8, 109–12); the Royal Commission on Aboriginal Peoples (1996: vols. 2 and 3); and Schouls (2003).

CHAPTER 7

1. This is especially evident in Taylor's discussion (1994: 30–2) in which he locates the modern notion of recognition in a politics of authenticity derived from Herder.
2. I share this worry with Kymlicka (2007: 101).

Bibliography

Cases cited

Canada:

A.-G. Canada v. Lavell – Isaac v. Bédard (1974) SCR 1349.
Delgamuukw v. British Columbia (1997) 3 SCR 1010.
Hartshorne v. Hartshorne (2004) 1 SCR 550.
Mitchell v. M.N.R. (2001) 1 SCR 911.
R. v. Van der Peet (1996) 2 SCR 507.
R. v. Powley (2003) SCR 207.
R. v. Sappier; R. v. Gray (2006) 2 SCR 686.
Syndicat Northcrest v. Amselem (2004) 2 SCR 551.

India:

Mhd. Ahmed Khan v. Shah Bano Begum AIR 1985 Supreme Court 945.

United States:

Employment Division, Human Resources of Oregon v. Smith 485 US 660 (1988).
Employment Division, Human Resources of Oregon v. Smith 494 US 872 (1990).
Martinez v. Santa Clara Pueblo 402 F. Supp. at 18 (DNM 1975).
Martinez v. Santa Clara Pueblo 540 F2d 1039 (CA 1976).
People v. Moua No. 315972-0, Fresno County Superior Court (7 February 1985).
Reynolds v. United States 98 US 145 (1878).
Santa Clara Pueblo v. Julia Martinez 56 L Ed 2nd 106 (1978).

International:

Diergaardt et al. v. Namibia (760/1997), ICCPR, A/55/40 vol. II (25 July 2000) 140.
Hopu and Tepoaitu Bessert v. France (549/1993), U.N. Doc. CCPR/C/60/D/549/1993/Rev.1 (1997).
Ivan Kitok v. Sweden. Communication 197/1985, Official Records of the Human Rights Committee 1987/88, vol. II.
Kitok v. Sweden (197/1985), U.N. Doc. CCPR/C/33/D/197/1985 (1988).
Länsman et al. v. Finland (511/1992), UN Doc.CCPR/C/52D/511/1992 (1994).
Ominayak, Chief of the Lubicon Lake Band v. Canada (167/1984), Canada, 10/05/90, UN Doc. CCPR/C/38/D/167/1984.

Works cited

Abu-Laban, Yasmeen and Gabriel, Christina. (2002). *Selling Diversity: Immigration, Multiculturalism, Employment Equity and Globalization.* Peterborough, ON: Broadview.

Adhar, Rex. (2003). Indigenous spiritual concerns and the secular state: some New Zealand developments. *Oxford Journal of Legal Studies* 23/4: 611–37.

Alfred, Gerald. (1995). *Heeding the Voices of Our Ancestors: Kahnawake Mohawk Politics and the Rise of Native Nationalism.* Toronto, ON: Oxford University Press.

Anaya, S. James. (1996). *Indigenous Peoples in International Law.* New York: Oxford University Press.

Appiah, Kwame Anthony. (2005). *The Ethics of Identity.* Princeton, NJ: Princeton University Press.

Asch, Michael. (2000). The judicial conceptualization of culture after Delgamuukw and Van der Peet. *Review of Constitutional Studies* 2: 119–37.

Bannerji, Himani. (2000). *The Dark Side of Nation: Essays on Multiculturalism, Nationalism, and Gender.* Toronto, ON: Canadian Scholars' Press, Inc.

Barrett, Jerome T. and Barrett, Joseph. (2004). *A History of Alternative Dispute Resolution: The Story of a Political, Social, and Cultural Movement.* San Francisco, CA: Jossey-Bass Inc.

Barry, Brian. (2001). *Culture and Equality: An Egalitarian Critique of Multiculturalism.* Cambridge, MA: Harvard University Press.

Barsh, Russell and Henderson, James Youngblood. (1997). The Supreme Court's Van der Peet trilogy: naive imperialism and ropes of sand. *McGill Law Review* 42/4: 993–1009.

Beaman, Lori G. (2002). Aboriginal spirituality and the legal construction of freedom of religion. *Journal of Church and State* 44/1: 135–49.

—— (2008). *Defining Harm: Religious Freedom and the Limits of the Law.* Vancouver, BC: University of British Columbia Press.

Benhabib, Seyla. (2002). *The Claims of Culture: Equality and Diversity in the Global Era.* Princeton, NJ: Princeton University Press.

Berger, Benjamin. (2007). Law's religion: rendering culture. *Osgoode Hall Law Journal* 45/2: 277–314.

Bernier, I. (2005). Trade and culture, in Patrick F. J. Macrory, Arthur E. Appleton, and Michael G. Plummer (eds.), *The World Trade Organization: Legal, Economic and Political Analysis.* New York: Springer Science and Business Media, Inc., pp. 747–94.

Borrows, John. (1997–8). Frozen rights in Canada: constitutional interpretation and the trickster. *American Indian Law Review* 22: 37–64.

—— (2001). Listening for a change: the courts and oral tradition. *Osgoode Hall Law Journal* 39/1: 1–38.

—— (2002). *Recovering Canada: The Resurgence of Indigenous Law.* Toronto, ON: University of Toronto Press.

—— (2008). Living law on a living earth: Aboriginal religion, law, and the Constitution, in Richard Moon (ed.), *Law and Religious Pluralism in Canada.* Vancouver, BC: University of British Columbia Press.

Bouchard, Gérard and Taylor, Charles. (2008). Building the future: a time for reconciliation. *Report of the Commission de consultation sur les practiques d'accommodement reliées aux differences culturelles.* Québec, QC: Gouvernement du Québec, http://www.accommodements.qc.ca/documentation/rapports/rapport-final-integral-en.pdf

Bourke, Joanna. (1997). Women's business: sex, secrets and the Hindmarsh Island affair. *University of New South Wales Law Journal* 20: 333–51.

Boyd, Marion. (2004). *Dispute Resolution in Family Law: Protecting Choice, Promoting Inclusion.* Toronto, ON: Ministry of the Attorney General of Ontario, http://www.attorneygeneral.jus.gov.on.ca/english/about/pubs/boyd/

—— (2005). Religiously-based alternate dispute resolution: a challenge to multiculturalism. *Canadian Diversity* 4/3: 71–4.

Bramham, Daphne. (2008). *The Secret Lives of Saints: Child Brides and Lost Boys in Canada's Polygamous Mormon Sect.* New York: Random House.

Brom, Frans W. A. (2004). WTO, public reason, and food: public reasoning in the 'trade conflict' on GM-food. *Ethical Theory and Moral Practice* 7: 417–31.

Brown, Wendy. (2006). *Regulating Aversion: Tolerance in the Age of Identity and Empire.* Princeton, NJ: Princeton University Press.

Brubaker, Rogers and Cooper, Frederick. (2000). Beyond 'identity'. *Theory and Society* 29: 1–47.

Bruckner, Pascale. (2007). Enlightenment fundamentalism or racism of the anti-racists? *signandsight.com*, 24 January, http://www.signandsight.com/features/1146.html

Canadian Bar Association. (1989). Task force on alternative dispute resolution. *Report of the Canadian Bar Association Task Force on Alternative Dispute Resolution: A Canadian Perspective.* Ottawa, ON: Canadian Bar Association.

Carens, Joseph H. (1997). Liberalism and culture. *Constellations* 4/1: 39–47.

—— (2000). *Culture, Citizenship, and Community: A Contextual Exploration of Justice as Evenhandedness.* Oxford, UK: Oxford University Press.

Carlson, Brian. (2002). The bio-piracy of wild rice: genome mapping of a sacred food. *GeneWatch* 15/4, http:www.gene-watch.org/genewatch/articles/15-4wildrice.html

Carlson, Keith Thor. (1996). Stó:lō exchange dynamics. *Native Studies Review* 11/1: 5–48.

Casal, Paula. (2003). Is multiculturalism bad for animals? *Journal of Political Philosophy* 11: 1–22.

Chambers, Clare. (2007). *Sex, Culture, and Justice: The Limits of Choice.* University Park, PA: Pennsylvania State University Press.

Chan, Janet B. L. (1997). *Changing Police Culture: Policing in a Multicultural Society.* Cambridge, UK: Cambridge University Press.

Christie, Gordon. (1998). Aboriginal rights, Aboriginal culture, and protection. *Osgoode Hall Law Journal* 36/3: 447–84.

Cohen, Joshua, Howard, Matthew, and Nussbaum, Martha C. (eds.) (1999). *Is Multiculturalism Bad for Women*? Princeton, NJ: Princeton University Press.

Connolly, William. (1991). *Identity/Difference: Democratic Negotiations of Political Paradox.* Ithaca, NY: Cornell University Press.

Copp, David. (2002). Social unity and the identity of persons. *The Journal of Political Philosophy* 10/4: 365–91.

Coultard, Glen. (2007). Subjects of empire: indigenous people and the 'politics of recognition' in Canada. *Contemporary Political Theory* 6: 437–60.

Creppell, Ingrid. (2003). *Toleration and Identity: Foundations in Early Modern Thought.* London, UK: Routledge.

Dauvergne, Catherine. (2005). *Humanitarianism, Identity, and the Nation: Migration Laws in Canada and Australia.* Vancouver, BC: University of British Columbia Press.

Day, Richard. (2000). *Multiculturalism and the History of Canadian Diversity.* Toronto, ON: University of Toronto Press.

Deveaux, Monique. (2000*a*). *Cultural Pluralism and Dilemmas of Justice.* Ithaca, NY: Cornell University Press.

—— (2000*b*). Conflicting equalities? Cultural group rights and sex equality. *Political Studies* 48: 522–39.

—— (2006). *Gender and Justice in Multicultural Liberal States.* Oxford, UK: Oxford University Press.

Dhamoon, Rita. (2007). The politics of cultural contestation, in Barbara Arneil, Monique Deveaux, Rita Dhamoon, and Avigail Eisenberg (eds.), *Sexual Justice/ Cultural Justice: Critical Perspectives in Political Theory and Practice.* London, UK: Routledge, pp. 30–49.

Dworkin, Ronald. (1977). *Taking Rights Seriously.* Cambridge, MA: Harvard University Press.

Eisenberg, Avigail. (1994). The politics of individual and group difference in Canadian jurisprudence. *Canadian Journal of Political Science* 27: 3–21.

—— (2003). Diversity and equality: three approaches to cultural and sexual difference. *Journal of Political Philosophy* 11: 41–64.

—— (2007). Reasoning about the identity of Aboriginal people, in Stephen Tierney (ed.), *Accommodating Cultural Diversity.* Aldershot, UK: Ashgate Publishing.

—— and Jeff Spinner-Halev (eds.). (2005). *Minorities within Minorities: Equality, Rights and Diversity.* Cambridge, UK: Cambridge University Press.

Eltahawy, Mona. (2005). Ontario must say 'no' to *Shari'a. Christian Science Monitor* 2 February, http://www.csmonitor.com/2005/0202/p09s01-coop.html

Emon, Anver. (2009). Islamic law and the Canadian mosaic: politics, jurisprudence, and multicultural accommodation. *Canadian Bar Review* 87: 392–425.

Fanon, Frantz. (1963). *The Wretched of the Earth.* New York, NY: Grove Press.

Festenstein, Matthew. (2005). *Negotiating Diversity: Culture, Deliberation, Trust.* Cambridge, UK: Polity Press.

Flanagan, Thomas. (2000). *First Nations? Second Thoughts.* Montreal, QC: McGill-Queens University Press.

Fontes, Lisa Aronson. (2005). *Child Abuse and Culture: Working with Diverse Families.* New York: The Guildford Press.

Forst, Rainer. (1997). Foundations of a theory of multicultural justice. *Constellations* 4/1: 63–71.

Fraser, Nancy. (1997). *Justice Interruptus.* London, UK: Routledge.

—— (2000). Rethinking recognition. *New Left Review* 3: 107–20.

Fuss, Diana. (1989). *Essentially Speaking: Feminism, Nature and Difference.* New York: Routledge.

Gitlin, Todd. (1995). *The Twilight of Common Dreams.* New York: Henry Holt and Co.

Greenawalt, Kent. (2006). *Religion and the Constitution. Volume 1: Free Exercise and Fairness.* Princeton, NJ: Princeton University Press.

Gutmann, Amy. (2003). *Identity in Democracy.* Princeton, NJ: Princeton University Press.

Hall, Stuart. (1996). Introduction: Who needs, 'identity'?, in Stuart Hall and Paul Du Gay (eds.), *Questions of Cultural Identity.* London, UK: Sage, pp. 1–17.

Henderson, James Youngblood. (1999). The struggle to preserver aboriginal spiritual teaching and practices, in John McLaren and Harold Coward (eds.), *Religious Conscience, the State and the Law.* Albany, NY: State University of New York Press, pp. 168–88.

Johnson, James. (2000). Why respect culture? *American Journal of Political Science* 44/3: 405–18.

Jung, Courtney. (2000). *Then I Was Black: South African Political Identities in Transition.* New Haven, CT: Yale University Press.

—— (2003). The politics of indigenous identity: neoliberalism, cultural rights, and the Mexican Zapatistas. *Social Research* 70/2: 433–62.

—— (2008). *The Moral Force of Indigenous Politics: Critical Liberalism and the Zapatistas.* New York: Cambridge University Press.

Khan, Sheena. (2005). The *shari'a* debate deserves a proper hearing. *The Globe and Mail* 15 September: A19.

Kingsbury, Benedict. (1992). Claims by non-state groups in international law. *Cornell International Law Journal* 25: 481–513.

Knop, Karen. (2000). Here and there: international law in domestic courts. *NYU Journal of International Law and Politics* 32: 501–35.

Kompridis, Nikolas. (2005). Normativizing hybridity/neutralizing culture. *Political Theory* 33/3: 318–43.

Korsgaard, Christine. (1996). *The Sources of Normativity.* Cambridge, UK: Cambridge University Press.

Krakauer, Jon. (2003). *Under the Banner of Heaven: A Story of Violent Faith.* New York: Random House.

Krauss, Clifford. (2004). When the Koran speaks, will Canadian law bend? *The New York Times* 4 August: A4.

Kukathas, Chandran. (1998). Liberalism and multiculturalism: the politics of indifference. *Political Theory* 26/5: 686–99.

—— (2001). Is feminism bad for multiculturalism? *Public Affairs Quarterly* 15/2: 83–98.

—— (2003). *The Liberal Archipelago.* Oxford, UK: Oxford University Press.

Kymlicka, Will. (1995). *Multicultural Citizenship.* Oxford, UK: Oxford University Press.

—— (1997). Do we need a liberal theory of minority rights? Reply to Carens, Young, Parekh and Forst. *Constellations* 4/1: 72–87.

—— (2001). *Politics in the Venacular.* Oxford, UK: Oxford University Press.

—— (2005). Testing the bounds of liberal multiculturalism? Paper Presented at the Canada Council of Muslim Women's Conference on 'Muslim Women's Equality Rights in the Justice System: Gender, Religion and Pluralism'. Toronto, ON, 9 April.

—— (2007). *Multicultural Odysseys: Navigating the New International Politics of Diversity.* Oxford, UK: Oxford University Press.

—— and Patten, Alan. (2003). Introduction: Language rights and political theory: context, issues and approaches, in Will Kymlicka and Alan Patten (eds.), *Language Rights and Political Theory.* Oxford, UK: Oxford University Press, pp. 1–51.

Laegaard, Sune. (2007). The cartoon controversy: offense, identity oppression? *Political Studies* 55/3: 481–98.

Lambert, Hon. Mr. Justice Douglas. (1998). Van der Peet and Delgamuukw: ten unresolved issues. *UBC Law Review* 32/2: 249–70.

Levey, Geoffrey Brahm and Modood, Tariq. (2008). Liberal democracy, multiculturalism and the Danish cartoon affair, in Geoffrey Brahm Levey and Tariq Modood (eds.), *Secularism, Religion, and Multicultural Citizenship*. Cambridge, UK: Cambridge University Press.

Lithwick, Dahlia. (2004). How do you solve the problem of *shari'a*? Canada grapples with the boundaries of legal multiculturalism. *The Slate* 10 September, http://slate.msn.com/id/2106547/

Lopez, Ernesto Hernandez. (2008). Food and culture: Mexican corn's national identity cooked in 'Tortilla Discourses' post-TLC/NAFTA. *St. Thomas Law Review* 18. Available at SSRN: http://ssrn.com/abstract = 1108624

Macdonald, Roderick A. (2005). Rendering unto God: Islamophobia and religious tribunals. *Quid Novi*, Faculty of Law, McGill University, Montreal, QC, 4 October, http://www.law.mcgill.ca/quid/archive/2005/051004toc.html

Mackie, Gerry. (1996). Ending footbinding and infibulations: a convention account. *American Sociological Review* 61/6: 999–1017.

—— (2003). Female genital cutting: a harmless practice? *Medical Anthropology Quarterly* 17/2: 135–58.

Mackinnon, Catharine. (1987). *Feminism Unmodified: Discourses on Life and Law*. Cambridge, MA: Harvard University Press.

Macklem, Patrick. (2001). *Indigenous Difference that the Constitution of Canada*. Toronto, ON: University of Toronto Press.

—— (2008). Minority rights in international law, *Oxford Journal of Constitutional Law* 6/3–4: 531–52.

Macklin, Audrey. (2006). Multiculturalism in a time of privatization: faith-based arbitration and gender equality. *Canadian Diversity* 4/3: 75–9.

Macleod, Colin. (2006). Interpreting the identity claims of young children, in Avigail Eisenberg (ed.), *Diversity and Equality: The Changing Framework of Freedom in Canada*. Vancouver, BC: University of British Columbia Press, pp. 134–52.

Malloy, Tove. (2005). *National Minority Rights in Europe*. Oxford, UK: Oxford University Press.

Markell, Patchen. (2003). *Bound by Recognition*. Princeton, NJ: Princeton University Press.

McLaren, John. (1999). The Doukhobor belief in individual faith and conscience and the demands of the secular state, in John McLaren and Harold Coward (eds.), *Religious Conscience, the State and the Law*. Albany, NY: State University of New York Press, pp. 117–35.

McRanor, Shauna. (1997). Maintaining the reliability of Aboriginal oral records and their material manifestations: implications for archival practice. *Archivaria* 43: 64–88.

Minow, Martha. (1991). Identities. *Yale Journal of Law and the Humanities* 3/83: 97–130.

Modood, Tariq. (1998). Anti-essentialism, multiculturalism, and the 'recognition' of religious groups. *Journal of Political Philosophy* 6/4: 380–99.

—— (2005). *Multicultural Politics: Racism, Ethnicity and Muslims in Britain.* Minneapolis, MN: University of Minnesota Press.

—— (2007). *Multiculturalism: A Civic Ideal.* London, UK: Polity Press.

Monture-Angus, Patricia. (2003). *Thunder in My Soul: A Mohawk Woman Speaks.* Halifax, NS: Fernwood Publishers.

Moore, Margaret. (2006). Identity claims and identity politics: a limited defence, in Ignor Primoratz and Aleksandor Pavković (eds.), *Identity, Self-Determination, and Secession.* London, UK: Ashgate, pp. 27–44.

Mumtaz Ali, Syed. (1994). The review of the Ontario civil justice system: the reconstruction of the Canadian Constitution and the case for Muslim personal/family law. *A Submission to the Ontario Civil Justice Review Task Force.* Toronto, ON: Canadian Society of Muslims, http://muslim-canada.org/submission.pdf

—— (2004). An update on the Islamic Institute of Civil Justice (*Darul Qada*). *The Canadian Society of Muslims,* http://muslim-canada.org/news04.html

Nahanee, Teressa Anne. (1997). Indian women, sex equality and the *Charter,* in Caroline Andrew and Sandra Rodgers (eds.), *Women and the Canadian State.* Kingston and Montreal, QC: McGill Queen's University Press, pp. 89–103.

Narayan, Uma. (1997). Contesting cultures: 'Westernization', respect for cultures, and third-world feminists, in Linda Nicholson (ed.), *The Second Wave.* London, UK: Routledge, pp. 396–414.

NAWL (National Association of Women and the Law). (2007). *No Religious Arbitration Coalition: What Have We Learned*? www.nawl.ca/ns/en/documents/2007ReligiousArbitBestPractices.doc

Nnaemeka, Obioma. (2005). African women, colonial discourses, and imperialist interventions: female circumcision as impetus, in Obioma Nnaemeka (ed.), *Female Circumcision and the Politics of Knowledge: African Women and Imperialist Discourses.* Westport, CT: Praeger, pp. 27–46.

Nussbaum, Martha. (1999). *Sex and Social Justice.* Oxford, UK: Oxford University Press.

—— (2000). *Women and Human Development: The Capabilities Approach.* Cambridge, UK: Cambridge University Press.

Okin, Susan Moller. (1998). Feminism and multiculturalism: some tensions. *Ethics* 108: 661–84.

Ontario. (1991). *Arbitration Act, 1991* SO 1991, c17.

Ontario bill bans faith-based tribunals. (2005). *The Globe & Mail* (online edition), 15 November.

Ontario. (2005). Bill 27: An Act to amend the Arbitration Act, 1991, the Child and Family Services Act and the Family Law Act in connection with family arbitration and related matters, and to amend the Children's Law Reform Act in connection with the matters to be considered by the court in dealing with applications for custody and access. Toronto, ON: Office of the Legislative Assembly of Ontario, http://www.ontla.on.ca/documents/Bills/38_Parliament/session2/b027_e.htm

Phillips, Anne. (2007). *Multiculturalism without Culture.* Princeton, NJ: Princeton University Press.

—— and Saharso, Sawitri (eds.) (2008). *Ethnicities: Special Issue on the Rights of Women and the Crisis of Multiculturalism* 8/3.

Portelli, Alessandro. (1998). What makes oral history different, in Robert Perks and Alistair Thomson (eds.), *The Oral History Reader.* London, UK: Routledge, pp. 63–74.

Postero, Nancy Grey and Zamosc, Leon (eds.) (2004). *The Struggle for Indigenous Rights in Latin America.* Eastbourne, UK: Sussex Academic Press.

Povinelli, Elizabeth. (1998). The state of shame: Australian multiculturalism and the crisis of Indigenous citizenship. *Critical Inquiry* 24: 575–610.

Prins, Baukje and Saharso, Sawitri. (2008). In the spotlight: a blessing and a curse for immigrant women in the Netherlands. *Ethnicities* 8: 365–84.

Quong, Jonathan. (2002). Are identity claims bad for deliberative democracy? *Contemporary Political Theory* 1/3: 307–28.

Rawls, John. (1985). Justice as fairness: political not metaphysical. *Philosophy and Public Affairs* 14/3: 223–51.

Renteln, Alison Dundes. (2004). *The Cultural Defense.* Oxford, UK: Oxford University Press.

Ross, Michael Lee. (2005). *First Nations Sacred Sites in Canada's Courts.* Vancouver, BC: University of British Columbia Press.

Royal Commission on Aboriginal Peoples. (1996). *Final Report of the Royal Commission on Aboriginal Peoples.* Ottawa, ON: Queen's Printer.

Rutledge, David. (2005). *Shari'a* for Canada? *Religion Report,* Radio National, 2 February, 8.30 am; repeated at 8.00 pm.

Scheinin, Martin. (2000). The right to enjoy a distinct culture: Indigenous and competing uses of land, in Theodore S. Orlin, Allan Rosas, and Martin Scheinin (eds.), *The Jurisprudence of Human Rights Law: A Comparative Interpretive Approach.* Turku, Finland: Institute for Human Rights Abo Akademi University, pp. 159–222.

Schouls, Tim. (2003). *Shifting Bourndaries: Aboriginal Identity, Pluralist Theory, and the Politics of Self-Government.* Vancouver, BC: University of British Columbia Press.

Scott, David. (2003). Culture in political theory. *Political Theory* 31/1: 93–116.

Sen, Amartya. (1999). *Development as Freedom.* New York: Anchor Books.

—— (2006). *Identity and Violence: The Illusion of Destiny.* New York: WW Norton and Co.

Shachar, Ayelet. (1998). Group identity and women's rights in family law: the perils of multicultural accommodation. *The Journal of Political Philosophy* 6/3: 285–305.

—— (2001). *Multicultural Jurisdictions.* Cambridge, UK: Cambridge University Press.

Shapiro, Samantha M. (2008). Kosher wars. *New York Times Magazine* 12 October: 50–5.

Simons, Margaret. (2003). *The Meeting of the Waters: The Hindmarsh Island Affair.* Sydney, Australia: Hodder Headline Australia Pty Ltd.

Smith, Andrea. (2005). *Conquest: Sexual Violence and American Indian Genocide.* Cambridge, MA: South End Press.

Song, Sarah. (2007). *Justice, Gender and the Politics of Multiculturalism.* Cambridge, UK: Cambridge University Press.

Spinner, Jeff. (1994). *The Boundaries of Citizenship: Race, Ethnicity and Nationality in the Liberal State.* Baltimore, MD: Johns Hopkins University Press.

Spinner-Halev, Jeff. (2001). Feminism, multiculturalism, oppression and the state. *Ethics* 112: 84–113.

Stabinsky, Doreen. (2002). Transgenic maize in Mexico: two updates. *GeneWatch* 15/4, http://www.gene-watch.org/genewatch/articles/15-4maize.html

Sullivan, Winnifred Fallers. (2005). *The Impossibility of Freedom of Religion.* Princeton, NJ: Princeton University Press.

Taylor, Charles. (1985). Understanding and ethnocentricity, in Charles Taylor (ed.), *Philosophy and the Human Sciences: Philosophical Papers 2.* Cambridge, UK: Cambridge University Press, pp. 116–33.

—— (1991). *The Ethics of Authenticity.* Cambridge, MA: Harvard University Press.

—— (1994). *Multiculturalism and the 'The Politics of Recognition'.* Princeton, NJ: Princeton University Press.

Thornberry, Patrick. (1991). *International Law and the Rights of Minorities.* Oxford, UK: Oxford University Press.

Tibbetts, Janice. (2004). Courts come to grips with Islamic justice. *Ottawa Citizen* 20 September: A5.

Tilley, Viriginia Q. (2002). New help or new hegemony? The transnational indigenous peoples' movement and 'being Indian' in El Salvador. *Journal of Latin American Studies* 34: 525–54.

Tully, James. (1995). *Strange Multiplicity: Constitutionalism in the Age of Diversity.* Cambridge, UK: Cambridge University Press.

Turpel-Lafond, Mary Ellen. (1997). Patriarchy and paternalism: the legacy of the Canadian state for First Nations women, in Caroline Andrew and Sandra Rodgers (eds.), *Women and the Canadian State.* Montreal, QC: McGill-Queen's University Press, pp. 64–78.

Vallance, Neil. (2006). The misuse of 'culture' by the Supreme Court of Canada, in Avigail Eisenberg (ed.), *Diversity and Equality: The Changing Framework of Freedom in Canada.* Vancouver, BC: University of British Columbia Press, pp. 97–113.

Van Cott, Donna Lee. (2006). Multiculturalism versus neo-liberalism in Latin America, in Keith Banting and Will Kymlicka (eds.), *Multiculturalism and the Welfare State.* Oxford, UK: Oxford University Press, pp. 272–96.

Van den Bossche, P. and Dahrendorf A. (2006). *Selected Bibliography on International Law and the Protection of Cultural Diversity,* http://www.cupore.fi/documents/SelectedBibliographyforHelsinkiConferencefinal1.pdf

Van Ginkel, Rob. (2004). The Makah whale hunt and leviathan's death: reinventing tradition and disputing authenticity in the age of modernity. *Ethnofoor* 17/1–2: 58–89.

Volpp, Leti. (2000). Blaming culture for bad behaviour, *Yale Journal of Law and the Humanities* 12: 89–116.

Waldron, Jeremy. (2000). Cultural identity and civic responsibility, in Will Kymlicka and Wayne Norman (eds.), *Citizenship in Diverse Societies.* Oxford, UK: Oxford University Press, pp. 155–74.

Weinstock, Daniel. (2006). Is 'identity' a danger to democracy? in Igor Primoratz and Aleksandar Pavkovic (eds.), *Identity, Self-Determination and Secession.* London, UK: Ashgate, pp. 15–26.

Wente, Margaret. (2004). Life under *shari'a*, in Canada? *The Globe and Mail* 29 May.

Whyte, John. (1974). The Lavell case and equality in Canada. *Queen's Quarterly* 81/1: 28–42.

Woehrling, José. (1998). L'obligation d'accommodement raisonnable et l'adaptation de la société a la diversité religieuse. *McGill Law Journal* 43: 325–46.

Yashar, Deborah. (2005). *Contesting Citizenship in Latin America: The Rise of Indigenous Movements and the Postliberal Challenge.* Cambridge, UK: Cambridge University Press.

Young, Iris Marion. (1990). *Justice and the Politics of Difference.* Princeton, NJ: Princeton University Press.

—— (1997*a*). Difference as a resource for political communication, in James Bohman and William Rehg (eds.), *Deliberative Democracy: Essays on Reason and Politics.* Cambridge, MA: MIT Press.

—— (1997*b*). A multicultural continuum: a critique of Will Kymlicka's Ethnic-Nation Dichotomy. *Constellations* 4/1: 48–53.

—— (2000). *Democracy and Inclusion.* Oxford, UK: Oxford University Press.

Žižek, Slavoj. (1997). Multiculturalism, or the cultural logic of multinational capitalism. *New Left Review* 225: 28–51.

Index

Aboriginal peoples 46, 72, 124, 155 n. 5
- assimilation 133
- entitlements 123, 125, 127, 133
- land claims 30, 95
- recognition of self-determination 126
- rights 121, 122, 123, 125, 126
- women and sexual equality 69
- *see also* Indigenous peoples
- *see also* Royal Commission

Abu-Laban, Yasmeen 8
accommodation 1, 43, 46, 54, 68, 126–7
- cultural 2, 6, 13, 59, 65–7

accountability 46, 48
- democratic 78

Adhar, Rex 3
administrative costs 40, 102
Africa, *see* East Africa; Namibia; Senegal; South Africa
agency 31, 59, 127
- identity and 20
- respect for 24

Ahmed Khan (Mhd.) v. Shah Bano Begum (India 1985) 146 n. 8
Akwesasne 122, 156 n. 13
Alfred, Gerald 136
alienation 95
American Indian Religious Freedom Act (1978, amdt. 1994) 102
American Indians 98
Amish people 97, 153 n. 8
Amselem, see *Syndicat Northcrest*
Anaya, S. James 130, 135, 158 n. 21, 159 n. 27
animals 7
- artificial growth hormones 17
- cruelty 16, 132
- slaughter 16

Appiah, Kwame Anthony 19, 20
Arbitration Act (Ontario 1991) 45, 47, 148 n. 2
Arjomand, Homi 47
arranged marriages 57
Asch, Michael 3
assimilation 2, 12, 55, 75, 76, 131, 133, 141
Attorney-General of Canada v. Lavell (1973) 83, 84, 85–6, 89, 146 n. 8, 152 nn. 15, 17
Australia 31, 66, 94
- Aboriginal land claims 95, 97

authenticity 13, 60–1, 67, 80, 141, 142
- and identity claims 44, 60, 92
- religious identity and 91–117

autonomy 52–5
- individual 25, 53, 55
- legitimate claims to 66
- meaningful 53
- minority 68
- tribal 87
- *see also* cultural autonomy

Bannerji, Himani 58
Barrett, Jerome T. & Joseph 148 n. 3
Barry, Brian 2, 24, 25, 28, 59, 60, 80, 100–1, 153 n. 6, 155 n. 2

Barsh, Russell 126, 127
Beaman, Lori G. 3, 147 n. 25, 152–3 n. 2
Bédard, Yvonne 84, 86, 152 nn. 15, 17
Benhabib, Seyla 2, 7, 34, 35, 59, 75, 76, 78, 150 nn. 13, 17
Berger, Ben 154 n. 12
Bernier, I. 16
bias 12, 25, 41, 44, 50, 74, 90, 115, 140
  cultural 56, 73
  ethnic 18, 26
  gender-based 73
  institutional 3, 10, 43, 110–11, 116
  perspective from which to reveal 11, 15, 27
  political 73
  rules of evidence 17
  structural 10
  unfair 26, 43, 103, 109
Binnie, Ian, Justice 156–7 n. 14
Black, Galen 99
Blackmun, Harry, Justice 98, 99, 153 n. 3
blasphemy 94–5
Borneo 135
Borrows, John 33, 106, 125, 126, 136, 155 n. 7
Bouchard, Gérard 6
Bountiful, British Columbia 83
Bourke, Joanna 152 n. 1
Boyd Report (Canada 2004) 46, 47, 48, 51, 148–9 n. 5, 150 n. 10
Bramham, Daphne 82
Brennan, William J., Justice 153 n. 3
Brazil 157 n. 16
Britain 4, 16
  multiculturalism 6, 7, 58, 155 n. 4
British Columbia 32, 33, 83, 123
  fishery regulations 122, 147 n. 20
  Supreme Court 123
  see also Bountiful, British Columbia
Brubaker, Rogers 19, 20, 21, 149 n. 10
Bruckner, Pascale 6

California 153 n. 4
Canada 4, 6, 146 n. 8
  identity claims by national minorities 5
  import of goods duty-free across the border between United States and 122
  Indigenous peoples 31, 66, 71, 75, 84, 85–6, 135
  multiculturalism 7, 58
  peyote rituals 97
  religious arbitration 13, 45–51, 139
  religious freedom 17, 93, 147 n. 25
  religious minorities 124
  see also British Columbia; DCT; Lubicon; Nova Scotia; *Ominayak*; Ontario; Quebec; Supreme Court of Canada; Sto:lo *Syndicat Northcrest*
Canadian Bar Association 148 n. 3
Canadian Bill of Rights 84, 86
Canadian Charter of Rights and Freedoms (1982) 152 n. 14, 154 n. 11
Canadian Muslim Women's Council 47, 148–9 n. 5
Canadian Society of Muslims 45, 46
Carens, Joseph 53, 67, 150 n. 13
Carlson, Brian 146 n. 6
Carlson, Keith Thor 33, 147 n. 20
casinos 127, 135

Catholic Church 72–3, 100–1, 151 n. 6
Catholics 45, 98
  living out of wedlock 113
celestial marriages 152 n. 12
Chambers, Clare 147 n. 16
Chan, Janet 146 n. 10
Charlottetown Accord (Canada 1992) 145 n. 1(1)
Charter of Fundamental Rights of the European Union (2000) 16, 145 n. 1(2)
children 35, 36, 38, 55
  abuse of 81
  apprehended by social services 82
  harm 40
  membership status 84
  see also girls
choice 19, 54, 56, 57
  autonomous 53
  incommensurable 60
  individual, importance of 108
  women 26, 69
Christianity 95, 97, 145 n. 4(1)
Christie, Gordon 126
circumcision:
  female 6
  male 39, 113
  see also FGC
citizenship 19
  boundaries of 28
Clayquot Sound 135
Coast Salish peoples 23
  see also Sto:lo people
coercion 39, 41, 48, 49, 51, 56, 82
  and indoctrination 83
collective action 35, 36, 37, 82, 113
collective identity 19, 108, 112
collectivism 5
  individualism and 4
colonialism 4, 62, 74, 86, 125, 131
  assimilative policies 76
  history of domination 5
  continuation of 120–1
  destructive effects of 5, 135
Colorado 153 n. 4
communities 10, 95, 108
  Aboriginal peoples 156–7, n. 14
  cultural 53, 73
  economic 124
  ethnic 72
  healthy 128–9, 133
  Indigenous peoples 4–5, 23, 29, 62, 72, 75, 83–6, 121–2, 124, 126, 128–9, 133–7, 146 n. 8, 147 n. 18, 151 n. 7, 152 n. 13, 157 n. 18
  insularity of 82
  marginalized 45
  minority 46, 50, 55, 59, 62
  viability of 54
  religious 45–6, 72, 73, 96
  tribal 88
compelling interest test 17, 102, 153 n. 3
compossibility, *see* norm of compossibility
conflict resolution 9, 55, 65, 69, 70, 74
  community 77
  deliberative approach to 76
Connolly, William 147 n. 17
consensus 56
consent 39, 46, 50
Constitution Act (Canada 1982) 154 n. 11, 155 n. 5
constitutions 16, 119, 146 n. 6
  Canada 4, 122, 123, 126, 134, 152 n. 14, 156 n. 11
  US 96, 102

controversial practices 33, 34–5, 81, 82, 92, 106, 122, 135, 137
Convention Concerning Indigenous and Tribal Peoples (ILO 1989) 145 n. 3(2), 146 n. 5, 158 n. 21
Cooper, Frederick 19, 20, 21, 149 n. 10
Copp, David 19, 20
Coulthard, Glen 151 n. 9
Creppell, Ingrid 19, 20
cultural autonomy 29, 46
 claims to 66, 67, 70, 75, 76
 rights to 69, 77, 85, 89
 sexual equality and 65, 66, 70, 71, 74–8, 83, 84, 90
cultural differences 28, 38, 67, 73
 heightening 6
 respect for 39, 71
cultural enclavism 6
cultural identity 30, 122, 130, 137
 construction of 30
 jeopardy and 88, 128
 practice central to 129
 preservation of 141
 protection of 16, 29, 131
 shaping 8
cultural minorities 3, 8, 17, 28, 41, 43, 69, 127, 128
 accommodation of 2, 13, 59
 claims to autonomy 66
 options and choices 56
 rights of 130
cultural practices 1, 8, 28, 29–30, 54–5, 62, 120, 124, 126, 128, 129, 142
 construction of 129, 133
 controversial 6–7, 34–5, 122, 135, 137
 fishing 126, 128
 gambling and casinos 127, 135
 gender and 8, 11, 13, 18–20, 27
 hunting 126, 128
 protection of 50, 141
 reindeer herding 134
 respect for 38
 trade in goods 123–4
culture 20, 52, 54
 autonomy-based interest in 53, 57
 critics of 7
 distinctive 128, 130
 interests 71
 protection for 16
 sexist 70
 static 120
 symbolic forms of 25
 worries about survival of 5
 see also DCT
cultural loyalty 38–9

Dahrendorf, A. 16
Danish Cartoon Affair 94–5
Dauvergne, Catherine 146 n. 12
Day, Richard 8, 59
DCT (distinctive culture test) 17, 121, 122–7, 129, 131, 132, 133, 156 nn. 11, 13, 157 n. 15
decision-making processes 34, 59, 85, 115, 121
 communal 35, 74, 77
 essentialism and 62
 internal 79
 legal 92, 93, 96, 110
 pragmatic 43, 101–2
 participatory 79
 see also public decision-making
Delgamuukw v. British Columbia (Canada 1997) 147 n. 21
deliberation 65, 74–8, 139

Denmark 4, 16
determinism 58
Deveaux, Monique 34–5, 69, 75, 76, 77–8, 151 n. 7
disadvantage 5, 10, 26, 110
 historical 41
 structural and relational 24
discrimination 72–3, 84
 employment 101
 impact on identity 87
 religious 4, 56
 sexual 6, 78, 86
diversionary effect 49
diversity 7, 12, 141, 142
 responses to 57, 58
 sexual equality and 65–90
divorce 46, 49, 51, 75
 women at risk of being coerced into 49
 see also religious arbitration
domestication 8, 12, 13, 44, 62–3, 120–1, 130, 131, 134–6
 identity and 141
 in the distinctive culture test 125–7
dominant groups 1–5, 10, 25, 26, 40, 49, 58, 61, 72, 116, 138
 institutions and 1–5, 11
 norms of 50
 power of 8, 117
 practices distasteful to 82
 practices viewed in terms of risk 114
 religious 101
 standards imposed on marginalized groups 37
dress codes 6, 29
Dworkin, Ronald 68

East Africa 36
education 82
egalitarian reciprocity 34, 78
Eisenberg, Avigail 8, 73
El Salvador 147 n. 18
elites 4
 conservative 141
 religious 107
entitlements 3, 4, 9, 10, 11, 14, 15, 18, 19, 21, 22, 23, 29, 30, 33, 49, 61, 63, 91, 92, 99, 101, 102, 109, 112, 119, 122, 125, 130, 139, 140
 Aboriginal 123, 125, 127, 133
 abstract 4, 5
 claims to 60
 constitutional 97, 100, 127
 cultural 70, 124, 137, 143
 identity claims 20, 120
 Indigenous 61–2, 131
 non-negotiable 69
 relevance of culture to 61–2
 religious 93, 143
 rights-based 73
equality 7, 25
 cultural 8
 gender 47, 66, 67
 individual, abstract 59
 normative commitments to 32
 public decision-making and 10
 see also sexual equality
essentialism 2, 8, 13, 120–1, 130, 131–4
 distinctive culture test and 125–7
 identity claiming and 44, 61, 119–20, 141
ethnic minorities
 unjust exclusion of 3
 see cultural minorities
ethnicity 18, 19, 26, 29, 37
ethnocentricism 2, 140
Europe:
 gender equality 66
 multiculturalism 58, 59

Evatt, Elizabeth 158 n. 18
evidence
 inscrutable 99, 110
 opaque 99
 sincerity as 33, 105, 106, 110, 115
exclusion 3, 15, 28–30, 112, 117
 commemorated in the face of adversity 31
 historical 31, 106
external protections 55–6

fairness 25, 27, 28, 41, 85, 123
 background social conditions 29
 procedural 75
 public practices 10, 11, 15, 140
false consciousness 11, 30, 41
family law 46, 47, 51
 see also religious arbitration; marriage; divorce
Fanon, Frantz 151 n. 9
Fatah, Tarek 47
feminism 48–9, 69
Festenstein, Matthew 146 n. 13, 155 n. 3
FGC (female genital cutting) 6, 36, 38, 39, 147 n. 24
Finland 33, 133
 see also *Länsman*; Sami
First Nations 124, 127
 see also Aboriginal peoples; Indigenous peoples; Cree; Inuit; Lubicon; Maliseet; Mi'kmaq; Mohawk; Sto:lo
Flanagan, Thomas 133
FLDS (Fundamentalist Latter Day Saints) 30, 33, 81, 82, 83, 152 n. 12
 see also Bountiful, British Columbia; *Reynolds v. United States* (1878); celestial marriages; polygamy
Fontes, Lisa Aronson 38, 146 n. 10
food and culture 17
forced marriages 58
Forst, Rainer 53, 54
France 4, 6, 129, 158 n. 20
Fraser, Nancy 2, 59
freedom of association 34, 72, 78, 101
freedom of choice 6, 7, 52
freedom of conscience 106
freedom of exit 34, 78
freedom of speech 4, 22, 72, 97
freedom of thought 106
French language 43

Gabriel, Christina 8
gender 19, 27, 49, 73
gender equality 47, 66
 see also sexual equality
genetically modified foods 17
genomics research 16
Germany 4
girls 70
 circumcised 6
 practices that deny 56
 underage, marriages 82
Greenawalt, Kent 92, 101–2
group identity 1, 21, 23, 27, 82
 impact of discrimination on individual and 87
groups
 bounded 7
 cultural or ethnic 5, 17, 27, 34–5, 46, 71
 human rights 28–9

marginalized 37, 66
plurality or hybridity of 21
racial(ized) 27, 58
self-determining 77
see also culture, dominant groups; minorities/minority groups; religious groups
Guatemala 147 n. 18
Gutmann, Amy 146 n. 13

Hall, Stuart 19, 147 n. 17
harm 35–41, 52, 82–3, 100
potential 41, 100
risk of 114, 115
Henderson, James Youngblood 3, 126, 127
Herder, J. G. von 159 n. 1
Hindmarsh Island, Australia 97
homosexuals 72–3
Hopu and Tepoaitu Bessert v. France (1993) 129
Hughes, Bethany 152 n. 2
human rights 28–9, 36
attentiveness to 139
internationalization of 72
tribunals 13
hunting 126, 128, 132, 134
hybridity 7, 21

ICCPR (*International Covenant on Civil and Political Rights*) 17, 128, 129, 130
identification 20–1
identity approach 15–16, 32–40, 41, 79–89
identity claims 5, 8–11, 14, 15–16, 21, 55, 62, 72, 85, 87, 88, 89, 120–1
adjudicating 103
assessing 18, 25, 27, 28, 33–5, 37, 40, 41, 43–5, 57, 58, 63, 65, 66, 86, 90, 93, 96, 104, 111, 115, 117, 139, 140, 141, 143
assimilation and 75
authenticity of 60, 92
avoiding 3, 13, 45, 119, 140
compossibility and 69–70, 72
defining characteristics of 60
distinction between individual and group 23
domestication and 62–3, 120, 125–7, 131, 134–6
essentialism and 120, 121, 125–7, 130, 131–4
fraudulent 61, 92–6, 103, 107, 112–13, 116, 141
indigenous 119–38
moral force of 24–32, 43
opaque 80, 81
political legitimacy of 68
problems with interpreting 18
proliferation of 69–70
public decision-making and 14
recognition of 44
religious arbitration as 51
religious 61, 91, 95, 104, 107, 110, 114
scepticism about 12, 44, 60, 67, 74, 141
weak 32, 35, 39
see also minority claims
identity politics 2, 12, 13, 16–18, 44, 51, 66, 69, 119–20
camouflages racism 63
complexities 20
identity quietism 13, 43–5, 51–8, 63, 65
identity scepticism 13, 43–4, 45, 58–63, 65, 67, 73, 92, 111, 141
IICJ (Islamic Institute of Civil Justice) 46

impartiality 27, 50
inclusion 28–32, 59
incommensurability 12, 60, 65–90
India 146 n. 8, 151 n. 7
  Muslim minorities 78
Indian Act (Canada 1876) 84, 86, 152 nn. 13, 16
Indian Civil Rights Act (United States 1968) 88
indigenous identity 28, 89
Indigenous peoples 3, 4, 5, 29, 31, 34, 71, 88
  adjudicating conflicts 72
  covertly assimilating and domesticating 12
  identity claims 119–38, 140
  land claims 30
  protection of identities 17
  relevance of culture to entitlements 61–2
  right to self-government 85
  sexist rules of membership 75
  distinctive from settler majority 83–4
  see also Aboriginal peoples
Indigenous women, see *Attorney General of Canada v. Lavell* and *Santa Clara* cases
individual rights 4, 8, 24, 71–2, 74, 79
  collective and 23
  conventional understanding of 90, 140
  cultural bias of 57, 73–4
  historical development of 22
  liberal interpretation of 7, 52
individualism 5, 71
  collectivism and 4
indoctrination 37, 82, 83
  socialization and 36
inequality 11, 15
  gender 66
  group 4
  structural 41
injustice 14
  economic 136
  historical 29
  social 8
  structural 28, 29, 30, 31
institutional humility 25–8, 29, 32, 35, 38, 41, 43, 49–50, 52, 91, 103, 112, 119, 140
integration 6, 59
integrity 20
intellectual property 16
Inter-American Commission on Human Rights 157 n. 16, 158 n. 21
intermarriage 75, 86
internal restrictions 55–6
International Labour Organization 16, 28, 158 n. 21
Inuit language 128
Inuit people 155 n. 5
Islam 6, 49, 50
  blasphemy 94–5
  religious arbitration 45–51, 58
  see also IICJ; shari'a law; Muslims
Islamophobia 6, 49
Ismaili Muslims 45
Israel 78

Jackson, Robert H., Justice 153–4 n. 8
jeopardy condition 32–3, 35, 41, 80, 81, 83, 91, 111, 112, 115, 116, 137, 142, 143
Jehovah's Witnesses 153 n. 8
Jewish holidays 30, 95, 108–9
Jews/Judaism 45, 46, 105, 106, 154 n. 9
  circumcision 39, 113

collective identity 108
kosher practice 107–8
minyans 23
observant 32, 33, 93, 108, 115
orthodox 104
religious holidays 32, 108, 115
see also succahs
Johnson, James 25, 120, 147 n. 15
Judaism, *see* Jews
Jung, Courtney 28, 29, 30–1, 59, 136
justice 25–6, 28
procedural 78, 87, 88

Kingsbury, Benedict 158 n. 19
kirpans 43, 55, 57
Knop, Karen 158 n. 21
Kompridis, Nikolas 158 n. 25
Korsgaard, Christine 146 n. 11
kosher practice 55, 107–8
Krakauer, Jon 82
Kukathas, Chandran 69, 151 n. 2, 154 n. 16
Kymlicka, Will 2, 6, 52–7, 141, 150 nn. 12, 13, 14, 158 nn. 22, 23, 159 n. 2

Laegaard, Sune 95
Lambert, Douglas, Justice 123, 156 n. 8
language 19, 87, 128
differences of 28
right to use 23, 128
survival of 5
Länsman et al. v. Finland (1992) 129
Laskin, Bora, Justice 85, 86
Latin America 28, 31, 136
Lavell, Jeanette. 84, 85–6, 89, 152 nn. 15, 17
see also *Attorney-General of Canada v. Lavell*
legal tests 17
distinctive culture test 17, 121, 122–7
compelling interest test 17, 87, 99, 102, 153 n. 3
reasonable limits test 106
sincerity test 107
legislatures 92, 99–100, 102, 121
legitimacy 2, 3, 6, 11–12, 14, 15, 18, 26, 34, 44, 48, 62, 66, 68, 75, 80
democratic 35
self-governing institutions 79, 89
Levey, Geoffrey Brahm 95
Lévi-Strauss, Claude 19
L'Hereux-Dubé, Claire, Justice 156 n. 12
liberal multiculturalism 56, 57, 72, 141
identity quietism and 51
Kymlicka's arguments for 52–7
liberalism 22, 53, 71, 74
linguistic identity 16
London transport bombing (2005) 6
Lubicon people 128, 129, 130, 157 n. 17, 158 n. 24
see also *Ominayak, Chief of the Lubicon Lake Band v. Canada*

Macdonald, Roderick A. 149 n. 6
Mackie, Gerry 36
Mackinnon, Catharine 152 n. 18
Macklem, Patrick 158 nn. 19, 20
Macklin, Audrey 149 n. 9
McLachlin, Beverly, Chief Justice 156 n. 12
McLaren, John 3
Macleod, Colin 35, 36
McRanor, Shauna 33
Makah community 43, 132, 134, 135
Maliseet First Nation 122, 124, 125

Malloy, Tove 155 n. 2
Markell, Patchen 8, 59
marriages 55, 75, 82, 84
arranged 57, 82
celestial 152 n. 12
forced 58
membership and 84
prenuptial agreements and 50, 149 n. 9
see also divorce; polygamy; monogamy
Marshall, Justice 153 n. 3
Martinez, Audrey see *Santa Clara Pueblo Indians v. Julia Martinez*
Martinez, Julia see *Santa Clara Pueblo Indians v. Julia Martinez*
Mayan people 147 n. 18
membership rules 55, 75, 85–7
Mennonites 45
Métis people 155 n. 5, 156 n. 11
Mexico 17, 31, 97
Mi'kmaq First Nation 122, 124, 125
minorities/minority groups 11, 12, 18, 26, 101
accommodation of 59, 67
assimilation of 2
authenticity and 99
illiberal 56
integration of 6
linguistic 16, 128, 150 n. 14
officials refuse to recognize their practices 3
resolution to conflicts internal to 76–7
stereotyping of 140
see also Aboriginal peoples; cultural minorities; Indigenous peoples; minority claims; minority rights; national minorities; religious minorities
minority claims:
decision-making about 41, 54, 59
denied a fair hearing 103
moral force of 28
stereotypes and 3, 9
minority rights 1, 2, 17, 53, 57
means of responding to 5–6
societies that protect 9
two leading approaches to 25
Minow, Martha 67, 68
misrecognition 24
Mitchell, Michael, Mohawk Grand Chief 124, 156 n. 13
Mitchell v. MNR (Canada 2001) 124, 156 n. 13
Modood, Tariq 95, 145 n. 4(1), 150 nn. 13, 17, 155 n. 4
Mohawk people 122, 124, 156 n. 13
monogamy 83
Monture-Angus, Patricia 67
Moore, Margaret 19–20
multiculturalism 9, 10, 46–56, 60–2, 141, 142
backlash against 5, 6, 44, 63
critics of 2, 6, 8, 43
defenders of 2, 13
feminism and 69
incomplete nature of 139
normative commitments of 13, 43, 57, 58, 59, 65
official policy 7–8
public anxiety against 5, 7, 45
see also liberal multiculturalism
Mumtaz Ali, Syed 46, 47, 149 nn. 5, 7, 8
municipal codes of conduct 6
Muslim Canadian Congress 47
Muslims 47–9, 66, 78
accommodation of practices 2
blasphemy 94–5

cultural enclavism 6, 58
forced marriages 58
racism or anti-Muslim sentiment 58
religious arbitration 45–9, 50–1, 55, 58, 149 n. 8, 150 n. 11
restrictions on women 6, 55
veiling 2, 30, 55, 57, 58
see also Islam; religious arbitration; shari'a law

Nahanee, Teressa Anne 67, 76, 85, 152 n. 17
Namibia 157 n. 18
Narayan, Uma 151 nn. 7, 9
narcotics 6, 92, 96–7, 98, 99
national minorities 4–5, 16, 133
Native American Church 97–9, 100, 102, 103, 112, 115
NAWL (National Association of Women and the Law, Canada) 48–9
Netherlands 6, 7, 16
Neumann, Steffen 154 n. 15
New Mexico 153 n. 4
Ngarrindjeri women 94
NIB (National Indian Brotherhood) 84–5
Nnaemeka, Obioma 39
norm of compossibility 69–70, 72
norm of cultural integrity 130
North American Free Trade Agreement 16
Nussbaum, Martha 69, 70–1, 72–3, 151 n. 3

O'Connor, Sandra Day, Justice 102, 153 nn. 5, 8–9
Okin, Susan 2, 69, 70
Ominayak, Chief of the Lubicon Lake Band v. Canada (1984) 128, 129, 158 n. 24
oppression 11, 15, 26, 27, 29, 30, 31, 52
Oregon v. Smith (US 1988) 92, 94, 96–103, 109, 110, 112, 114–15, 153 nn. 3, 7, 8

pacificists 96
parental authority 6, 7, 35–6, 38
Patten, Alan 150 n. 14
patriarchy 49, 76, 83, 86–7
People v. Moua (California 1985) 146 n. 8
peyote ritual 96–9, 102, 109, 115, 153 n. 4
Phillips, Anne 2, 6, 7, 38, 58, 59, 60, 66, 145 n. 3(1), 150 nn. 11, 17, 155 n. 1
pluralism:
radical legal 47
religious 49
polygamy 30–4, 57, 81–3
Polynesians 129
Portelli, Alessandro 147 n. 21
Postero, Nancy Grey 136
Povinelli, Elizabeth 8, 29, 59, 95, 96, 152 n. 2
pre-contact criterion 123–4, 125, 126, 127, 129, 132–3
prenuptial agreements 50, 149 n. 9
Prins, Baukje 150 n. 1
process-based approach 74–9, 85, 89, 90
public decision-making 1, 3, 9, 12, 13, 43, 50, 52, 58, 61, 68, 73, 82, 120, 136, 140, 141, 143
authenticity and 91–5, 99, 103, 111, 113, 115, 117

public decision-making (*cont.*)
avoidance of identity claims 142–65
diverse societies 15–42, 59
group practices 133
identity and 2
majority identity 11
rights-based approach and 74
role of identity claims 14
public institutions 1–4, 15, 17, 20, 39, 63, 81, 114, 121, 133, 139, 142
access to and treatment by 27
attempts to define or assess cultures 7
burdens on 70, 102
dominant groups and 3
elite and hegemonic 9
experience with identity claims 107, 117, 143
just 26, 27, 28
legitimacy 68
prayer rooms in 30
see also institutional humility
public officials 1, 3, 143
Pueblo Indians 34, 56, 77, 83, 87–9, 146 n. 8
Purcell, Megan 147 n. 26

Quaker belief 97
Quebec/Québécois 6, 148 n. 1, 156 n. 13
Quiroga, Cecilia Medina 158 n. 18
Quong, Jonathan 81

R v. Sappier (Canada 2006) 124, 125
R v. Van der Peet (Canada 1996) 4, 49, 50, 122, 123, 124, 125, 137, 155 n. 6, 156 nn. 8–10, 12, 156 nn. 9–10, 12
race 19, 28
racism 8, 12, 45, 56, 140
identity politics camouflages 63
multiculturalism gives rise to 6, 8, 58
see also Islamophobia
Rawls, John 150 n. 12
reasonable limits test 106
Rehoboth Basters community 157–8 n. 18
reification 15, 20
see also essentialism
reindeer herding 33, 129, 130, 133, 134
relativism 7
cultural 57, 72
religious arbitration 6, 43, 55, 57, 149 n. 9
access to 30
coercively imposed on women 39, 48
public debate over 45–51, 58, 139
religious beliefs:
authenticity of 92, 94, 97, 111, 114
centrality of 32, 97
importance of a practice to 93
normal and abnormal 117
personal nature of 103, 104, 105, 109, 112
peyotism and 96
sincerity and 17, 93, 103–11, 114
subjective nature of 107, 111, 112
religious dissent 56, 112, 113, 114, 115
religious doctrine 94, 104–5, 109–15
interpretation of 107–9
judicial interference in 97
religious freedom 17, 71–3, 91, 106–7
conflicts over 1
constitutional protection of 103
fraudulent claims and 113
legislative rather than judicial adjudication of 102
reasonable limit on 106, 109

Religious Freedom Restoration Act (US 1993) 102, 153 n. 3
religious fundamentalism 49
 see also FLDS
religious groups 27, 35, 71, 96, 101, 117
 identity claims by 61, 91, 95, 104, 107, 110, 114
 see also Jews/Judaism, Muslims, FLDS
religious identity 16, 32–3, 48
 authenticity and 91–117
 claims about 61
 importance of practice to 17, 23, 83
religious liberty 71, 73
religious minorities 17, 96, 128
 entitlements of 93, 114
 identity claims of 43, 48, 92, 111, 115
 practices of 1, 82, 103, 106–7, 117
 state suspicion 61
religious practices 1, 6–7, 37, 102, 107, 110, 112–14
 accommodation of 94, 99, 104
 assessment of 94, 100, 103–7, 117
 centrality of 23, 82, 100
 controversial 33, 51, 57, 81, 92, 106
 genuine as opposed to fraudulent 100
 harm and 115, 152 n. 2
 hostile 103
 choice in 108
 peyote ritual 97, 98, 115
 polygamy 32, 34, 81, 82–3
 Sabbath observance 32, 33, 55
 spirit dancing 23
 succahs 104, 105, 115
Renteln, Alison Dundes 38, 146 n. 9
respect 28–32, 38–9, 71, 78
 claims worthy of 70
 equal 123
 identity and 19, 20
 inclusion and 28–32
Reynolds v. United States (1878) 82–3
rights 16, 33, 71, 125, 126
 abstract 86, 89
 choosing between 85
 collective 4, 5, 23, 24, 69, 71
 constitutional 17, 121, 122, 123, 124
 cultural 53, 61, 69, 128, 130
 fidelity to 7
 fundamental 50, 71, 73, 86, 89, 91
 Indigenous 6
 respect for 70
 women's 47, 69
 see also human rights; ICCPR; individual rights; minority rights
rights-based approach 65, 68–74, 76, 79, 84, 86
rituals 97, 98
Roma lifestyle 30
Ross, Michael Lee 126
Royal Commission on Aboriginal Peoples (Canada 1996) 94, 145 n. 2(1), 159 n. 27
Rutledge, David 46

Sabbath observance 32, 33, 55
safeguard condition 35, 37–40, 41, 80, 82, 91, 111, 114, 138, 142, 143
Saharso, Sawitri 66, 145 n. 3(1), 150 n. 1
salmon fishing/trading 32, 33, 122–3, 124, 134, 137

Sami community 33, 129, 130, 133–4, 159 n. 26
Santa Clara Pueblo Indians v. Julia Martinez (US 1978) 34, 56, 77, 83, 87–9, 146 n. 8
Sarawak 135
Saudi Arabia 56
Scalia, Antonin, Justice 92, 97, 153 n. 7
Scheinin, Martin 158 n. 20
Schouls, Tim 159 n. 27
self 19, 20
  fragmented 21
  individual's sense of 24, 31
self-determination 120, 127, 134
  appropriate recognition of 126
  claims for 136
  entitlement to 62, 63, 131, 135
  struggles for 77, 135
self-esteem 19, 20, 25, 67
self-government 66–7, 126
  entitlement to 62, 84–5, 135
  interference with 87–8
  legitimacy of 89
self-respect 25, 67
self-understanding 14, 18, 19, 20, 23, 27, 30, 52, 80, 110, 136, 140
  centrality/importance of authenticity to 60
  collective 21
  healthy 22
Sen, Amartya 19, 151 n. 5
Senegal 39
settler societies 76
sexism 4, 6, 13, 34, 49, 52, 89, 135
  community 66, 75
  cultural 70
  excusing 12
  religious practices 51, 66
sexual equality 47–52, 57
  criteria that deny 100
  diversity and 65–90
  multiculturalism and 47
sexual orientation 72–3
Shachar, Ayelet 55, 77, 154 n. 17
Shapiro, Samantha M. 154 n. 13
shari'a law 45, 46, 47, 48, 49, 50, 146 n. 8
Simons, Margaret 152 n. 1
sincerity approach 93, 95, 103–11, 112, 114, 115
Singh, Jakeet 150 n. 16
Smith, Alfred, see *Oregon v. Smith*
Smith, Andrea 67
social construction 24, 25, 28, 29–32
social context 19, 24
social movements 31
social services 82
socialization 35, 36
societal cultures 53, 54, 57
solidarity 20
Song, Sarah 49, 75
South Africa 30–1, 34
Spain 16
speech:
  freedom of 4, 22, 72, 97
  hateful 7
Spinner, Jeff 55
Spinner-Halev, Jeff 75, 78, 151 n. 9
Spirit Dancing 23
spirituality 128
stereotypes 2, 9, 18, 61, 110, 115
  cultural 58
  decision-making avoids questioning 116
  dominant 111
  false 140
  minority claims assessed according to 3
  nurturing 7
  racial 45, 48, 49, 57, 58

stigmatization 59
Sto:lo First Nation 32, 33, 122–3, 134, 137, 138, 147 n. 20
succahs 93, 95, 104, 105, 106, 108, 115–16, 154 nn. 9, 14
Sullivan, Winnifred Fallers 153 n. 6
Supreme Court of Canada 84, 104, 108, 121, 123, 146 n. 12, 149 n. 9
Syndicat Northcrest v. Amselem (Canada 2004) 93, 95, 96, 103–11, 112, 113, 114, 115–16, 154 n. 14, 155 n. 18

Tahiti 129
Taylor, Charles 6, 19, 24, 93, 140, 159 n. 1
Tewa language 87
Thornberry, Patrick 158 n. 22
Tibbetts, Janice 46
Tilley, Virginia Q. 29, 147 n. 18
TOSTAN (international NGO) 36, 38, 39
trade disputes 16–17
transparency 93, 110, 115, 121, 138, 139
Tully, James 3
turbans 57
Turpel-Lafond, Mary Ellen 76, 151 n. 7

UN (United Nations) 17, 28, 128
UNESCO (UN Educational, Scientific and Cultural Organization) 28
UNHRC (United Nations Human Rights Committee) 17, 128–31, 138, 157 nn. 17–18, 158 nn. 20, 24
  Convention on the Rights of the Child (1990) 16
  Declaration on the Rights of Persons Belonging to National or Ethnic, Religious and Linguistic Minorities (1992) 16
  Draft Declaration on the Rights of Indigenous Peoples (1994) 16, 130, 145 n. 2(2)
United States
  Indigenous peoples 31, 66, 84
  kosher food 108
  peyote rituals 97
  polygamy laws 33, 83
  see also *Oregon v. Smith*; *Religious Freedom Restoration Act*; *Reynolds*; *Santa Clara*; US Supreme Court
universalism 50
  false 56
US Congress 102, 153 n. 3
US Supreme Court 34, 77, 87, 88, 92, 96

validation condition 33–7, 41, 80, 82, 91, 111, 113, 115, 116, 137, 142, 143
Vallance, Neil 146 n. 12
values 4, 6, 20, 25, 27, 28, 30, 54, 57, 60, 75, 87, 90, 133
  abstract 49, 50, 71, 74
  cultural 3, 72
  fundamental 68, 74, 86
  identity-related 3, 23, 29, 132
  incommensurable 69, 73, 74, 79–80, 86
  non-negotiable 69
  priority of 71
  religious 107, 112
  sexual equality 48

Van Cott, Donna Lee 136
Van den Bossche, P. 16
Van der Peet, Dorothy Marie, see *R. v. Van der Peet*
Van Ginkel, Rob 134
Van Gogh, Theo 6
veils 2, 30, 55, 57, 58
voluntary self-ascription 34, 78

Waldron, Jeremy 60, 67, 69–70, 72, 80
Washington State 132
Weinstock, Daniel 60, 67, 147 n. 15
Wente, Margaret 47, 149 n. 5
whale hunting 132, 134, 135
  regulation of 43
Whyte, John 152 n. 15
Woehrling, José 154 n. 10
women 6, 47, 66, 70
  abuse of 81
  barriers for 6, 47
  choices faced by 69
  genital cutting 36
  identities of 86
  membership rules 75, 78, 84, 85
  multiculturalism and 47
  restrictions on 39, 48–9, 55
  secret business' of a spiritual nature 94
  see also Ngarrindjeri women
World Trade Organization 16–17

xenophobia 38

Yanomami people 157 n. 16
Yashar, Deborah 136
Young, Iris 2, 3, 26, 27, 146 n. 14, 147 n. 16, 150 n. 13

Zamosc, Leon 136